NESTLED WITHIN THE Carolinian Forest in southwestern Ontario, Langdon Hall is one of Canada's most gorgeous country house hotels. Renowned for exquisite cuisine that changes with the seasons to reflect the reaps of the harvest—wild produce growing in abundance on the property and the bounty of the kitchen gardens—Chef Jason Bangerter ...the spring this might mean Sw... ...wheat, and the summer might ... Cream. Upon the arrival of fi... ...ash Soup with Sweetbreads, C... ...Caramel with Brown Butter ... ...of winter offer comforting dis... ...e and Madeira Jus, or a decade... ...uit.

Langdon Ha... ...ed recipes with notes on techni... ...g, farmers, and purveyors. Feat... ...ut, readers will be transported ... ...ambitious and others are simp... ...home cook.

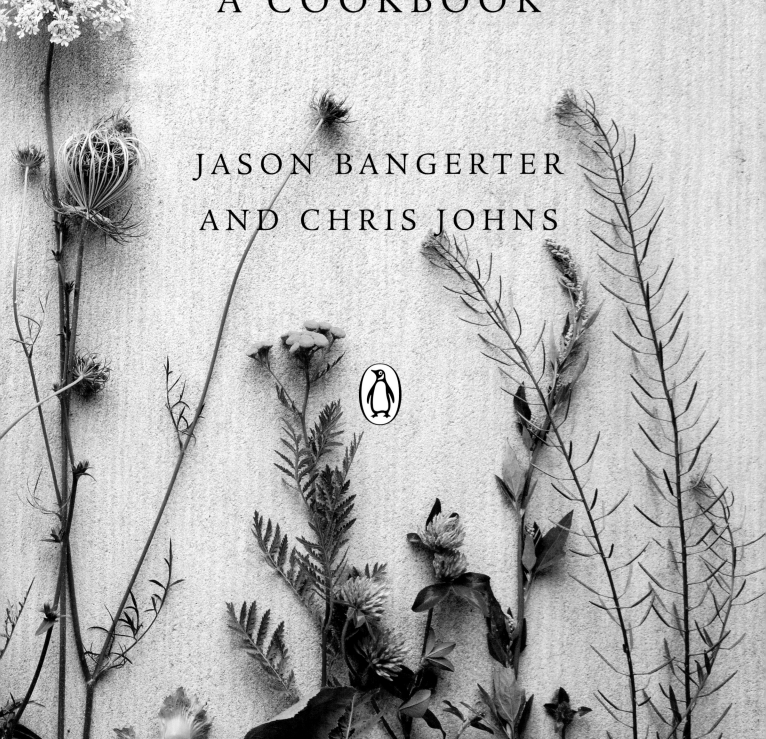

LANGDON HALL

A COOKBOOK

JASON BANGERTER
AND CHRIS JOHNS

PENGUIN
an imprint of Penguin Canada,
a division of Penguin Random House Canada Limited

Canada • USA • UK • Ireland • Australia • New Zealand • India • South Africa • China

First published 2022

Copyright © 2022 by Langdon Hall Country House Hotel and Spa

www.penguinrandomhouse.ca

Library and Archives Canada Cataloguing in Publication

Title: Langdon Hall : the cookbook / Jason Bangerter and Chris Johns.
Names: Bangerter, Jason, author. | Johns, Chris (Food writer), author.
Identifiers: Canadiana (print) 20200406574 | Canadiana (ebook) 20200406582 |
ISBN 9780735237223 (hardcover) | ISBN 9780735237230 (EPUB)
Subjects: LCSH: Langdon Hall. | LCSH: Seasonal cooking. | LCSH: Cooking. |
LCGFT: Cookbooks.
Classification: LCC TX714 .B358 2021 | DDC 641.5/64—dc23

Cover and interior design by Kelly Hill
Cover and interior photography by Colin Faulkner
Food styling by Jason Bangerter
Prop styling by Lara McGraw

Printed and bound in China

10 9 8 7 6 5 4 3 2 1

Penguin
Random House
PENGUIN CANADA

For Stacey, who has always supported my
dreams and aspirations, and to our two
beautiful children, Sebastian and Christian,
who sometimes eat the food I cook, and to our
family, for their unwavering love and support.
—JASON BANGERTER

For Jillian, Harper Grace and Bowie.
—CHRIS JOHNS

CONTENTS

INTRODUCTION

CROSS THE LITTLE BRICK BRIDGE that leads to Langdon Hall. Follow the black ribbon of road as it winds up through the small patch of Carolinian forest that separates the hotel from the outside world. In spring, new shoots of goldenrod, buckthorn and thistle bring the first touches of green to the understorey. Turn another corner, in summer, and lofty maples, towering poplars and broad-leafed American chestnuts explode in shades of green from the vast expanse of manicured lawn. Approach the grand portico of the house in autumn, when the air is filled with the resinous perfume of pine trees and chimney smoke, and the white columns and red bricks of the mansion glow with reflected light from the almost comical bedlam of fall foliage.

William Bennett and Mary Beaton first made this same winding journey through the forest in the late 1980s. The driveway was broken gravel back then, the gardens overgrown and ill defined, and the house neglected and unloved. "It was a twenty-five-thousand-square-foot home," Bill recalls, "with maybe two and a half million bricks, and most of them were cracked."

Nonetheless, something in their hearts told them that the grand old building, with its Ionic columns and perfectly balanced facade, could one day join the ranks of the world's great hotels. Truly a family endeavour, son Braden Bennett runs the day-to-day operations as managing partner and his wife, Jennifer Houghton, gallery director, oversees the featured artist series at the inn. In the four decades since Bill and Mary acquired the country mansion, courtesy of their hard work, unfailing eye for detail and ability to inspire in others the level of hospitality they themselves embody, one of the world's great hotels is precisely what Langdon Hall has become.

And that's why generations of visitors, from all around the world, have made the trek over the little brick bridge, up the long, and now beautifully finished, driveway to find themselves similarly enchanted.

One of those people was Jason Bangerter, a Toronto chef who started on his culinary journey with John Higgins at the King Edward Hotel and went on to study in some of Europe's finest kitchens, staging and working under the tutelage of legends like Pierre Koffmann, Jean-Georges Vongerichten and Anton Mosimann. He didn't come deliberately looking for a job so much as to see the property and get a feel for the place, but Langdon Hall had other plans.

"The first day I drove up the driveway I almost fell out of my seat," he recalls. "I was amazed by what I was seeing. I had no idea something like this existed in Ontario. I could not believe the beauty and the majesty of the property, and when I got out of my car and heard the roosters crowing and smelled the aroma of the wood-burning fireplaces, the freshness of the surrounding forest air and the smell of pastries and bread baking from the chimney, this huge rush, a huge wave of emotion came over me. It was just so magical, but it was also very intoxicating. I was actually pretty nervous as I walked up to the front door and realized this place was way more than I had ever imagined."

That was back in 2013. Bill met the awestruck chef in the reception and the two went for a stroll. "We walked along the flower gardens," Jason recalls, "over to the apple orchard and down to the garden, and the feeling of the place was just really warm and welcoming."

On the drive back into the city, stuck in traffic, his phone rang. The job was his if he wanted it. Bill and Mary stipulated two rules: "Cook from our land, and make sure the guests are happy." He accepted.

Up until that day, Jason had been on the path to becoming a corporate chef, working in downtown Toronto, managing staff, running numbers, designing kitchens, training chefs. Langdon Hall offered him the opportunity to apply those skills, but also to rediscover the things that had drawn him to cooking in the first place: a connection to the land and farmers and to raw, wild ingredients. In some ways, it would be a reinvention.

"Sustainable seafood and farm-to-table, that wasn't the way I was trained," he says. "Europeans taught me to cook, and that meant using monkfish and orange roughy and all that stuff, so when I came back to Canada I wanted to cook like I'd cooked in England and France and Germany. I was ordering langoustines from Scotland and oysters from Brittany, sole from the English Channel. But it didn't feel right. The products when they arrived in Toronto were poor quality, not what I had used while cooking in Europe. That's when I realized I needed to tap into what was here, what was close to home. That was 2003. I worked hard at developing relationships with nearby farmers, foragers and fishers, with the focus on connecting with like-minded, passionate suppliers to work with. Ten years later, Langdon Hall provided me the opportunity to be even closer to the source, to develop an even deeper relationship with the land and ingredients."

The chef started to learn about what was available around him and when—what was in our own waters, what different areas nearby produced best, and what wild ingredients were available in each season.

"The first little while I was focused just on trying to understand all the moving parts. That was a huge education for me. Learning to understand where wild stuff grew. Knowing that was a big component of what was available to me on the property. It took me about a year, maybe a year and a half, to really get control of it. I still miss things, but the beauty of this place is that it's an ongoing process and Mother Nature changes things up almost every year, so it's never quite the same."

He had one distinct and crucial advantage when it came to understanding the cycle and maximizing the property: the garden. The garden's role is so central to the property's cuisine and philosophy that it should be considered an extension of the kitchen, and the gardeners an al fresco element of the kitchen brigade.

The Wilks family felt the powerful draw of this piece of nature a century ago and set about building Langdon Hall as a summer home. At the time, the kitchen garden would have primarily been used to feed the staff. Room and board was expected, so it only made sense to grow as much for yourself as possible. The family would come and enjoy the produce during the summer, of course, but most of what was grown would be preserved for later in the season to sustain the staff who lived and worked on the property year-round.

That tradition is honoured, maintained and expanded today by the gardening team, a group of individuals as important to Langdon Hall's success as the kitchen brigade. The Olmstead-designed vegetable garden is a production garden first and foremost, although the kitchen draws ingredients from throughout the grounds, but it also serves an important role as a teaching garden. At just a little over a hundred square metres, the vegetable garden is generously proportioned, but not exactly sprawling for a kitchen as busy as Langdon Hall's and the gardeners strive to grow as much as possible in the space. Beyond that, they emphasize full flavour over abundance and include a selection of traditional, heirloom varieties that might well have grown in the plot since the house's earliest days.

For Jason, his immersion in the gardens has changed his understanding of ingredients, the way he creates dishes, indeed his entire culinary philosophy. "The training that I've received by working with the gardening team and being immersed in the garden every day is incredible," he says. "Intimately knowing the life cycle of a plant or a herb, how much of it can be used and when. No one ever taught me this stuff and I probably never would have learned these things if I wasn't in a position where I have them at my fingertips. Not many chefs have the luxury of a large garden. The whole experience of cooking in a property like this and working with knowledgeable gardeners completely changes your role as a chef."

For guests as well, spending part of an afternoon wandering through the gardens also changes their perception. To see that potato freshly dug out of the rich soil, dirt still clinging to its skin, transformed in the dining room by the skill of the chefs into something elegant and elevated, brings another layer of understanding to the meal.

Jason says, "As our cuisine has developed and grown over the years, I think we've established a philosophy that's about a connection to the ground and to the terroir that creates an experience that is as exciting for the guests as it is for the whole culinary team."

There's something reassuring when everyone on staff shows the same pride in knowing where those morel mushrooms were found or that the marigolds have just begun to flower or that the lemongrass in dessert was just picked from the greenhouse.

"We have the opportunity to put something on the plate that no one has ever seen before," Jason says, "where you're eating something that's truly connected to here and unique. It's a true taste of place. That's what drives us, and that's why even now, eight years after I first arrived, every time I drive up the driveway I get that same feeling of excitement I had the very first time I came here."

A NOTE FROM
BILL BENNETT AND MARY BEATON
Founders/Owners of Langdon Hall Country House Hotel and Spa

WE COULD NEVER HAVE imagined Langdon Hall would take us on such a journey of historical discovery and culinary creation. Our ambition was to renovate the spaces and create places in the gardens to offer a respite from city life in the countryside. After thirty-five years, we are left with a sense of pride and gratitude for all those who have joined us on this journey.

When developing Langdon Hall, we tried to understand its sense of place and to respect the past pride of an American summer house created by Eugene and Pauline Wilks—including the gardens, lawns and woodlands. We were fortunate to retain Dr. Leslie Laking, who had retired from the Royal Botanical Gardens, to consult and hire our first head gardener, Mathew Smerek, to renovate the gardens and revive the past purpose of providing a vegetable and herb supply to the hotel's kitchen.

Several years after opening the hotel, original letters and plans of the gardens from 1902 were discovered. We were pleased to learn that Langdon Hall was the work of John Charles Olmsted, son of Frederick Law Olmsted, the father of nineteenth-century American landscape architecture. This significant historical discovery was a pivotal piece in our story.

For us, it was a natural progression to pair the gardens with the kitchen, and over time we witnessed culinary acclaim grow for the dining room at Langdon Hall. The woodlands were explored and foraged by our chefs Nigel Didcock, Louise Duhamel, James Saunders, Neil McCue, Andrew Taylor, Frank Dodd and Jonathan Gushue. Their innate passion and respect for the gardens and woodlands, coupled with the committed kitchen brigades and dining room personnel—many of whom have gone on to receive critical acclaim—are notable qualities.

Writers and photographers told stories of how chefs at Langdon Hall created cuisine using harvested ingredients before farm-to-table was a trend. As seeds continued to be sown and talented chefs continued to reap the harvest, the gardens evolved over the decades, evoking the spirit of the past but very much growing for the present.

Today, the garden and landscape still exude the original essence of the Olmsted plans in the skilful hands of the gardening team. The great green lawns glisten, favourite herbs and vegetable varieties grow, and the purposeful woodland paths are groomed, guiding the way for the cuisine of Chef Bangerter.

Born locally, world travelled, Chef Jason Bangerter beautifully pairs his culinary creations and skill with the Langdon Hall terroir. Since he joined us on our journey, we have enjoyed watching him discover the garden gifts offered at Langdon Hall and witnessing his recipes change through the seasons. As he enthusiastically explores the woodland, floral and vegetal offerings, a new breath has entered the kitchen, and his passion for the local lands and suppliers around us is evident. Our journey continues with culinary acclaim as Chef Bangerter and his brigade lead us into the next chapters.

A NOTE FROM
CHEF JASON BANGERTER

I HAVE OFTEN BEEN ASKED, "When are you going to write a book?" and I have always replied, "I would love to, but I am far too busy." And yet, here we are. Back in the early moments, I pondered what I could cut out of my day or how I would balance the time and energy needed to accomplish such a project. I knew one thing for sure: if I was going to create a book about my cuisine, it would have to include the property and people at Langdon Hall.

Our cuisine is inspired by this place, by foraging wild edibles, by a kitchen garden pollinated and enriched by the property's own honeybees, which also supply extraordinary honey. The region and local farm community is also very important, giving us pasture-raised heritage breeds of pork, poultry, lamb and longhorn cattle, and organic and heirloom vegetables and eggs. These ingredients, nurtured with care, are used to create our dishes with passion and purpose, dishes that tell stories about source and inspiration. In this way we aim to provide an unexpected journey for our guests and forge memories throughout their experience, memories enhanced by a special feeling, a sense of this place. This is what we have tried to capture in the pages of this book. We want to share the process and the results of our hard work and ethos, while showcasing the beauty of the property and an in-depth look at some of the relationships with our food community.

We wanted to include some of the unique art at Langdon Hall in the images throughout this book, showing the juxtaposition between the history of the property and the rustic raw earth of the garden and ingredients that are then transformed into the beautiful pieces of work on the plate. The painting on page 244 was the first of the series and probably my favourite one. It is an eighteenth-century painting of the lady of the house in a hunting gown. If you look closely you might be able to see that the pheasant in her arms is actually not part of the painting and is in fact a fresh bird that has been laid on the canvas. The perfect backdrop for Champagne eggs.

My hope is that this book not only inspires you but also helps to share our story, providing insight into the philosophy of our cuisine and the diversity of our terroir. I wish to share with you a little of my journey, my joy and my passion for the beautiful cuisine at Langdon Hall.

HOW TO USE THIS BOOK

The cuisine at Langdon Hall is very personal and intimately connected to the land, to the local terroir, and that's something we really wanted this book to convey. Consequently, there are some ingredients that you probably won't find at your local grocery store and a few recipes that require specialized equipment or specialized techniques. Please don't be daunted. We made a decision to keep the recipes as true to their original incarnation as possible, without cutting corners or compromising on our vision, but we've also made sure they work for home cooks.

Where there are especially challenging steps or esoteric ingredients, I've made suggestions for shortcuts or substitutions that can turn even the most complex recipe into something surprisingly accessible.

The important thing to remember when you're cooking from this cookbook is to try to not get discouraged if you can't find the exact products I'm using in the recipes. I highly doubt everyone will have the same access to the unique ingredients I harvest from the property at Langdon Hall. That is okay. Almost every dish in this book will be fine without the flowers and wild garnishes, but we felt it was important to include them to give a true sense of our philosophy. Similarly, a number of recipes that at first appear daunting contain shortcuts that will make them really quite straightforward. Adjust and adapt to ingredients or techniques or a pace you enjoy. Create your own dishes. You don't have to make all the components of a dish. Maybe take the sauce or the vegetable and be creative with it.

Remember, cooking good food should bring joy and pleasure. The purpose of cuisine and the act of eating is twofold: to nourish the body and the soul, and to bring family and friends together. It is a key component of the art of living.

Expand your horizons, build your confidence. Above all, have fun!

A NOTE ABOUT SALT
In the kitchen we use Diamond Crystal kosher salt and in any recipe in the book where salt is called for, that's the brand we use as a measuring guide. If you are using Morton kosher salt, reduce the given Diamond Crystal amount by one-third.

EIGHT
DEGREES

EASTER IS ON THE horizon, and all around the grounds at Langdon Hall there's a feeling something fundamental has shifted. It's eight degrees above freezing today. Not warm, exactly, but a milestone that always serves as a special marker for the gardens. Something in the air feels different. You can almost smell the ground starting to thaw and the soil come back to life.

The first intense magenta-coloured buds have appeared on the eastern redbuds, presaging the blushing pink flowers that will soon detonate like soft fireworks from the branches. High up in the tallest reaches of the tulip trees, new growth prepares to transform into spectacular yellow-and-orange flowers eager to fatten up plump bees. Before long, the sweet, citrusy, almond-milk aroma of lilac blossoms will drift through open bedroom windows.

Already, tulip mania has started in the perennial gardens behind the cloister building, the bright, showy flowers joined by a riot of effusive crocuses. In the kitchen garden, the team, having tidied up the beds and finished their first shallow till, are planting some of the earliest vegetables: radishes, tatsoi, celery root. If the weather holds, they'll be able to get in an early round of carrots and bring in some of the Paris Market Atlas variety that were planted last year and left in the ground over the winter, rendering them deeply flavourful and intense.

"Everyone gets excited about the arrival of spring," Jason says. "Everyone in the kitchen, everyone in the dining room. Everyone. Because they know that it means new menus are coming, a season has ended and we're pushing forward. I think we do a good job through the winter of keeping the food really colourful, by preserving and keeping things looking beautiful and delicate, and I love those dishes, but when you get into the full push of spring, it's a whole new look on the plate. It's all fresh, delicate and green, you've got all these little shoots and leaves that really define the vibrant flavour of the season."

Rhubarb, fiddleheads, ramps, morels—there's a very short window when these ingredients are perfect, making spring the most ephemeral season. Summer produce sticks around, but the best spring flavours tend to be fleeting and all the more special because of it.

For the kitchen brigade, one ingredient truly personifies the season: white asparagus. "The whole team is just so happy when that first delivery of white asparagus arrives," Jason says. "It's such a beautiful ingredient, and it's only around for such a brief time, so every year it's special."

Most of the white asparagus served in the dining room comes from places like Janssen Produce, a remarkable little farm about an hour's drive south that has specialized in white asparagus for twenty-six years and still washes each spear by hand. Langdon Hall also grows a tiny amount of the precious crop, covering the delicate spears with a terracotta cloche to prevent the sun from turning them green. "We don't produce a lot and it's not around for a long time," Jason explains, "but a few lucky guests who happen to be here just at the right time get to sample both the white and the green asparagus from our own garden."

Across the country, at almost the exact same time the gardeners are carefully cutting the asparagus out of the soil, the harvesting of another iconic seasonal ingredient is under way. Just off the west coast of Vancouver, Steve Johansen and his fishing crew at Organic Ocean fishery—who practise sustainable, environmentally responsible harvesting—are busy hauling in the first spot prawns of the year. With the boat's hold full, the fishers race back to the harbour in order to get the plump, sweet creatures to Langdon Hall's kitchen door so fresh they're still wriggling.

Closer to home, on the edge of the seventy acres of forest surrounding the hotel, sous chef Philippe de Montbrun leads a few cooks on a foraging expedition. "This is wild ginger," he says, passing around a handful of the aromatic heart-shaped leaves. "It pairs well with fats, so we'll dry some of it for infusing into cream and infuse some of it into oils. It's a beautiful ingredient, fragrant, but without any of the sharpness of cultivated ginger."

He gently lifts up a clump of the wild ginger with a trowel and points out where the plants are connected by underground rhizomes. "Early spring and late fall are the best time to harvest these," he explains, "because that's when the plants are dormant. If we try to harvest them when they're growing, it can damage them." He severs one of the rhizome connections by making a cut close to the plant's base while leaving the roots intact, and then he replants them, ensuring they'll be here again next year. Knowing how to sustainably harvest these ingredients is as important as knowing where to find them.

When it comes to foraged ingredients, the kitchen at Langdon Hall thinks in terms of two-week windows, so everything is harvested, used and preserved at the same time. The buds of the wild dog roses that the cooks are busy harvesting will get grilled and show up on the lunch menu as part of a foraged salad. The petals get steeped in oil, turning it bright red, ready for use throughout the year.

These foraging excursions are more than just a chance to harvest some pristine seasonal ingredients, however. They provide an opportunity for the team to bond, and also to decompress. "What's the best thing to do after a high-pressure day at work?" Phil rhetorically asks the assembled chefs. "Go for a walk in the forest. Ground yourself. Breathe some fresh air. Spending time out here getting to understand the land and the seasons is important for what we do as cooks, but I also want you to share these lessons with your friends. Tell your family. Show your kids. It's important to pass this information along."

CULTURED BUTTER
with Canadian flaky sea salt

WE USE THIS BUTTER FOR everything, from sauces to roasting, poaching or brushing meat, fish and vegetables to glazing desserts and pastries. And we love to flavour it with different ingredients—herbs, spices, vegetables, honey from our bees or pollen from the flowers in the garden or around the property. The sky is the limit, really. But the one thing that is a common standout experience for every guest at Langdon Hall is this butter in its natural form spread on some of our fresh-baked sourdough bread, with just a sprinkle of Canadian flaky sea salt on top.

MAKES ABOUT 1 POUND

Cultured Butter
4 cups whipping (35%) cream
½ cup plain natural full-fat yogurt

Garnish
Canadian flaky sea salt

FOR THE CULTURED BUTTER
The day before you would like the butter, whisk together the whipping cream and yogurt in a stand mixer bowl. Cover with a kitchen towel and let stand at room temperature overnight. Attach the bowl to the mixer and fit with the whisk attachment. Cover the mixer with a kitchen towel or plastic wrap to prevent the cream splashing once you start the mixer. Whip on high speed until the cream is at a medium peak, about 5 minutes. Reduce the speed to medium and mix until the cream overwhips and splits. You'll know when this happens because the butterfat milk solids will separate from the buttermilk and start to clump around the whisk. Reduce the speed to low and continue to whip until all the butterfat has separated from the buttermilk, about 3 more minutes. Strain the mixture through a fine-mesh sieve, reserving the buttermilk for another recipe. Transfer the butterfat to a stainless steel or ceramic bowl.

Rinse the butterfat under cold running water while kneading it with your hands. Once you see no more milky fluid when you squeeze the butterfat, you have "washed" it enough. It is important to remove all

the milky liquid to prevent the butter from spoiling. Turn the water off, drain the bowl and continue to knead and squeeze the butterfat until you can't extract any more liquid from it. At this time you can shape or form the butter into blocks or cylinders or press it into a mould or dish. Store in the refrigerator for up to 1 week or in the freezer for up to 3 months.

TO SERVE
Remove the butter from the fridge about 1 hour before using. Garnish with flaky sea salt.

JB'S TIP
For me, radishes with butter is one of the best ways to taste butter. The peppery crunch of fresh radishes is incredible, and when you combine it with the sweet, salty, rich, creamy butter, it's a match made in heaven. One of my favourite ways to serve this is to bring guests down into the garden and pull some radishes right out of the ground together. We wash them and dip them in some of our freshly made butter whipped with a taste of Langdon Hall estate honey. There's hardly anything better.

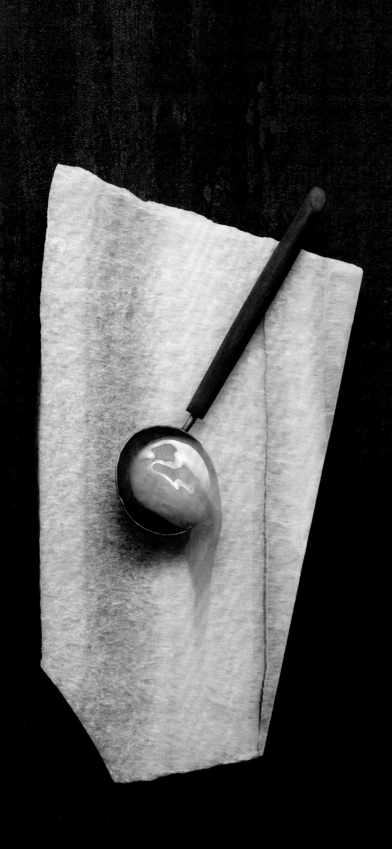

WELL-DRESSED PEEWEE HEN EGGS

with caviar, greenhouse flowers and herbs

CAVIAR SERVICE IS OFTEN ACCOMPANIED by snipped chives, mounds of minced shallots and boiled egg yolks and egg whites. For this dish, I wanted to have some fun and bring the whole egg and garden favourites to the party instead. Working so closely with the gardening team and farmers in our area has introduced me to many new ingredients and interesting characters that inspire new ideas and playful creations. It was through our relationship with farmer Murray, for example, that I learned young adolescent chicks lay eggs, too. Peewee eggs, they're called. You don't usually see them at the market or in the grocery store, but every once in a while we get them at Langdon Hall. They are the perfect size for a canapé or fun modern twist on caviar service. Here we use heritage hen peewee eggs from Murray's farm in a playful nod to the devilled egg, alongside Canadian caviar and the ever-changing beautiful garden garnishes harvested from the Langdon Hall greenhouse.

SERVES 6 TO 12

Aïoli (makes extra)

2 large egg yolks

1 garlic clove, finely minced or grated with a microplane

½ tablespoon fresh lemon juice

1 teaspoon white wine vinegar

1 teaspoon Dijon mustard

1 cup vegetable oil

½ tablespoon olive oil

1 teaspoon kosher salt

Devilled Eggs

6 peewee or regular eggs, simmered for 10 minutes, cooled and peeled

2 tablespoons aïoli (recipe at left)

1 teaspoon Dijon mustard

1 teaspoon kosher salt

Garnishes (any or all)

Shiso leaves

Basil leaves

Chervil leaves and flowers

Bachelor's button petals

Nasturtium leaves and flowers

Dill leaves and flowers

Fennel fronds

Marigold leaves and flowers

Canadian sturgeon caviar, for serving

FOR THE AÏOLI

In a medium bowl, whisk the egg yolks with the garlic, lemon juice, white wine vinegar and mustard to mix well. While whisking, add the vegetable oil in a thin stream, followed by the olive oil, whisking continuously to emulsify. The aïoli will thicken to the texture of a silky mayonnaise. If it becomes too thick, thin it with a few drops of room-temperature water. Stir in the salt. Transfer the aïoli to a covered container and refrigerate for up to 5 days.

FOR THE DEVILLED EGGS

With a sharp knife, cut a thin slice from the top and bottom of each egg so they will sit upright once halved. Evenly slice the eggs in half crosswise. Remove the yolks and reserve for the filling. The egg white should have a cup shape. Rinse the egg whites in water to clean out any remaining yolk and dry them on paper towel.

In a food processor, purée the reserved egg yolks with the aïoli and mustard until you have a smooth, creamy texture without lumps. If there are lumps, pass the mixture through a fine-mesh sieve. Season with the salt.

TO SERVE

Using a teaspoon or a piping bag fitted with a plain tip, fill each egg white cup with the yolk mixture. Garnish the top with soft herbs and edible flowers. To finish, place a generous spoonful of Canadian sturgeon caviar on the side.

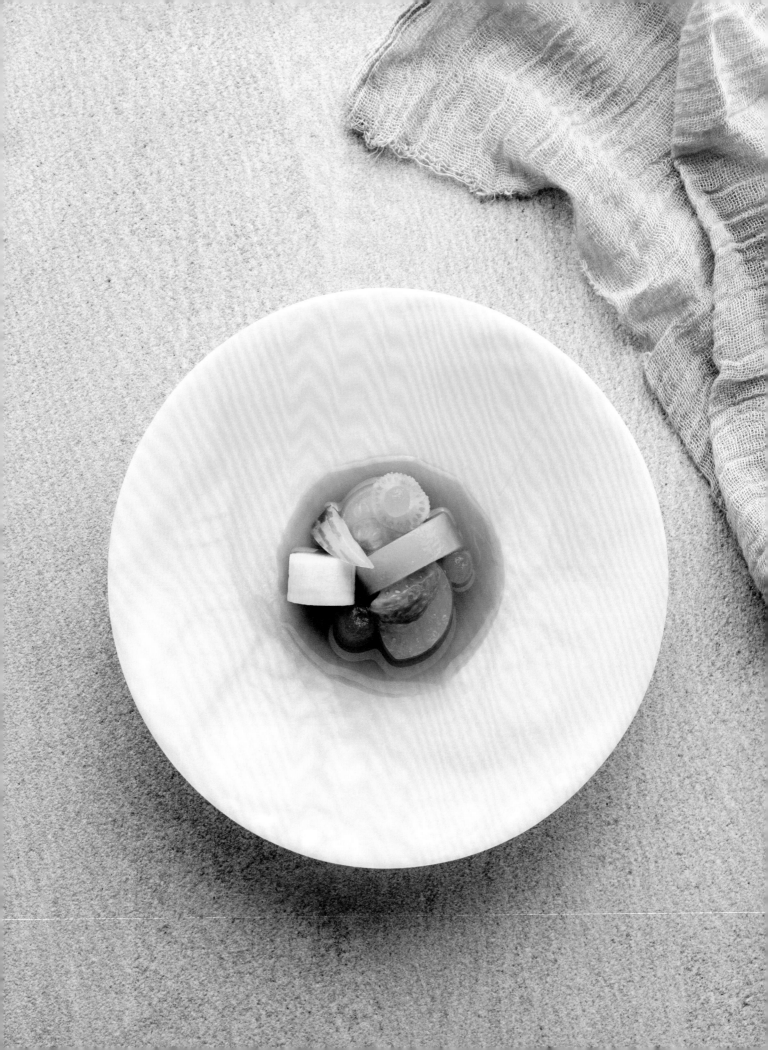

GREEN GARDEN VEGETABLES
heirloom cucumbers with melon, green tomato and dill

I WANT THE FOOD AT Langdon Hall to offer a true sense of place, a one-of-a-kind dining experience inspired by what is growing here on the property, and I build balance in these dishes using ripe and unripe ingredients, sweet and sour. In my search for simplicity, I hit on this idea of building dishes around one colour. This dish, for example, was created by simply taking everything that was green in the garden and building it all around three varieties of cucumber that are ideal for this dish. Tomatoes have been very successful in our garden the last few years. Green Zebra is an heirloom variety that is becoming very popular.

With the cucumbers, green tomatoes, green melon and a juice made from cucumber infused with dill, this is definitely an example of not trying to make a dish extra flashy with different heights and crisps and powders. It's all about the natural essence of the fruits and vegetables.

The dish will work just as well with only the common English cucumber. The juice is also great on its own or used in a garden-inspired cocktail.

SERVES 4

Green Garden Vegetables

1 Armenian cucumber

1 lemon cucumber

1 Boothby's Blonde heirloom cucumber

1 small honeydew melon

2 Green Zebra tomatoes

1 teaspoon kosher salt

Green Garden Juice

1 cup sliced peeled Granny Smith apples

4 cups sliced English cucumbers

1 cup chopped fresh dill

1 teaspoon kosher salt

1 teaspoon white balsamic vinegar

FOR THE GREEN GARDEN VEGETABLES

Peel the cucumbers and cut them into bite-size rectangles using a knife or shaped cookie cutters. Place the cucumbers in a medium bowl. Reserve the trimmings for the green garden juice.

Slice the melon in half and scoop out and discard the seeds. Using a small melon baller (½ to 1 inch in diameter), scoop out 12 melon balls (3 per person) and add them to the bowl with the cucumbers.

Cut the tomatoes into wedges small enough to fit onto a soup spoon and add them to the bowl with the other prepared vegetables. Season them all with the salt and mix gently.

FOR THE GREEN GARDEN JUICE

In a high-speed blender, combine the apple, cucumber, dill, salt, white balsamic vinegar and reserved cucumber trimmings. Purée until juiced and smooth. Strain the juice through a fine-mesh sieve into a juice jug. Cover with plastic wrap and refrigerate until chilled. This juice should be made on the day you are serving the dish to ensure it has fresh and vibrant colour and flavour.

TO SERVE

Arrange the prepared cucumber, tomato and melon in chilled shallow bowls. Pour the chilled green garden juice over the top to finish at the table.

CHILLED PEA SOUP
with fine herbs and blossoms

THERE ARE ABOUT SIX WEEKS of the year when peas are absolutely peaking, just bursting with that really green, earthy, fresh new-season flavour that shouts spring. That's my favourite time to make this soup. Essentially, it's a very simple chilled spring pea soup that's flavoured with garlic, shallot, delicate fine herbs and a little dry white wine. To set the whole dish off, I take all the blooming flowers from things that make sense with peas—mint, marjoram, citrus-flavoured marigold, pea flowers and borage with its fresh sea salt/oyster flavour—and scatter them around as garnish.

This recipe is beautiful as a soup, but it also works as a sauce for a piece of fish or even as a hearty healthy vegetable smoothie.

SERVES 6

Chilled Pea Soup

1 tablespoon olive oil

1 cup thinly sliced shallots

½ cup thinly sliced fennel

2 garlic cloves, thinly sliced

½ teaspoon minced peeled fresh ginger

½ teaspoon kosher salt

1 cup dry white wine

4 cups water, Chicken Stock (page 286) or Vegetable Stock (page 285)

5 cups shucked fresh peas

½ cup lightly packed fresh flat-leaf parsley

¼ cup lightly packed fresh basil leaves

¼ cup lightly packed fresh dill

¼ cup lightly packed fresh mint leaves

¼ cup lightly packed fresh tarragon leaves

Garnishes

1 cup lightly packed fresh edible flowers

Extra-virgin olive oil, to drizzle

FOR THE CHILLED PEA SOUP

In a medium saucepan, heat the olive oil over medium-low heat. Add the shallot, fennel, garlic and ginger and gently cook without browning, stirring often, until tender, about 5 minutes. Season with the salt. Add the white wine and reduce by two-thirds. Add the water or stock, bring to a simmer and cook for 5 minutes to infuse the flavour and build the stock. Add the fresh peas and continue to simmer for 2 minutes. Remove from the heat and stir in the parsley, basil, dill, mint and tarragon.

Strain the stock into another container, reserving it for adjusting the consistency of the soup. In a high-speed blender, purée the vegetables and herbs, adding enough of the stock in a slow, steady stream while blending to achieve a smooth, velvety consistency. Once processed, adjust the seasoning with salt, if required. Strain the soup through a fine-mesh sieve into a medium bowl and chill completely over ice before serving.

TO SERVE

Pour the soup into chilled bowls. Garnish with edible flowers and drizzle with olive oil.

CANAPÉS INSPIRED
BY GARDEN FLOWERS

with bouquet cornet, marigold madeleine and cilantro cucumber

THESE FRESH, DELICATE BITES OF SPRING are an ideal way to enjoy the taste of the gardens. Flowers and flowering herbs pair superbly with a glass of Champagne or an herbal inspired cocktail. Here the blossoms steal the spotlight. Flowers have some serious flavour and some can even pack a punch! I've used spicy mustard varieties in the cornet, fresh cilantro in the cucumber and citrusy marigold in the madeleine, but you can easily substitute any delicate herb or edible flowers.

MAKES ABOUT 20 REGULAR OR 40 MINI MADELEINES AND 4 CORNETS, SERVES 4

Marigold Madeleines

1⅓ cups cake flour

2 teaspoons baking powder

½ teaspoon kosher salt

4 large eggs

1 tablespoon honey

¾ cup sugar

1 tablespoon minced marigold leaves

1 tablespoon lemon zest

¾ cup unsalted butter

Bouquet Cornets

1 large egg yolk, for brushing

Pinch of kosher salt

1 sheet brik pastry (feuille de brick)

1 cup Crème Fraîche (page 281), in a piping bag fitted with a small plain tip

Cilantro Cucumber

1 English cucumber

1 tablespoon white balsamic vinegar

1 teaspoon extra-virgin olive oil

¼ teaspoon kosher salt

½ cup loosely packed roughly chopped cilantro leaves and stems

½ teaspoon coriander seeds

Garnishes

Lemon Gel (page 284)

Lime Leaf Powder (page 283)

For the madeleines: marigold leaves and flowers

For the cucumber: cilantro leaves and flowers

For the cornets: mix of radish flowers, horseradish greens, ground elder, mustard flower, wild dame's arugula flower

FOR THE MARIGOLD MADELEINES

In a medium bowl, sift together the cake flour, baking powder and salt.

In a separate medium bowl, whisk together the eggs, honey, sugar, marigold leaves and lemon zest until light and frothy, about 2 minutes.

In a small saucepan, melt the butter over low heat, then remove from the heat. Using a spatula, fold the sifted flour mixture into the egg mixture in 2 additions, being careful not to overwork the batter. When combined, slowly incorporate the melted butter until emulsified. Transfer to a piping bag fitted with a large plain tip and rest overnight in the refrigerator.

Preheat the oven to 325°F (160°C).

Brush the moulds of a madeleine pan with some melted butter and dust with flour, tapping off any excess. Pipe the madeleine batter into the moulds. Place the pan on a baking sheet and bake for 12 minutes, rotating front to back halfway through, until the madeleines are lightly golden to golden brown on top. Allow to cool for 5 minutes, then remove the madeleines from the moulds and cool on racks. Repeat if needed to make about 20 regular or 40 mini madeleines.

FOR THE BOUQUET CORNETS

Reduce the oven temperature to 300°F (150°C). Line a baking sheet with parchment paper.

In a small bowl, whisk together the egg yolk and salt. Using a 3-inch round cookie cutter, punch out

RECIPE CONTINUES . . .

4 discs of brik pastry. Wrap each disc around a cornet (cone) mould, brushing the seam with the egg yolk to glue together. Arrange standing up on the prepared baking sheet and bake for 7 minutes or until golden brown. Allow to cool before removing the cornets from the moulds.

FOR THE CILANTRO CUCUMBER

Peel the cucumber and cut into 1-inch × 4-inch rectangular bars. In a large bowl, whisk together the white balsamic vinegar, olive oil and salt to form a dressing. Add the cucumber and toss together. Transfer the cucumber with the dressing, chopped cilantro and coriander seeds to a sous vide bag. Vacuum-seal on full pressure and allow the cucumber to marinate for 1 hour. Remove the cucumber from the bag and cut into 1-inch cubes. (No vac pack? No problem. Just marinate the cucumber in a covered container for 1 hour.)

TO SERVE

Using a squeeze bottle or spoon, dot a couple of small spots of the lemon gel on top of a madeleine to glue the flowers to it. Dust with lime leaf powder and garnish with marigold leaves and flowers. Garnish the cucumber with cilantro leaves and flowers, using some lemon gel if needed to hold the flowers in place. Half-fill a cornet with the thick crème fraîche. Build a mini bouquet with the spicy herb leaves and flowers and set in the cornet.

MARINATED SHRIMP

with puffed quinoa, lemon gel and crème fraîche

HERE WE TAKE THE IDEA of a shrimp cocktail, something traditional and familiar, and rethink it in a way that makes it luxurious and extraordinary. Instead of serving the shrimp whole, we mince them more like a tartare, and rather than a cocktail dipping sauce, we scatter around all these aromatic, citrusy herbs and flowers and dot the dish with candied lemon peel and some lemon gel and crème fraîche. Finally, we dust the whole thing with powdered lime leaf so every bite of this fragrant, fresh-tasting marinated shrimp is different.

SERVES 4

Candied Lemon Peel

1 cup lemon peel, white pith removed

5 cups water, divided

1 cup sugar

Garden Court Bouillon (makes about 3 quarts)

1 cup sliced white onion

½ cup sliced leek (white part only)

¼ cup sliced celery

¼ cup sliced carrot

2 garlic cloves, crushed

1 teaspoon sliced peeled fresh ginger

1 lemongrass stalk, tough outer leaves and stems discarded, roughly chopped

4 star anise

1 tablespoon coriander seeds

2 tablespoons kosher salt

1 teaspoon black peppercorns

8 cups water

1 cup dry white wine

½ cup white wine vinegar

¼ cup lightly packed fresh dill

¼ cup lightly packed fresh flat-leaf parsley

¼ cup lightly packed fresh tarragon leaves

1 fresh bay leaf

Puffed Quinoa

2 cups water

½ cup dry red quinoa

4 cups vegetable oil, for frying

1 teaspoon kosher salt

Shrimp

1 pound (450 g) extra-large shrimp (size 16–20), peeled and deveined

1 tablespoon extra-virgin olive oil

1 tablespoon Lemon Gel (page 284)

1 teaspoon kosher salt

Garnishes

1 cup Crème Fraîche (page 281)

Lemon Gel (page 284)

Pansy flowers

Lemon verbena leaves

Lemon balm leaves

Fresh dill

Lime Leaf Powder (page 283)

FOR THE CANDIED LEMON PEEL

Cut the lemon peel into thin strips. Bring 2 cups of the water to a boil in a small saucepan over high heat. Add the sliced lemon peel and boil for 1 minute. Using a slotted spoon, transfer the lemon to a small bowl set over ice water to cool. Drain the pot of water, rinse and repeat the process once more. This will remove some of the bitterness from the lemon. Once the lemon peel is blanched, add the remaining 1 cup water and the sugar to the saucepan and bring to a boil over medium heat, stirring until the sugar has dissolved completely. Add the blanched lemon peel and continue to cook for 1 minute. Remove from the heat and allow the

lemon peel to cool to room temperature in the syrup. Transfer the peel and syrup to an airtight container and store in the refrigerator until ready to use or for up to 2 weeks.

FOR THE GARDEN COURT BOUILLON

In a medium saucepan, combine the onion, leek, celery, carrot, garlic, ginger, lemongrass, star anise, coriander seeds, salt and black peppercorns. Add the water and bring to a boil over high heat, then reduce the heat to a simmer and cook until the vegetables are tender, about 8 minutes. Add the white wine, white wine vinegar, dill, parsley, tarragon and bay leaf and continue to simmer for another 8 minutes. Strain

RECIPE CONTINUES . . .

through a fine-mesh sieve into a clean medium saucepan. Discard the vegetables and herbs.

FOR THE PUFFED QUINOA

In a small saucepan, bring the water to a boil. Add the quinoa, reduce the heat to low and simmer, covered, for 15 minutes. The quinoa is ready once it is tender. Drain the quinoa in a sieve and spread it on a baking sheet lined with parchment paper. Pat dry and let cool.

In a medium saucepan over medium heat, bring the vegetable oil to 360°F (185°C). Add the quinoa and fry until golden brown and crispy, stirring occasionally, about 2 minutes. Using a spider or small wire-mesh strainer, remove the fried quinoa from the oil and transfer to a baking sheet lined with paper towel to absorb excess oil. Season with the salt.

FOR THE SHRIMP

Bring the garden court bouillon to a simmer. Plunge in the shrimp and simmer for 1 minute, then remove the saucepan from the heat and leave the shrimp to poach for 2 minutes. Using a slotted spoon, transfer the shrimp to a medium bowl of ice to cool rapidly. When cool, using a sharp knife, mince the shrimp. Transfer to a medium bowl and season with the olive oil, lemon gel and salt.

TO SERVE

Using a funnel, fill a piping bag fitted with a small plain tip with the crème fraîche. Repeat to fill a separate piping bag with the lemon gel.

Set a 3-inch ring mould or round cutter on a plate and lightly pack the seasoned shrimp into the mould. Pipe dots of crème fraîche and lemon gel randomly over the shrimp. Sprinkle with the puffed quinoa. Place 4 pieces of candied lemon peel on top and decorate with the herbs in a pattern that resembles plants growing out of the puffed quinoa. Dust with lime leaf powder. Carefully remove the ring mould. Repeat to assemble the remaining 3 plates.

JB'S TIPS

This dish can be whipped together quickly if you have some good-quality peeled and cooked shrimp on hand.

Candied ginger or even the kind of pickled ginger that you have with sushi would be a great substitute for the candied lemon peel.

There are a million uses for the puffed quinoa. It's fantastic just popped in a salad or topping a piece of cooked fish. We add it to granola as well. You could easily use puffed rice or fried crispy shallots in its place.

The candied lemon peel is also extremely versatile. Add it and its syrup to fruit salad, cocktails or to add a sweet hint of lemon to marinated olives.

PICKLED WHITEFISH

with nasturtium purée and flowers

THIS SIMPLE ONTARIO WHITEFISH IS poached in a light pickle brine, similar to a Mediterranean escabeche. We start with a quick and easy pickling liquid—coriander seed, shallot and white wine vinegar—and just pour that over the fish to gently cook it. To offset the acidity, we roll the fish in crème fraîche (or sour cream) to give it a nice clean, creamy, fatty coating. In the dining room, we serve it on a purée of nasturtium greens garnished with nasturtium flowers from the garden.

If you can't find nasturtiums, watercress works fine here, or you could serve it with the Chilled Pea Soup (page 28). Similarly, bass, perch or small pickerel or trout would all be good Ontario Great Lakes substitutes for the whitefish in this preparation.

SERVES 4

Pickled Whitefish

1 cup white wine vinegar

1 cup Fish Stock (page 287) or water

¼ cup sliced shallots

2 tablespoons chopped fresh dill

2 tablespoons chopped fresh tarragon

1 tablespoon coriander seeds

1½ teaspoons kosher salt, divided

1 skinless whitefish fillet (1 pound/450 g)

¼ cup Crème Fraîche (page 281)

Nasturtium Purée

4 cups Fish Stock (page 287) or water

2 cups lightly packed nasturtium leaves

1 cup lightly packed baby spinach

Garnishes

12 whole nasturtium flowers, individual petals separated

Freshly ground grains of paradise or coriander seeds

FOR THE PICKLED WHITEFISH

To make the pickling liquid, place the white wine vinegar, fish stock, shallots, dill, tarragon, coriander seeds and 1 teaspoon of the salt in a small saucepan and bring to a boil over medium heat.

Place the whitefish in a small baking dish big enough to hold the fish flat and deep enough to hold enough of the pickling liquid to completely cover the fish. Pour the hot pickling liquid over the whitefish to cook it, and let it marinate while it cools. Keep the fish in the liquid until ready to serve.

When ready to serve, remove the whitefish from the pickling liquid, transfer it to paper towel and pat dry. Discard the pickling liquid.

Place the crème fraîche in a medium bowl. Break the whitefish into large flakes and season with the remaining ½ teaspoon salt. Gently roll the whitefish in the crème fraîche to coat evenly.

FOR THE NASTURTIUM PURÉE

Fill a medium bowl with ice water. In a medium saucepan, bring the fish stock to a boil over high heat. Drop the nasturtium leaves and spinach into the stock and cook for 20 seconds. Using a slotted spoon or spider, remove the blanched leaves from the stock and plunge them into the ice water, stirring to cool rapidly. (Do not discard the stock.) Once cooled, remove the nasturtium and spinach from the ice water and squeeze as much liquid as possible from the leaves. Place on a paper towel and squeeze again to absorb any additional moisture. Roughly chop the nasturtium and spinach and place in a high-speed blender. Blend until a thick purée is formed, adding fish stock as needed to adjust the consistency. Pass the purée through a fine-mesh sieve.

TO SERVE

Place a tablespoon of nasturtium purée in the centre of the plate. Arrange 3 pieces of the prepared whitefish on and around the purée. Layer nasturtium petals on the whitefish. Dust with grains of paradise or coriander seeds.

SALMON AND LEEKS
with ox-eye daisy, brown butter and hazelnuts

I REMEMBER AS A KID visiting my relatives in Victoria, British Columbia, and going salmon fishing with my dad and uncle and my little brother, Tim. The seals would come up and try to get the salmon off the line, and it seemed like we were very close in our little tin boat to extremely large killer whales. For a kid from Ontario it was quite the experience.

One thing I was excited about with this recipe was featuring the daisies from the garden, so we took the flower heads from the ox-eye daisies just as they were budding and pickled them, and also used the leaves as garnish. The flower heads serve in the caper role, but they're much more floral than regular capers. The leaves are quite juicy and pungent, almost like coriander, so it all works really nicely with the oily, rich and fatty flavour of the salmon.

SERVES 4

Leek-Top Purée

1 tablespoon unsalted butter

4 cups leeks (green part only) sliced crosswise into 1-inch rounds

¼ cup sliced shallots

1 teaspoon minced garlic

1 teaspoon kosher salt

2 cups whipping (35%) cream

Ox-Eye Daisy Caper Butter

1 cup unsalted butter

¼ cup roughly chopped ox-eye daisy capers

¼ cup roughly chopped toasted blanched hazelnuts

1 tablespoon sherry vinegar

2 tablespoons minced fresh chives

1 tablespoon chopped fresh dill

1 tablespoon chopped fresh flat-leaf parsley

Roasted Leeks

2 tablespoons vegetable oil

2 cups leeks (white part only) sliced crosswise into ¼-inch rounds

½ cup unsalted butter

½ cup Vegetable Stock (page 285) or Fish Stock (page 287)

½ teaspoon kosher salt

Salmon

4 skinless salmon fillets (5 ounces/140 g each), at room temperature

2 teaspoons kosher salt

1 tablespoon vegetable oil

2 tablespoons unsalted butter

½ fresh lemon

Garnish

1 cup ox-eye daisy leaves

FOR THE LEEK-TOP PURÉE

In a medium saucepan, melt the butter over medium-low heat. Add the leeks, shallots and garlic and gently cook without browning, stirring often, until tender, about 5 minutes. Season with the salt. Add the cream, bring to a simmer and cook for 5 minutes.

Strain the cream into another container, reserving it for adjusting the consistency of the purée. In a high-speed blender, purée the vegetables, adding enough of the cream in a slow, steady stream while blending to achieve a smooth, velvety consistency. Once processed, adjust the seasoning with salt, if required. Strain the purée through a fine-mesh sieve into a small saucepan. Warm gently and keep covered.

FOR THE OX-EYE DAISY CAPER BUTTER

In a wide heavy medium saucepan, melt the butter over medium-low heat. As it melts, continuously swirl the butter around the pan. The milk solids will separate from the butterfat and begin to colour. The solids will go from brown to burnt quickly, so watch closely. Keep swirling the butter over the heat until it is light brown in colour and starts to smell nutty. Strain the brown butter through a fine-mesh sieve or several layers of cheesecloth into a small saucepan.

RECIPE CONTINUES . . .

Discard the milk solids. Stir in the ox-eye daisy capers, hazelnuts and sherry vinegar. Keep warm until ready to serve.

Just before serving, stir in the chives, dill and parsley.

FOR THE ROASTED LEEKS

In a medium frying pan, heat the vegetable oil over medium-high heat. Carefully add the leeks so the rounds don't break up and roast, adjusting the heat accordingly, until golden brown on the bottom, about 2 minutes. Turn the leeks, add the butter and continue to cook until the butter is foaming and starting to brown, about 1 minute. Add the vegetable stock, bring to a simmer and allow the leeks to glaze until tender. Remove from the heat, season with the salt and keep warm.

FOR THE SALMON

Season the salmon with the salt on both sides. In a medium frying pan, heat the vegetable oil over medium-high heat. Carefully lay the salmon in the pan and reduce the heat to medium. Cook the salmon on the one side for 2 minutes. Add the butter and allow it to melt and start foaming. Baste the salmon with the hot butter to just barely cook through the top side of the fish. This should take no longer than 1 minute. Using a fish spatula, remove the salmon from the pan and place on paper towel, then squeeze the lemon juice over the salmon to finish.

TO SERVE

Place the salmon on warmed plates or in coupe bowls. Spoon a mound of leek-top purée beside the salmon. Scatter pieces of the roasted leeks around the salmon. Spoon the daisy caper butter over the fish. Garnish with the daisy leaves.

JB'S TIP

If you don't have access to ox-eye daisy capers, this recipe works well with regular salted or brined capers, and the daisy leaves can be easily replaced with baby spinach, arugula or young dandelion.

HALIBUT

with new-season onions and white wine butter sauce

HERE WE'RE FOCUSING ON SHADES of white, starting out with the beautiful, sustainably sourced halibut from our fisher friends at Organic Ocean in Vancouver, British Columbia. To complement that gorgeous fish, we bring in different elements of allium along with sweet baby turnips. In some ways, though, this recipe isn't even about the halibut. The fish is there to add some substance, but the real character is derived from the charred wild garlic that brings a touch of smokiness, as well as the onion flowers with their sweet garlic chive intensity, along with the tender, juicy turnips. Everything is held together with a nice buttery sauce so that you end up with this delicate, beautifully balanced, gorgeously monochromatic dish of springtime alliums.

SERVES 4

White Wine Butter Sauce

½ cup sliced shallots

1 teaspoon minced garlic

¼ cup loosely packed fresh tarragon leaves

1 fresh bay leaf

½ teaspoon black peppercorns

⅔ cup dry white wine

⅓ cup white wine vinegar

¼ cup Fish Stock (page 287), Vegetable Stock (page 285) or Chicken Stock (page 286)

1 cup unsalted butter cut into ½-inch dice

1 teaspoon fresh lemon juice

½ teaspoon kosher salt

Baby Turnips

8 baby white turnips

1 sprig fresh thyme

2 cups Vegetable Stock (page 285)

¼ cup Tio Pepe or other dry sherry

2 tablespoons kosher salt

Halibut

1 tablespoon unsalted butter

½ tablespoon sliced shallot

¼ cup dry vermouth

¼ cup Fish Stock (page 287)

4 skinless centre-cut halibut fillets (5 ounces/140 g each)

1 tablespoon kosher salt

½ cup sliced spring onions

Wild Garlic

8 wild garlic plants

1 tablespoon Garlic Confit oil (page 282)

1 teaspoon kosher salt

Garnish

Spring onion or chive flowers

FOR THE WHITE WINE BUTTER SAUCE

Place the shallots, garlic, tarragon, bay leaf and black peppercorns in a small saucepan. Add the white wine, white wine vinegar and fish stock and bring to a boil over medium-high heat. When the liquid is boiling, reduce the heat to low and gently simmer until the liquid is reduced to about ¼ cup and has the consistency of a thick sauce or glaze. Whisk in the butter, a cube at a time, until all the butter has melted and an emulsified sauce has formed. Be careful not to let the sauce simmer. Season with the lemon juice and salt. Pour the sauce through a fine-mesh sieve into a small saucepan, cover and keep in a warm place until ready to use.

FOR THE BABY TURNIPS

In a small saucepan, combine the turnips, thyme, vegetable stock, sherry and salt. Bring to a rolling simmer over medium-high heat, then reduce the heat to a low simmer and cook until the turnips are just fork-tender, 12 to 15 minutes. Cooking time may vary depending on the size of the turnips. Remove from the heat and hold in the cooking liquid until ready to serve. Just before serving, gently warm if needed.

RECIPE CONTINUES . . .

FOR THE HALIBUT

Preheat the oven to 350°F (180°C).

In a large frying pan with a tight-fitting lid or a casserole dish large enough to hold the fillets in one layer without touching, gently cook the shallots in the butter over low heat, stirring occasionally, until tender, about 4 minutes. Increase the heat to medium, add the vermouth and cook until reduced by half. Add the fish stock and bring to a simmer.

Season the halibut with the salt and cover each piece with a layer of sliced spring onions. Place the fillets in the pan, ensuring that they are not touching, and cover with the lid. Transfer to the oven and bake for 6 to 8 minutes or until just cooked through. Cooking time may vary depending on the thickness of the fish. When cooked, spoon some of the liquid in the pan over the fish.

FOR THE WILD GARLIC

Brush the wild garlic with the garlic confit oil and season with the salt. Heat a large frying pan over high heat until smoking. Add the wild garlic and cook for 30 seconds per side to lightly char and wilt.

TO SERVE

Place the halibut on warm plates. Arrange the warm baby turnips on the fish. Spoon the white wine butter sauce over the top and garnish with spring onion flowers and the charred wild garlic.

JB'S TIP

There are many varieties of onion and leek, and you could use any here. Wild garlic grows like a weed on the property, so we always have it. Wild leek, spring baby leek and spring onion will all work in place of the wild garlic. You may just need to adjust cooking times.

CURED WILD SALMON

with bronze fennel, lemon verbena, anise hyssop and cucumber juice

CURING IS A METHOD OF fish preparation I really love, because the flesh comes out so fresh and light while retaining the beautiful inherent flavour of the fish. I like to use this technique throughout the year and just change up the herbs, spices and garnishes as they evolve with the seasons—tarragon in spring, coriander flowers in summer, whole pine cones and balsam fir or juniper in winter. This is a very versatile recipe and can be served as an elegant canapé, a light appetizer or a main course.

My favourite fish to use for this dish is wild Pacific coho, but it will work with any species of salmon as well as tuna, trout and halibut. Curing times will vary depending on the thickness of the fillet.

SERVES 8

Cured Salmon

3 cups sugar

2 cups kosher salt

1 lemongrass stalk, tough outer leaves and stems discarded, roughly chopped

1 tablespoon lemon zest

1 tablespoon orange zest

½ cup lightly packed fresh dill

1 cup chopped fennel stems and fronds

2 cups lightly packed chopped fresh cilantro leaves, stems and roots

12 fresh lemon verbena leaves

2 fresh lime leaves

12 star anise

3 tablespoons coriander seeds

1 teaspoon fennel seeds

½ teaspoon white peppercorns

1 skinless wild salmon fillet (2 pounds/900 g)

Fennel Oil

¼ cup lightly packed fresh basil leaves

¼ cup lightly packed fresh fennel fronds

¼ cup lightly packed fresh mint leaves

¼ cup lightly packed fresh flat-leaf parsley

¼ cup lightly packed fresh tarragon leaves

1 cup vegetable oil

Poached Fennel

1 fennel bulb

4 star anise

1½ teaspoons kosher salt, divided

1 teaspoon extra-virgin olive oil

Cucumber Juice (makes extra)

4 cups cucumber juice (from about 4 English cucumbers)

½ cup lightly packed chopped fresh mint leaves and stems

½ cup lightly packed chopped fresh dill fronds and stems

½ cup lightly packed chopped fennel fronds and stems

2 lemongrass stalks, tough outer leaves and stems discarded, chopped

¾ cup fresh lemon juice

¾ cup Lemongrass Syrup (page 284)

Garnishes

Lemon Gel (page 284)

English cucumber (for the balls)

Salmon roe

Bronze fennel fronds and flowers

Wood sorrel

Lemon verbena

Lemon balm

Anise hyssop

Cilantro

Dill

FOR THE CURED SALMON

In a large bowl, combine the sugar and salt. In a food processor, combine the lemongrass, lemon and orange zest, dill, fennel, cilantro, lemon verbena, lime leaves, star anise, coriander seeds, fennel seeds and white peppercorns. Pulse to roughly chop. Add the chopped mixture to the bowl of sugar and salt and stir well.

Spread one-third of the cure mixture in a baking sheet or casserole dish large enough to hold the salmon flat. Lay the salmon on the cure mixture, ensuring that all the flesh is in contact with the cure. Pour the remaining mixture over the fish to cover it completely. Press gently to firmly pack the mixture around the fish. Cover the dish

RECIPE CONTINUES . . .

with plastic wrap and place in the refrigerator to cure for 24 hours.

Remove the salmon from the cure mixture and rinse gently under cold running water. Discard the cure mixture. Pat the salmon dry with paper towel. Slice the fillet lengthwise down the centre into 2 halves. Wrap each half into a tube, tightly in plastic wrap to smooth the exterior of the cured salmon, twisting the ends to resemble a sausage shape. Place in the refrigerator until ready to serve.

When ready to serve, with the plastic wrap still on to help maintain the shape of the salmon, slice each half of the salmon crosswise into sixteen 2-ounce (57 g) slices. Remove the plastic wrap.

FOR THE FENNEL OIL

Fill a medium bowl with ice water. In a small saucepan of boiling salted water, blanch the basil, fennel fronds, mint, parsley and tarragon for 20 seconds. Drain the blanched herbs and transfer to the ice water to stop the cooking. When cooled, squeeze out excess water so the blanched herbs are as dry as possible. In a high-speed blender, purée the blanched herbs with the vegetable oil until you've achieved a smooth green purée, about 3 minutes. Pour the purée into a medium jar and store, covered, in the refrigerator for 2 hours.

Strain the oil through a fine-mesh sieve or several layers of cheesecloth. You will be left with a bright green herb-flavoured oil. The fennel oil can be made the day before and stored in the refrigerator in a mason jar or another small sealed container.

FOR THE POACHED FENNEL

Pull off and discard the outer layer of the fennel bulb to remove any damaged or blemished spots. Cut the fennel lengthwise into ¼-inch-thick slices.

Fill a medium bowl with ice and water. In a small saucepan, cook the fennel slices in boiling water with the star anise and 1 teaspoon of the salt until tender, about 8 minutes. Drain the fennel and plunge it into the ice water to stop the cooking. When cooled, drain the fennel again, pat dry, remove the core and cut into bite-size pieces. Store in a covered container in the refrigerator until ready to use.

FOR THE CUCUMBER JUICE

In a high-speed blender, combine the cucumber juice, mint, dill, chopped fennel and lemongrass. Blend until smooth. Stir in the lemon juice and lemongrass syrup. Strain the juice through a fine-mesh sieve into a juice jug and cover with plastic wrap. Refrigerate until ready to use. This juice should be made on the day you are serving the dish to ensure it has fresh and vibrant colour and flavour. (This recipe makes more than required; enjoy on its own for a refreshing summer sip or add a splash of sparkling wine for a garden-inspired cocktail.)

TO SERVE

Place 2 slices of salmon in a shallow bowl or coupe plate. Dot the lemon gel on and around the salmon. Peel the cucumber and, using a small melon baller (½ inch in diameter), scoop out 5 cucumber balls per serving. Season the poached fennel and cucumber balls with the olive oil and remaining ½ teaspoon salt. Decorate the salmon with the fennel, cucumber balls, salmon roe and all the citrus- and anise-flavoured garden herbs and flowers. Pour in a few tablespoons of the cucumber juice and finish by drizzling the fennel oil around the fish. Repeat to assemble the remaining bowls.

JB'S TIP

Most important for this dish is simply using the freshest sustainably sourced fish you can find. The longer you leave the fillet in the cure, the more it will take on the flavour of the herbs and spices and the firmer it will become. I suggest 24 hours, but even at 16 hours you'll still end up with a delicious finished dish. Play with the curing times to find your preference.

SPRING LAMB TARTARE
with black radish, wild leek and lamb fat aïoli

WHEN I FIRST ARRIVED AT Langdon Hall, I'll always remember the owners, Bill and Mary, telling me to, "Be yourself. Be inspired by the property, and create food that has a taste and a sense of this place and don't feel like you have to cook anything that chefs in Toronto, or anywhere else for that matter, are cooking."

That always stuck with me. And when it came down to creating this dish, I really wanted to do a tartare—I love steak tartare, and anywhere I've ever worked there's been steak tartare on the menu—but I wondered, how could I do something different that met that final requirement? This is what I came up with. It is nothing like a traditional tartare. It doesn't have all the usual ingredients in it. Instead, what I've done is introduce elements of the property and the spring season, so I have some black radish, chive flowers and wild leeks, ingredients that speak to spring that are also really great in combination with lamb.

SERVES 4

Wild Leek Powder

4 cups loosely packed wild leek (ramp) leaves

Pickled Wild Leeks

1 cup wild leek (ramp) bulbs

1 cup white wine vinegar

¼ cup water

⅔ cup sugar

1 teaspoon coriander seeds

½ teaspoon black peppercorns

½ teaspoon fresh thyme leaves

¼ teaspoon kosher salt

Roasted Lamb Fat

Lamb bones and trimmings removed from the rack (see lamb tartare at right)

½ tablespoon vegetable oil

½ cup sliced shallots

¼ cup sliced garlic cloves

½ tablespoon fresh rosemary leaves

½ cup pre-rendered lamb fat or all the fat cap and trimmings from the rack

Lamb Fat Aïoli

1 cup Mayonnaise (page 280), at room temperature

1 teaspoon Dijon mustard

1 teaspoon fresh lemon juice

¼ cup roasted lamb fat (recipe at left), at room temperature

Kosher salt, if needed

Lamb Vinaigrette

¼ cup Lamb Jus (page 51), warm

2 tablespoons roasted lamb fat (recipe at left), warm

1 teaspoon sherry vinegar

½ teaspoon kosher salt

½ teaspoon freshly ground black pepper

Lamb Tartare

1 cleaned rack of lamb (1¾ pounds/790 g), fat and bones removed and reserved for the roasted lamb fat

½ cup minced shallots

2½ tablespoons rinsed and minced capers

1½ tablespoons Pickled Mustard Seeds (page 283)

1 tablespoon chopped fresh chives

2 teaspoons chopped fresh rosemary

½ tablespoon Dijon mustard

1½ tablespoons Lamb Jus (page 51), warm

2 teaspoons roasted lamb fat (recipe at left), warm

1 teaspoon kosher salt

1 teaspoon freshly ground black pepper

Garnishes

2 or 3 black radishes

1 teaspoon extra-virgin olive oil

Pinch of kosher salt

Chive flowers

RECIPE CONTINUES . . .

FOR THE WILD LEEK POWDER

Set a dehydrator to 120°F (50°C).

Wash the leek leaves under cold running water and dry well on paper towel. Lay the wild leek leaves on the dehydrator tray or on a rack on a baking sheet. Do not overlap the leaves. Dehydrate for 4 hours or until the leaves are completely dry and brittle. Transfer to a high-speed blender or spice grinder and process to a fine powder. Pass the powder through a fine-mesh sieve and store in an airtight container in a dry area for up to 3 days.

FOR THE PICKLED WILD LEEKS

In a small saucepan, combine the wild leek bulbs, white wine vinegar, water, sugar, coriander seeds, black peppercorns, thyme and salt. Bring to a simmer over medium heat and simmer for 2 minutes. Transfer the leeks and the pickling liquid to a 2-cup mason jar. Allow to cool, seal the jar and keep in the refrigerator for at least 48 hours before using.

FOR THE ROASTED LAMB FAT

Preheat the oven to 350°F (180°C).

Place the lamb bones in an ovenproof frying pan or small baking sheet. Roast for 10 minutes or until golden brown and caramelized.

In a small saucepan, heat the vegetable oil over medium heat. Add the reserved lamb trimmings and fry, stirring occasionally, until lightly caramelized. Reduce the heat to low and add the shallots, garlic and rosemary. Cook for 2 minutes, stirring occasionally, until the vegetables are tender and starting to colour. Add the roasted lamb bones and the lamb fat. Increase the heat to medium-low and allow the fat to melt. Continue to gently cook just under a simmer for 10 minutes, until the fat is rendered and has taken on the flavour of the lamb trimmings, shallots, garlic and rosemary. Strain the fat through a fine-mesh sieve or coffee filter into a small bowl. Discard the solids. Reserve ¼ cup of the lamb fat and let cool to room temperature for the lamb fat aïoli. Keep the remaining lamb fat warm.

FOR THE LAMB FAT AÏOLI

In a small bowl, whisk together the mayonnaise, mustard, lemon juice and roasted lamb fat. Season with salt, if needed.

FOR THE LAMB VINAIGRETTE

In a small bowl, whisk together the warm lamb jus, warm roasted lamb fat, sherry vinegar, salt and pepper until well combined. Keep in a warm area of the kitchen.

FOR THE LAMB TARTARE

Finely dice the lamb and place it in a medium bowl. Add the shallots, capers, pickled mustard seeds, chives, rosemary, mustard, warm lamb jus, warm roasted lamb fat, salt and pepper. Mix with a rubber spatula or a large spoon until all the ingredients are well incorporated. Taste and adjust the seasoning, if needed.

TO SERVE

Shave the black radish into thin rounds with a sharp knife or mandoline, 5 to 6 slices per portion. Using a 1-inch ring cutter, punch a disc out of the centre of each radish slice. Place them in a small bowl and season with the olive oil and salt. Slice the pickled wild leeks into thin rounds, 7 to 8 slices per portion.

Divide the lamb into 4 equal portions and spoon a portion onto each plate. Garnish with enough black radish rounds to cover the lamb. Spoon 1 teaspoon of the lamb fat aïoli onto each plate next to the tartare.

Decorate the radishes with the chive flowers and the pickled wild leeks. Dust the plate with the wild leek powder. Finish with a tablespoon of the lamb vinaigrette.

JB'S TIPS

Always be sure to use fresh meat for a tartare preparation. It is a good idea to let the butcher know what you're planning so they can help you select the best product they have to offer.

At the restaurant, we forage for wild leeks in the spring and preserve them for year-round use. One thing to remember is that any wild product, especially the popular ones, should be harvested with respect and purpose. We harvest with the rule that for every one leek we harvest, we leave ten behind: five to feed wildlife, five to go to seed.

You can use regular salted or brined capers and pickled onions instead of the pickled wild leeks. In place of the black radish, you can use valentine, daikon or breakfast radish.

LAMB AND FRESH TEA
with mint, chamomile and English peas

HERE WE BRING TOGETHER ALL of the things that are perfect with lamb and also bring in something that's unexpected, but really tasty. When I started at Langdon Hall there were a lot of fresh ingredients I had never worked with before, including chamomile. We found a huge patch of the stuff in the garden and felt that we needed to do something with it beyond just making tea. When I rubbed some between my fingers, inhaling its aroma, the first thing that popped into my mind was lamb. I went back to the kitchen right away and made an interesting and delicious lamb stock flavoured with chamomile. From that time on, I've always done some kind of lamb-and-chamomile creation in the springtime. Chamomile works well with lamb for the same reason mint and rosemary do. Lamb has a fairly strong, musky flavour, and something that's fresh and floral complements the meat beautifully.

SERVES 4

Lamb Jus

Lamb bones and trimmings removed from the lamb racks (see lamb at right)

1 teaspoon vegetable oil

1 cup sliced shallots

¼ cup sliced garlic

s½ tablespoon fresh rosemary leaves

½ tablespoon fresh thyme leaves

1 fresh bay leaf

½ teaspoon kosher salt

½ cup roughly chopped ripe tomato

½ cup dry white wine, divided

4 cups Veal Jus (page 289)

¼ cup loosely packed chamomile leaves and flowers

English Pea Purée

6 cups Vegetable Stock (page 285)

1 teaspoon kosher salt

2 cups shucked fresh peas

Lamb

2 cleaned racks of lamb (1½ pounds/675 g each), trim and bones removed and reserved for the lamb jus

1 teaspoon kosher salt

1 teaspoon freshly cracked black peppercorns

2 tablespoons vegetable oil

¼ cup unsalted butter

3 garlic cloves, crushed

¼ cup loosely packed fresh chamomile leaves and flowers

1 tablespoon fresh thyme leaves

1 teaspoon fresh rosemary leaves

Pinch of flaky sea salt

Fresh Peas

¾ cup Vegetable Stock (page 285)

1 cup shucked fresh peas

1 tablespoon unsalted butter

½ teaspoon kosher salt

Garnishes

Wild mint

Chamomile leaves and flowers

Wild pea tendrils

FOR THE LAMB JUS

Preheat the oven to 350°F (180°C).

Spread the lamb bones in a medium roasting pan. Roast, stirring occasionally, for 15 minutes or until golden brown and well caramelized.

In a medium saucepan, heat the vegetable oil over medium heat. Add the reserved lamb trimmings and fry, stirring occasionally, until lightly caramelized. Reduce the heat to low and add the shallots, garlic, rosemary, thyme, bay leaf and salt. Cook, stirring occasionally, until the vegetables are tender and starting to caramelize, 3 minutes. Add the roasted lamb bones and the tomato and cook for another 3 minutes. Pour ¼ cup of the white wine into the roasting pan and with a wooden spoon or rubber spatula scrape all the roasted bits off the bottom of the pan. Add this to the saucepan with the lamb trimmings, then add the remaining ¼ cup white wine. Reduce to almost dry. Add the veal jus and chamomile. Bring to a simmer, then reduce the heat to medium-low and gently cook for 10 minutes or until the jus is well flavoured with the lamb and chamomile. Strain through a fine-mesh sieve into a small saucepan, cover and keep warm. Discard the bones and vegetables.

RECIPE CONTINUES . . .

FOR THE ENGLISH PEA PURÉE

Fill a medium bowl with ice water. In a medium saucepan, bring the vegetable stock and the salt to a boil. Add the peas and blanch for 1½ minutes. Strain the peas, reserving the stock, and plunge them into the ice water to cool rapidly. This will stop the cooking and preserve their bright green colour. When the peas are cool, remove from the ice water and transfer to a high-speed blender. Purée the peas, adding just enough vegetable stock in a slow, steady stream while blending to achieve a smooth, velvety consistency. When processed, adjust the seasoning with salt, if required. Strain through a fine-mesh sieve into a small saucepan. Warm gently before serving.

FOR THE LAMB

Preheat the oven to 350°F (180°C).

Season the lamb with salt and pepper. Heat the vegetable oil in a large cast-iron skillet or ovenproof frying pan over high heat. Place the lamb in the pan and sear the meat on all sides until golden brown, about 30 seconds per side. Add the butter, crushed garlic, chamomile, thyme and rosemary and baste the lamb with the floral garlic butter for another minute. Transfer the pan to the oven and roast for 2 minutes. Turn over the meat, baste with the butter and aromatics again, and roast for an additional 2 minutes. Remove the lamb from the pan, place on a wire rack over a plate or small baking sheet, and let the meat rest for 8 minutes.

FOR THE FRESH PEAS

In a small saucepan, bring the vegetable stock to a simmer over medium-high heat. Add the peas, butter and salt and cook for 1 to 2 minutes, until the peas are cooked through and tender. Remove from the heat.

TO SERVE

Slice the rested lamb and arrange on warm plates. Sprinkle the lamb with the flaky sea salt. Add the pea purée and a mound of peas to each plate, and finish with wild mint, chamomile, pea tendrils and some lamb jus.

BEEF SHORT RIB AND CAVIAR
with toasted brioche and spring onion flowers

YOU COULD COMPARE THIS TO a surf and turf, but instead of the traditional lobster or scampi with a piece of beef, we crank up the luxurious factor with caviar. I especially love how the butteriness and pop of the caviar bring texture while adding that salty ocean flavour to the beef. When I first made this, it was pretty clear right away that it was a winning combination, but I still knew I could make it better. That's when the idea of searing and adding the trimmed beef fat came in. Then we discussed how much caviar there should be. Was it too much and overwhelming or did its flavour get lost? Ultimately, brioche fried in butter with braised short rib and caviar makes an excellent snack. It's made even better if you have a little fresh truffle lying around to grate over the top.

SERVES 4

Beef Short Rib
1 boneless Wagyu beef short rib
(6 ounces/170 g)
½ tablespoon kosher salt
½ tablespoon freshly cracked black
peppercorns
1 tablespoon vegetable oil
3 tablespoons unsalted butter

½ tablespoon fresh thyme leaves
1 garlic clove

Brioche Batons
Two ½-inch-thick slices of brioche
¼ cup unsalted butter, softened
½ teaspoon kosher salt

Garnishes
Caviar
Snipped fresh chive tips
Chive or fresh spring onion flowers

FOR THE BEEF SHORT RIB
Set a sous vide water bath to 149°F (65°C).

Trim the short rib of any excess exterior fat and connective tissue. Season the short rib and the trimmings with salt and pepper. In a large cast-iron skillet or frying pan, heat the vegetable oil over high heat. Sear the beef on all sides until golden brown, 1 to 2 minutes per side. Remove the beef from the pan and rest on a small baking sheet. Add the beef trimmings to the pan and fry until golden brown, about 3 minutes.

Transfer the caramelized trimmings, rendered cooking fat and the short rib to a sous vide bag. Vacuum-seal on full pressure. Add the beef to the water bath, reduce the temperature to 133°F (56°C) and cook for 48 hours. (If not using immediately, chill in an ice bath and store in the refrigerator until ready to serve or for up to 1 week.)

FOR THE BRIOCHE BATONS
Remove the crust and cut four 2-inch × ½-inch × ½-inch rectangles from the brioche slices. In a medium frying pan over medium heat, melt the butter until frothing. Fry the brioche in the butter until golden brown, turning to fry evenly on all sides, about 30 seconds per side. Season with a few grains of salt and transfer to paper towel to absorb excess butter.

FINISH THE BEEF SHORT RIB
Remove the beef from the sous vide bag and dry with paper towel. Reserve the rendered cooking liquid. Trim the beef into 1-inch-thick slices. Season the short rib with salt and pepper. In a medium frying pan over medium-high heat, melt the butter. Add the short rib, the reserved rendered cooking liquid, the thyme and garlic and cook, basting constantly, until the beef is golden brown on all sides, about 30 seconds per side. Transfer to a cutting board and slice the beef ¼ inch thick against the grain and trim the edges to the size of the brioche batons to cover the top perfectly. Lay each slice on top of the fried brioche, brush some of the butter from the frying pan onto the beef, and spoon a nice helping of caviar to cover. Garnish with chive tips and flowers or spring onion flowers.

WHITE ASPARAGUS

with wild leek pickles, green elderberry capers and sweet woodruff

THE ARRIVAL OF THE WHITE asparagus is always a big deal in the kitchen. It is a true celebration of the coming season. White asparagus is available for such a short time and is so special that most chefs jump on it as soon as it pops through the earth. The most common ways to serve white asparagus are cold, simply poached, accompanied by mayonnaise, a simple vinaigrette and a fresh herb salad or warm with hollandaise and a poached egg on top. With this dish, I wanted to take a slightly different approach and find a way to make something new and exciting that spoke to the terroir. I start by peeling off all the fibrous peel so the flesh of the vegetable is delicate when cooked, then I poach the spears slowly in salted water until they are so soft that they melt in your mouth. For garnish, I add green elderberry capers and wild leek pickles to bring in a little acidity without overpowering the delicate flavour of the asparagus. Finally, I introduce an aromatic floral component with a taste of wild sweet woodruff leaves and flowers from the Langdon Hall property.

SERVES 4

Green Elderberry Capers
1 cup green elderberries
1 cup water
1 teaspoon kosher salt

Wild Leek Pickles
1 cup wild leek (ramp) bulbs

1 cup white wine vinegar
¼ cup water
⅔ cup sugar
1 teaspoon coriander seeds
½ teaspoon black peppercorns
½ teaspoon fresh thyme leaves
¼ teaspoon kosher salt

Poached White Asparagus
12 jumbo white asparagus spears

Garnish
Woodruff leaves and flowers

FOR THE GREEN ELDERBERRY CAPERS
Place the green elderberries in a 2-cup mason jar. In a small bowl, stir the water and salt until the salt is dissolved. Pour the salt water over the elderberries and seal the jar with the lid. Ferment at just above room temperature, between 73 and 82°F (23 and 28°C), for 14 days. During the first 10 days, open the jar once a day to release the carbon dioxide produced by the bacteria that help along the fermentation process. After the first week the brine will start to turn cloudy, which is a good sign, and the pickle flavour will start to develop. After 14 days the capers will start to taste good. At this time they can be stored in the refrigerator. The cooler temperature will slow the fermentation and the berries will be ready to eat. They are best consumed within 1 month. They will last much longer, but will become mushy and lose their lustre over time.

FOR THE WILD LEEK PICKLES
In a small saucepan, combine the wild leek bulbs, white wine vinegar, water, sugar, coriander seeds, black peppercorns, thyme and salt. Bring to a simmer over medium heat and simmer for 2 minutes. Transfer the leeks and the pickling liquid to a 2-cup mason jar. Allow to cool, seal the jar and keep in the refrigerator for at least 48 hours before using.

FOR THE WHITE ASPARAGUS
Trim off the woody ends of the asparagus with a paring knife. Using a vegetable peeler, peel the asparagus completely from the base of the tip to the bottom of the spear.

Fill a medium bowl with ice water. Bring a medium saucepan of salted water to a boil over high heat. When the water is boiling, reduce the heat to medium-low. Gently drop the prepared asparagus into the saucepan and simmer for 7 minutes or until a paring knife slides into the asparagus stem with no resistance. Using a slotted spoon or tongs, gently remove the cooked asparagus from the saucepan and plunge the spears into the ice water to cool rapidly. Once cool, remove from the ice water and dry on paper towel.

TO SERVE
Slice the cooked white asparagus into rounds ½ to 1 inch long. Slice the wild leek pickles into 1-inch-long slivers. Arrange the asparagus rounds on the plates in a tight cluster. Spoon a small amount of the green elderberry capers and wild leek pickles into a small bowl with some of the pickling juice. Garnish the asparagus with the capers and pickles and a little of the pickling juice. Garnish with the woodruff leaves and flowers.

JB'S TIPS
If you do not have access to wild leeks, I suggest using pickled shallots or pearl onions. Regular salted or brined capers can be used in place of elderberry capers. If you can't find woodruff, a mix of delicate fine herbs such as chervil, tarragon, dill and chives will work just as well.

For a little added crunch, I like to add crushed toasted hazelnuts on this dish.

GREEN ASPARAGUS
with squid ink aïoli and Gem marigold

THIS DISH WAS DEVISED FOR our World Oceans Day menu. That whole tasting menu was designed to feature lesser known ocean species as well as lesser known ocean and fresh water lake ingredients. I first enjoyed this pairing prepared by chef David Kinch at Manresa in Los Gatos, California and loved the combination of the ocean flavour of squid ink with the asparagus. That was where the inspiration for the squid ink aïoli came from. At the same time, we had beautiful lemon verbena leaves in the garden, so we made a jam by infusing all the citrus-flavoured plants from the greenhouse and garden: the lemon verbena along with lemongrass, geranium, lemon balm and baby Gem marigold. The asparagus itself is just gently glazed in its own juice until tender. That technique goes back to the whole philosophy of Langdon Hall cuisine. If we just boiled the asparagus in water it would still be good, but we figured, why not take half the spears and juice them and then cook the remaining asparagus in its own juice? As a bonus, we discovered that the poaching liquid naturally reduces as it cooks, intensifying the flavour and raising the finished dish to a whole different level.

SERVES 4

Squid Ink Aïoli
1 cup Aïoli (page 281)
2 teaspoons squid ink

Glazed Asparagus
8 jumbo green asparagus spears, divided
1 tablespoon unsalted butter

Garnishes
Lemon Gel (page 284)
Tiny lemon verbena leaves
Gem marigold leaves and flowers

FOR THE SQUID INK AÏOLI
In a small bowl, whisk together the aïoli and squid ink. Transfer to a covered container and store in the refrigerator for up to 3 days.

FOR THE GLAZED ASPARAGUS
Using a juicer, juice 4 of the asparagus spears. Strain the juice through a fine-mesh sieve into a cup or small bowl and reserve.

Fill a medium bowl with ice water. Bring a medium saucepan of salted water to a boil. Trim the 4 remaining asparagus spears into 5-inch lengths. Using a vegetable peeler, carefully peel the fibrous bottom quarter of the asparagus. Place the prepared asparagus in the boiling water and cook for 1½ minutes. Using a slotted spoon or tongs, gently remove the blanched asparagus from the water and plunge them into the ice water. This will stop the cooking and preserve their bright green colour. When cool, remove from the ice water and dry on paper towel.

Melt the butter in a medium sauté pan over medium heat. Add the blanched asparagus spears and 2 tablespoons of the reserved asparagus juice. Bring to a boil and reduce to a glaze while basting the asparagus, 1 to 2 minutes. Using tongs, gently transfer the asparagus to paper towel to drain.

TO SERVE
Place the asparagus on plates. Garnish the spears with dots of the lemon gel. Top the asparagus and lemon gel with verbena leaves and marigold leaves and flowers. Spoon 1 teaspoon of the squid ink aïoli onto each plate.

SWEET PEA TART
with peas from the garden and buckwheat

SMALL TARTS ARE IDEAL FOR a canapé, as a light appetizer or as a nice lunch along with a soup or salad. They also make a great vehicle for celebrating the seasons. For this pea tart, we start by filling the shell with a spoonful of crème fraîche that we top with a thick pea purée and finish with lightly minted fresh peas that are briefly but perfectly cooked and then refreshed in ice water so they stay bright and green and pop with juicy green springtime flavour. It's a taste of the new season in one mouthful.

SERVES 4

Buckwheat Tart Shells
1 cup buckwheat flour

1 cup all-purpose flour

2 teaspoons sugar

¼ teaspoon kosher salt

1 cup chilled unsalted butter, cubed

2 large egg whites

2 teaspoons water, if needed

Mint Oil
1 cup lightly packed fresh mint leaves

½ cup vegetable oil

Fresh Spring Peas
1 cup shucked fresh peas

½ tablespoon mint oil (recipe above)

¼ teaspoon kosher salt

Garnishes
2 tablespoons Crème Fraîche (page 281)

2 tablespoons English Pea Purée (page 51)

Fresh mint leaves

Pea flowers

Pea tendrils

Flaky sea salt

FOR THE BUCKWHEAT TART SHELLS

In the bowl of a stand mixer fitted with the paddle attachment, mix together the buckwheat flour, all-purpose flour, sugar and salt. On low speed, add the chilled butter, a few pieces at a time, until the mixture resembles crumbly coarse sand with a few pea-sized pieces of butter still visible. Add the egg whites and continue to mix on low speed just until the dough forms a ball that holds together. Add the water if necessary to bring the dough together. Transfer the dough onto a work surface and flatten and shape it into a ½-inch-thick disc. Wrap in plastic wrap and chill for at least 2 hours in the refrigerator.

On a lightly floured surface, roll the dough out to ¹⁄₁₆-inch thickness. Cut out 4 circles with a 5-inch round cutter and fit each circle into a 3-inch tart pan with removable bottom, gently pressing it into the corners and up the sides. Trim the dough flush with the top of the pans. Chill the shells for 30 minutes before baking.

Preheat the oven to 350°F (180°C).

Arrange the tart pans on a small baking sheet. Prick the base of the pastry with a fork. Line each pan with parchment paper and fill with baking beans or rice. Blind bake the shells for 10 minutes, until the dough is baked and set. Remove the parchment and beans and continue to bake for another 5 minutes or until the dough is cooked through on the bottom and golden brown. Transfer to a rack and allow to cool completely. Remove the shells from the tart pans before serving.

FOR THE MINT OIL

Fill a medium bowl with ice water. Bring a medium saucepan of salted water to a boil. Blanch the mint in the pot of boiling water for 10 seconds. Drain the mint and plunge it into the ice water. When cool, drain the mint and squeeze out any excess water. In a blender, blend the mint and vegetable oil for 2 minutes. Strain through a fine-mesh sieve, several layers of cheesecloth or a coffee filter into a mason jar. Allow to cool, seal the jar with the lid and keep in the refrigerator until ready to use.

RECIPE CONTINUES . . .

FOR THE FRESH SPRING PEAS

Fill a medium bowl with ice water. Bring a medium saucepan of salted water to a boil. Add the peas and blanch for 1 minute. Drain the peas and add them to the ice water to cool rapidly. This will stop the cooking and preserve their bright green colour. When cool, drain and dry on paper towel.

In a small bowl, combine the blanched peas, the mint oil and the salt. Gently mix until the peas are coated with the oil.

TO SERVE

Spoon ½ tablespoon of crème fraîche into each tart shell and smooth it into a level puddle. Repeat with the pea purée. Carefully spoon the seasoned peas into the tart shell, filling it to the edge. Garnish the rim with mint, pea flowers and pea tendrils. Sprinkle with some flaky sea salt.

JB'S TIP

This recipe is very versatile and works with just about any ripe, seasonal vegetable: try peeled cherry tomatoes, grilled zucchini or confit eggplant. If you want to take it in a sweet direction, you could simply replace the peas with fresh berries.

PINK RHUBARB

with goat cheese mousse, yogurt meringue, sweet cicely and rose petal powder

DEPENDING ON HOW MUCH SUGAR you use in this recipe, it could end up being a dessert or a savoury appetizer. In this recipe it's an appetizer, and we're emphasizing the herbaceous, vegetal characteristics of rhubarb. It gets poached with a little bit of sugar but still has that hint of sour and is accompanied by a sweetened rhubarb jam, fresh goat cheese—which goes really well with rhubarb—sweet cicely, wild rose and a yogurt meringue. To turn this into a dessert, I'd simply candy the rose petals and blend with dehydrated raspberries and strawberries for the powder. Also, instead of using a seasoned goat cheese mousse underneath the meringue, I'd make a goat cheese cheesecake and maybe add some fresh fruits.

SERVES 4

Yogurt Meringue

½ cup thick fresh plain natural full-fat yogurt or labneh, at room temperature

¼ cup whipping (35%) cream, at room temperature

½ cup egg whites (about 4 egg whites)

1 cup icing sugar

Rhubarb Gel

2 cups juiced pink rhubarb

3½ tablespoons sugar

2 teaspoons (6.2 g) agar powder

Goat Cheese Mousse

½ cup soft fresh goat cheese, at room temperature

¼ cup whipping (35%) cream, at room temperature

½ teaspoon kosher salt

Pinch of freshly ground grains of paradise

Pink Rhubarb

1 cup sugar

¼ cup water

1 tablespoon fresh lemon juice

4 stalks pink rhubarb

Garnishes

Small wild rose petals

Sweet cicely leaves

Rose petal powder

FOR THE YOGURT MERINGUE

Set a dehydrator to 150°F (65°C).

In a small bowl, whisk together the yogurt and cream to make a smooth cream.

In the bowl of a stand mixer fitted with the whisk attachment, whisk the egg whites until frothy. While whisking on medium speed, gradually add the icing sugar and continue whisking until firm peaks are formed and the mixture starts to shine, about 3 minutes. Gently fold one-third of the egg whites into the yogurt mixture to lighten it, then fold in the remaining egg whites, being careful not to overwork the mixture.

On a baking sheet lined with parchment paper, evenly spread the meringue mixture to ⅛-inch thickness. Dehydrate for 16 hours, until you are left with a crunchy meringue. Break into 4-inch shards and store in an airtight container between layers of parchment paper. A silica pack will assist in keeping the meringue dry and crispy.

FOR THE RHUBARB GEL

In a small saucepan, whisk together the rhubarb juice, sugar and agar powder. Bring to a boil over high heat. Strain the liquid through a fine-mesh sieve into a small bowl and cool in the refrigerator until the jelly is firmly set, about 30 minutes. When set, remove the jelly from the bowl and cut into 1-inch cubes. In a blender, purée the jelly cubes until smooth. Pass through a fine-mesh sieve to remove any small lumps. Pour the gel into a squeeze bottle or piping bag and keep in the refrigerator until ready to use.

RECIPE CONTINUES . . .

FOR THE GOAT CHEESE MOUSSE

In a small bowl, whisk together the goat cheese, cream, salt and grains of paradise to form a smooth cream.

FOR THE PINK RHUBARB

In a small saucepan, combine the sugar, water and lemon juice. Bring to a simmer over medium heat to dissolve the sugar to make a syrup. Cut the rhubarb into 1-inch pieces cut on the bias. Place the rhubarb in the pan and reduce the heat to low, maintaining just under a simmer. Poach the rhubarb for 3 to 5 minutes, until it is tender. Remove from the heat and allow the rhubarb to cool in the syrup. You should get about 5 pieces from each stalk of rhubarb. Return the rhubarb to the syrup and reserve until ready to use.

FOR THE RHUBARB ROSE

For each serving, using a sharp paring knife, slice 2 pieces of poached rhubarb into thin lengthwise slivers. Line a plate with parchment paper. Starting in the middle of the plate, place slivers in a tight cluster and gradually add slivers to the outer layer to create a pattern that resembles a rose. Once all the slivers are used, insert small wild rose petals sporadically in the folds and gently squeeze the base to compress and hold the shape. Repeat to make 3 more roses.

TO SERVE

Spoon a couple of tablespoons of the goat cheese mousse onto each plate. Dot the rhubarb gel on and around the mousse. Using a small palette knife, carefully transfer a rhubarb rose to each plate. Arrange 3 poached rhubarb pieces on each plate. Garnish with sweet cicely, yogurt meringue and a dusting of rose petal powder.

FRESH EGG YOLK PASTA

with cheese custard, morel mushrooms and wild leek cream

THERE'S ALWAYS SOME KIND OF pasta on our menus. This one is a free-form cannelloni. We make sheets of fresh pasta, heavy on the egg yolk, and pipe a line of soft cheese similar to a flavoured mascarpone right down the middle of the pasta as soon as it comes out of the cooking water. The sauce is made from the wild leek leaves and morels that grow all over the property.

SERVES 8

Cheese Custard

1 tablespoon unsalted butter

1 cup sliced shallots

¼ cup sliced garlic

1 cup whipping (35%) cream

¼ cup whole milk

5 ounces (140 g) Brie

1 cup grated Parmigiano-Reggiano

¼ cup nutritional yeast

1 tablespoon kosher salt

12 egg yolks

Fresh Pasta

1¾ cups 00 flour

⅓ cup semolina flour

¼ teaspoon kosher salt

½ cup finely sliced fresh flat-leaf parsley

11 large egg yolks

1 large egg

1 teaspoon extra-virgin olive oil

2 tablespoons water

Wild Leek Cream

1 tablespoon unsalted butter

1 cup sliced shallots

2 tablespoons sliced garlic

1 fresh bay leaf

1 teaspoon crushed juniper berries

½ tablespoon fresh thyme leaves

½ cup dry white wine

3 cups whipping (35%) cream

2 cups loosely packed wild leek (ramp) leaves

1 tablespoon kosher salt, if needed

1 tablespoon fresh lemon juice

Morel Mushrooms

¼ cup vegetable oil

5 ounces (140 g) morel mushrooms, washed, patted dry, trimmed and sliced (2 cups sliced)

2 garlic cloves, crushed

1 teaspoon kosher salt

2 tablespoons unsalted butter

2 tablespoons minced shallot

½ cup Madeira

Garnish

Wild grape leaves from small tender vines

FOR THE CHEESE CUSTARD

Preheat the oven to 325°F (160°C).

Heat a medium saucepan over medium-low heat. Add the butter and allow to melt and bubble. Add the shallots and garlic, reduce the heat to low and cook gently, stirring frequently, until the shallots are tender and translucent, 3 to 4 minutes. Add the cream and milk and bring to a low simmer. Add the Brie and Parmigiano-Reggiano and simmer, stirring frequently, until the cheese is completely melted, about 5 minutes.

Transfer to a blender, add the nutritional yeast and salt and purée until smooth. Strain through a fine-mesh sieve into a medium bowl. In a separate medium bowl, whisk the egg yolks together. While whisking, add about 1 cup of the hot cheese purée to

combine well. Add the remaining cheese purée and whisk well to combine.

Bring 4 quarts of water to a simmer. Transfer the cheese mixture to a shallow casserole dish and cover with plastic wrap and foil. Place the prepared casserole in a larger roasting pan and transfer to the oven. Carefully pour enough simmering water into the larger pan to reach halfway up the side of the casserole dish. Cook for 35 minutes or until the custard has set and is no longer liquid. Remove the casserole from the water bath in the oven and allow to cool to room temperature. Store the custard, covered, in the refrigerator overnight.

The next day, transfer the custard to a food processor and purée on high speed until smooth. Store,

RECIPE CONTINUES . . .

covered, in the refrigerator. Bring to room temperature before using. You can spoon this directly onto the pasta or transfer to a piping bag and pipe a line down the pasta to finish the dish. Either will work fine.

FOR THE FRESH PASTA DOUGH

HAND METHOD

Sift the 00 flour, semolina flour and salt into a medium bowl. Stir in the parsley, then pour the flour mixture onto a work surface into a pile. Using your fingertips, make a well in the centre of the pile.

In a medium bowl, whisk together the egg yolks, egg, olive oil and water. Pour the wet mixture into the well in the flour mixture. Using your fingertips, begin to stir the liquid in the well, allowing the flour from the sides to slowly incorporate into the liquid, forming a dough. Once all the flour is incorporated, knead the dough for 15 minutes, adding a dusting of flour if the dough feels too wet or wetting your fingers with some water if the dough feels too dry. The finished dough should be smooth and elastic. It will appear firm but will soften while it rests. Wrap the dough in plastic wrap or a damp cloth and allow to rest for at least 1 hour but ideally overnight in the refrigerator for best results.

MIXER METHOD

Into the bowl of a stand mixer, sift the 00 flour, semolina flour, salt and parsley. In a separate bowl, whisk together the egg yolks, egg, olive oil and water. Attach the dough hook. With the mixer on low speed, slowly add the wet mixture to form a dough. Continue to knead the dough on low speed for 10 minutes, adding a dusting of flour if the dough feels too wet or a sprinkle of water if the dough feels too dry. The finished dough should be smooth and elastic. It will appear firm but will soften while it rests. Form the dough into a ball, wrap in plastic wrap or a damp cloth and allow to rest for at least 1 hour but ideally overnight in the refrigerator for best results.

TO ROLL AND CUT THE PASTA

Divide the dough into 4 pieces, cover lightly with a kitchen towel or plastic wrap and allow to come to room temperature. Using a pasta roller or a rolling pin on a lightly floured surface, roll one piece of dough at a time into a sheet about ⅝ inch thick. Cut the pasta into eight 5-inch × 3-inch rectangles, lightly dust with semolina or 00 flour and keep covered with kitchen towel or plastic wrap until ready to use Reserve the excess pasta dough for another use.

FOR THE WILD LEEK CREAM

Heat a medium saucepan over medium-low heat. Add the butter and allow to melt and bubble. Add the shallots and garlic, reduce the heat to low and cook gently, stirring frequently, until the shallots are tender and translucent without browning, 3 to 4 minutes. Meanwhile, tie the bay leaf, juniper berries and thyme into a sachet using cheesecloth and butcher's twine and add to the saucepan. Increase the heat to medium-high and add the white wine. Reduce the wine until almost completely evaporated. Add the cream and reduce the heat to a low simmer. Cook gently for 10 minutes to infuse all the flavours into the cream. Remove the spice sachet and squeeze any liquid into the saucepan. Discard the spice sachet. In batches, transfer the cream mixture along with the wild leek leaves to a high-speed blender and purée until smooth. Strain the sauce through a fine-mesh sieve into a clean saucepan. Taste and add salt, if needed. Whisk in the lemon juice. Keep warm.

Just before serving, give a quick whisk or buzz with an immersion blender to create some bubbles.

FOR THE MORELS

In a medium frying pan, heat the vegetable oil over medium heat. Add the mushrooms and crushed garlic, season with salt and fry for 1 minute, stirring occasionally. Reduce the heat to low, add the butter and shallots and cook for 1 minute longer, until the butter is foaming and starting to brown and the mushrooms are cooked through. Add the Madeira and continue to cook until the Madeira is almost completely evaporated. Using a slotted spoon, transfer the mushrooms to paper towel to absorb excess fat.

TO COOK THE PASTA AND SERVE

Bring a medium saucepan of salted water to a boil over high heat. Drop the pasta sheets into the boiling water and cook for 2 minutes. Drain the pasta and transfer to a work surface. Spoon or pipe a line of room-temperature cheese custard from one end of the pasta to the other. Roll the pasta into a log and carefully transfer it to a warm plate. Garnish with morels, wild leek cream and wild grape leaves.

FLATBREAD

WHEN ROLLED PAPER-THIN AND BAKED, unleavened dough, like this Armenian lavash, results in a bread with a crispy, almost cracker-like consistency that is extremely versatile. This is a very basic recipe, but feel free to add a sprinkling of herbs, spices, nuts or seeds just before the dough goes in the oven to transform this basic version into something extra-special.

The flavour and appearance of the dough can be changed and enhanced by the addition of ingredients such as pollens, curry, sumac, rosemary or thyme, or cumin, fennel, sesame or poppy seeds. Go wild. You can also colour the dough by adding flavoured colourings such as turmeric, beet juice or squid ink. If you're adding a purée or juice, just remember to reduce the amount of water in the recipe accordingly.

SERVES 4 TO 6

Flatbread Dough

1½ cups all-purpose flour

1 tablespoon sugar

1¼ teaspoons kosher salt

⅓ cup water, more if needed

3 egg whites, divided

2 teaspoons vegetable oil

FOR THE FLATBREAD DOUGH

In a medium bowl, whisk together the flour, sugar and salt. In a separate medium bowl, whisk together the water, 2 of the egg whites and the vegetable oil. Add the egg mixture to the flour mixture and, using your hands, stir until the dough comes together. Add additional water if the dough is dry. Knead the dough in the bowl 5 to 6 times, until smooth. The dough should be soft, silky and pliable but not at all wet.

Turn the dough out onto a work surface, divide it in half and roll each half into a ball. Cover with a kitchen towel and allow to rest for at least 30 minutes at room temperature, or wrap in plastic wrap and refrigerate overnight for best results. This allows all the built-up gluten to relax. Remove the dough from the refrigerator 2 hours before rolling to allow it to come up to room temperature.

BAKE THE FLATBREAD

Position a rack in the middle of the oven. Preheat the oven to 375°F (190°C). Line a baking sheet with a silicone mat or parchment paper.

On an unfloured work surface, roll out the dough ball into a ¼-inch-thick rectangle. Try not to handle the dough too much at this point; just a confident roll and stretch will do, otherwise you will have to knead the dough back together and rest again before stretching. The edges of the dough will be thicker than the middle; gently stretch them with your fingers. Lift the dough onto the prepared baking sheet. If a hole forms while you're stretching the dough, don't worry, the dough will still bake beautifully. Repeat with the remaining ball of dough.

In a small bowl, lightly whisk the remaining egg white. Brush the dough with the egg white just before baking to give it a nice shine. If you are so inclined, now is the time to sprinkle on any additional seasonings. Bake until golden brown, 10 to 15 minutes. Remove the flatbread to a rack and allow to cool completely.

JB'S TIP

In this recipe, the dough shrinks a bit as it bakes, resulting in a slightly thicker flatbread. If you prefer a thinner, crispier flatbread, spray the bottom (backside) of a baking sheet with nonstick spray. Stretch the rolled-out dough to cover, folding the dough edges under the rim of the baking sheet to hold it in place while baking. Bake for 6 to 10 minutes or until golden brown. Remove the flatbread to a cooling rack.

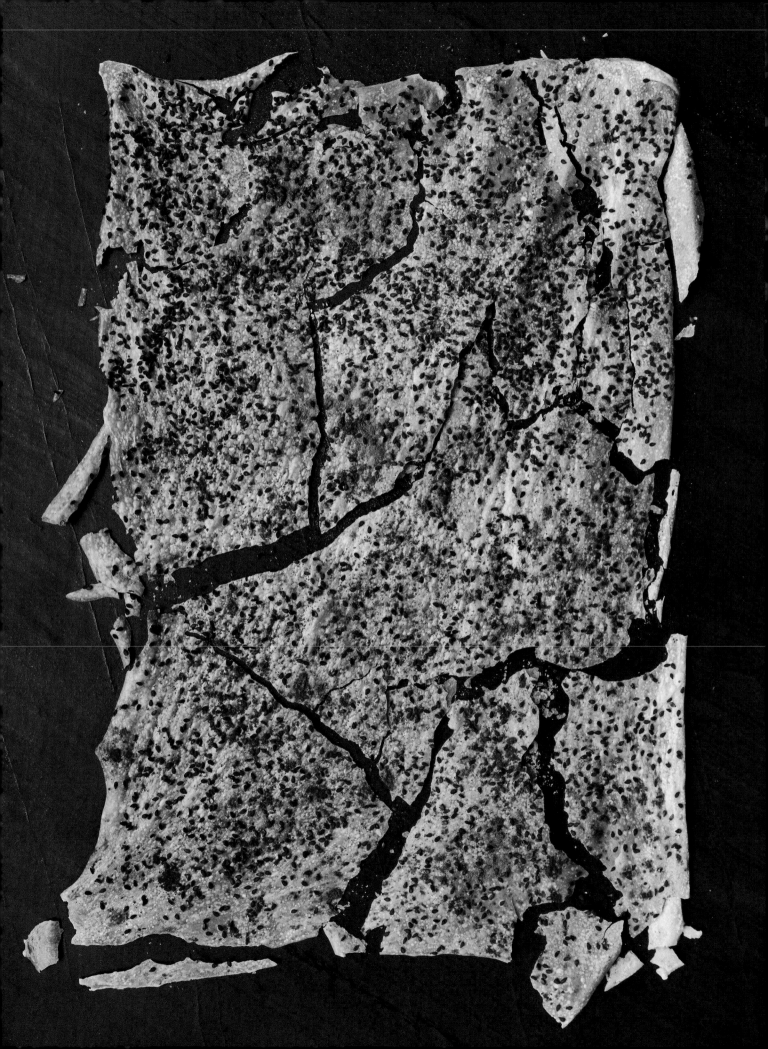

YOUNG SPRUCE TIP ICE CREAM
with foraged spruce tips

THIS IS AN EXCELLENT RECIPE for anyone who wants to try their hand at some entry-level foraging. The nice thing about spruce tips is that you know you're not going to poison yourself by picking the wrong thing! And spruce tips are abundant, so you're not going to damage the environment.

Lots of communities and cultures eat spruce tips. It's not so common in Ontario but you see them used quite often in Quebec, where they make things like spruce beer and an incredible forest-flavoured spruce soda. In this recipe we turn them into ice cream in a way that really showcases the natural, beautiful fresh flavour of young spruce tips. It's fantastic.

SERVES 4

Spruce Tip Ice Cream
2 cups whipping (35%) cream
2 cups whole milk, divided
1½ cups sugar
10 large egg yolks
2 cups young foraged spruce tips,
　rinsed and dried, divided

Garnish
Young foraged spruce tips
1 tablespoon of your favourite tree
　syrup to drizzle (optional)

FOR THE SPRUCE TIP ICE CREAM

In a small saucepan, combine the cream and 1 cup of the milk and bring to a simmer over medium heat. In a large bowl, whisk together the sugar, egg yolks and the remaining 1 cup milk. When the cream mixture is simmering, slowly pour it into the egg mixture while whisking continuously. Return the mixture to the saucepan and continue to gently whisk while heating to 180°F (82°C). Do not boil. Remove from the heat and strain through a fine-mesh sieve into a container. Stir in 1 cup of the spruce tips, allow the mixture to cool, cover and let steep in the refrigerator overnight.

The next day, with a rubber spatula, scrape the mixture into a high-speed blender. Add the remaining 1 cup spruce tips and blend until the spruce tips have broken down into small pieces, about 20 seconds. Strain the mixture through a fine-mesh sieve into an ice-cream maker and process according to the manufacturer's instructions until the ice cream has a soft-serve consistency. Scrape into a chilled airtight container and freeze until hard, about 4 hours. Keep frozen until ready to use.

TO SERVE

In a chilled bowl, arrange young spruce tips in a circle. Scoop the spruce tip ice cream and place in the centre. A drizzle of your favourite tree syrup and a glass of spruce beer would be a perfect finishing touch. Serve immediately.

HONEY CROISSANT

with raspberry milk chocolate ganache, garden flowers and herbs

WE MAKE CROISSANTS DAILY TO serve at breakfast, and believe it or not, sometimes there are leftovers. This is a great way to use them. This was one of the first dishes we created using our own chocolate that we developed in Paris. It's basically a raspberry ganache stuffed between two baked slices of croissant, so it's like a little chocolate-and-croissant Oreo. Because our chocolate is so herbaceous and earthy and has so many layers of flavour, the sweet fruitiness of the raspberry and the milk chocolate with fresh garden flowers and herbs really make this a next-level chocolate dish. Citrus and anise herbs are perfect here: try mint, lemon balm, basil, anise hyssop or tarragon.

SERVES 4

Raspberry Purée (makes about 1 cup)
2 cups fresh ripe raspberries

Raspberry Milk Chocolate Ganache
4½ ounces (130 g) milk chocolate, chopped (about ¾ cup)
⅛ teaspoon kosher salt
Raspberry Purée (recipe above)

1½ tablespoons glucose syrup
2 tablespoons unsalted butter, at room temperature

Honey Croissants
3 day-old croissants
¼ cup honey
¼ cup unsalted butter

Garnishes
Edible flowers
Mixed fine herbs

FOR THE RASPBERRY PURÉE

In a blender, purée the raspberries until smooth. Press the purée through a fine-mesh sieve into a small bowl to remove any seeds. Keep covered in the refrigerator until ready to use.

FOR THE RASPBERRY MILK CHOCOLATE GANACHE

In a medium bowl, combine the milk chocolate and salt.

In a small saucepan, heat the raspberry purée with the glucose syrup over medium heat until it boils. Pour the raspberry purée mixture over the milk chocolate and stir with a rubber spatula until the chocolate melts and the mixture is smooth and cohesive, with no lumps. Add the butter and stir until the butter is melted and fully incorporated. Strain into a container with a lid. Cool to room temperature, then cover and chill overnight in the refrigerator.

FOR THE HONEY CROISSANTS

Preheat the oven to 325°F (160°C). Line a baking sheet with parchment paper.

With a serrated bread knife, cut 8 crosswise ¼-inch-thick slices from the larger middles of the croissants. In a small saucepan, melt the honey and butter together over low heat and whisk to mix well. With a pastry brush, brush the honey-butter mixture onto both sides of the croissant slices. Arrange the slices on the prepared baking sheet, top with another sheet of parchment and weight them down with a second baking sheet to keep the slices flat while baking. Bake for 10 minutes, until the slices start to caramelize and are golden brown. Remove the pans from the oven, remove the top baking sheet and parchment and turn the croissant slices over. Bake, uncovered, for another 5 minutes or until the croissants are deep golden brown. Remove from the oven and allow to cool on the baking sheet. Store in an airtight container at room temperature for up to 2 days.

TO SERVE

Bring the raspberry milk chocolate ganache to room temperature. Transfer the ganache to a piping bag fitted with a small star tip. Just before serving (to prevent making the croissants soggy), pipe ganache onto one croissant slice, then place another slice on top to make a sandwich. Press the sandwich gently to expose the ganache along the seam of the croissants. Using a little ganache as glue, stand the croissant upright on a plate. Decorate the seam of the honey croissants with edible flowers and fine fresh herbs.

SOLSTICE

SPORTING A LACY AFTERNOON frock and a delicate parasol, the height of Edwardian fashion, Pauline Kingsmill, Langdon Hall's first chatelaine, takes a stroll in the orchard. The shade of an apple tree offers a break from the heat. She unwraps a tomato sandwich and takes a bite. A dragonfly sails past, drawing her focus higher up to where a Cooper's hawk carves wide circles in the deep blue sky. Beyond that a slice of moon hangs framed by billowing clouds.

One hundred years later, on a nearly identical afternoon, a group of friends in white summer dresses and wide-brimmed hats enjoys a picnic in the shade of that same apple tree. Even their basket seems little changed from one Pauline Kingsmill might have packed a century ago: house-baked sourdough with hand-churned butter, tender carrots and pickled turnips from the garden, fresh wild strawberries from the woods.

Summer unfolds in a timeless fashion at Langdon Hall. The ancient staccato beat of a red-bellied woodpecker still interrupts the electric drone of the cicadas. Children's laughter still carries over from the croquet court to the stables, their delight perfumed by the sweet, lush smell of freshly cut grass.

Langdon Hall was built for summer. Literally. Commissioned by Eugene Langdon Wilks as a summer home for himself and his family, the property absolutely glows during the long, warm days. That is as true today as it was a hundred years ago, maybe even more so, as everything about the place seems to revel in the hustle and bustle of the visitors who flock here to bask in its charms.

"It's a sensory overload up here in the summer," Jason says, watching a tractor tow a trailer full of snapdragons and lisianthus up to the summer house, the huge bouquets destined for a wedding celebration. "When you drive up the driveway and it's a ripe green summery landscape, automatically you're hit with this essence of floral and greenery, along with all the great smells that come with walking through the property, the baking and roasting and everything else. It's like a fairy tale."

The garden flowers: marigolds strain at their stems, fuzzy borage erupts in blue star-shaped flowers, tasty verbenas strain into the light. Herbs grow tall and flower—tender purple basil, pretty pink mint, delicate white coriander—their tiny arrangements just itching to be pinched. Honeybees and ladybugs, monarchs and painted ladies flit among the heaving produce. A sly bunny makes off with a tender carrot. Neither the gardeners nor the cooks mind, for the kitchen is spoiled for choice right now. To dine at Langdon Hall in the summer is to experience an almost overwhelming sense of abundance.

"Summer is the easiest of the seasons to not overcomplicate things," Jason says. "Everything in its natural state is just so delicious and beautiful and vibrant, it's when we do the least to the ingredients. That's something I can say I learned from my time at Langdon Hall, just to leave things alone. The quality of the ingredients enables us to do that."

Of course, that doesn't mean just putting a raw turnip on a plate. This is the time of year when the kitchen likes to, say, take a cucumber, slightly compress and barely pickle the flesh, place it in a seasoned bath of its own juice and dress it only with a few of those delicate herb flowers. Alternately, they might take vegetables of the same colour—gold or white or green—and bring them together into something monochromatic, the whole greater than the sum of its parts.

"I look at things now more than I ever have before for the beauty of the thing itself," Jason says. "Instead of looking for ways to change it, I analyze it to find out how to just let it be, and how I can, with little accents, make it extraordinary. Restraint is a sign of maturity."

Ripeness is a given, but in some cases it isn't the goal. Consider a plate of radishes, simultaneously tender and crisp, fading from red to white, peppery greens still attached. Most of the radishes the kitchen serves, like those guests are invited to dip in butter and sprinkle with sea salt at the start of the summer tasting menu, are harvested young and never reach maturity. The gardeners stagger plantings so there are always a couple of plots still coming while another is left alone and allowed to overgrow so the cooks can harvest the flowers and seed pods.

Summer's most iconic ingredient illustrates this multi-stage approach better than just about anything. "The tomato for me, when it's green and underripe, it's still wicked," Jason says. "It's crunchy, it's sour, it's great sliced, breaded and fried or diced and pickled. A ripe tomato is perfection, of course—you can eat them raw, or blanch them and peel them. A tomato without its skin is a whole different experience. Those same skins we'll dehydrate and buzz with salt to make tomato salt. Cooking them confit, slow-roasting or sun-drying them brings out completely different elements."

One of the kitchen's favourite preparations, and something guests will see used in myriad ways in the dining room and bar, is tomato water. Diced tomatoes are seasoned with herbs and salt and then strained to yield a clear, deeply flavourful liquid. The leftover seasoned tomatoes don't go to waste, but get cooked down into a sauce. Jason says that even the tomato leaves are used. "We blanch them and work them into pasta or dry them out into a powder that we dust on things to introduce a mysterious element of complexity."

Throughout the parade of warm, lazy, sun-filled days the garden is in constant flux. "Nothing is ever the same, even year to year," Jason says. "Sometimes you'll have a plant that will bolt and have these beautiful flowers that you've never seen before or a plant that will offer fruit that it didn't offer before. There's always something new and exciting."

SUMMER GARDEN CANAPÉS
roasted daylily, pattypan stuffed with ratatouille, heirloom tomato with herbs

CANAPÉS, BOTH SWEET AND SAVOURY, play a big role in setting the stage and giving us the opportunity to tell a story about the current season and of the meal to come. Here we create single bites of some ripe favourites from the garden in the peak of season.

Daylilies are not common in your local grocery store. So unless you grow them in your garden, you will need an alternative in this recipe. The flavour is very similar to asparagus, so lightly roasted green asparagus tips would be a perfect substitute. The pattypan filling is also a fantastic accompaniment to poached or grilled fish. Keep the tomato skins to make Tomato Salt (page 96), if you wish.

SERVES 4

Cherry Tomato

4 large perfectly ripe red cherry tomatoes

1 teaspoon olive oil

¼ teaspoon kosher salt

Ratatouille Filling and Pattypan Squash

2 plum tomatoes (blanched with the cherry tomatoes above)

1 shallot

2 garlic cloves

1 red bell pepper

½ green zucchini

3 tablespoons olive oil, divided

3 tablespoons dry white wine

1 teaspoon fresh thyme leaves

6 fresh basil leaves, finely chopped

2 teaspoons finely chopped fresh chives

1 teaspoon freshly ground black pepper

½ teaspoon kosher salt

4 bite-size pattypan squash

Pan Roasted Daylily

4 tight unopened daylily flower buds

2 tablespoons unsalted butter

1 garlic clove, crushed

2 sprigs fresh thyme

Pinch of kosher salt

Garnishes

For the tomatoes: bronze fennel fronds, lemon balm, nasturtium flowers, wood sorrel, fennel flowers, bachelor's button, basil, mint leaves

For the daylily: Orange Gem marigold leaves

Lemon Gel (page 284)

FOR THE CHERRY TOMATO

Fill a small bowl with ice water. Bring a medium saucepan of salted water to a boil over high heat. Using a paring knife, carefully score the cherry tomatoes and the plum tomatoes for the pattypan squash filling. The cherry tomatoes and plum tomatoes may blanch in different times depending on ripeness and size, so blanch them separately. Blanch the tomatoes in the boiling water for 10 seconds or until you see the skin split and start to peel away where you scored. Using a slotted spoon or spider, immediately remove the tomatoes from the boiling water and plunge them into the ice water to cool rapidly. When cool, remove the tomatoes from the ice water and peel away and discard the skin. Place the peeled cherry tomatoes in a small bowl. Place the plum tomatoes in a separate small bowl and reserve for the pattypan filling.

FOR THE RATATOUILLE FILLING

Cut the reserved blanched plum tomatoes lengthwise into quarters and remove the seeds. Dice the tomato flesh in a 1/16-inch dice and place in a small bowl. Dice the shallot, garlic, bell pepper and zucchini the same size as the tomato; keep them separate. In a medium saucepan, heat 1 tablespoon of the olive oil over low heat. Add the shallots and garlic and gently cook without browning, stirring occasionally, for about 3 minutes. Add the bell pepper and zucchini and continue to cook for 1 minute. Add the white wine,

RECIPE CONTINUES . . .

increase the heat to medium and allow the wine to reduce until almost dry, 1 to 2 minutes. Transfer to the bowl of diced tomatoes and add the thyme. Mix gently and allow to cool to room temperature. Mix in the basil and chives. Season with the black pepper, salt and the remaining 2 tablespoons olive oil.

FOR THE PATTYPAN SQUASH

Preheat the oven to 350°F (180°C). Line a baking sheet with parchment paper.

Slice the top third off each pattypan squash. Slice a small sliver off the bottom of each squash so it will sit upright. Using a melon baller or a small spoon, scoop some of the inside out of the squash, being careful not to go through the bottom. Halfway in is perfect. Brush the cut sides of the squash lightly with olive oil and season with a pinch of salt. Arrange the tops and bottoms of the squash cut sides down on the prepared baking sheet. Bake for 6 minutes, until just soft. The tops may take less time to cook, so check on them at the 3-minute mark and remove them if ready. Let cool to room temperature.

FOR THE PAN ROASTED DAYLILY

Wash the daylily flower buds in cold water. Dry on paper towel. In a small frying pan over medium heat, melt the butter with the garlic and thyme, stirring frequently until the butter is hot and foaming but not browning, 1 to 2 minutes. Add the daylily and carefully roll them in the pan for 30 seconds. If they are large and need more cooking, cook for another 30 seconds. They should be soft and lightly golden but still maintain their structure. Season with a pinch of salt. Remove the daylily from the pan and drain on paper towel.

TO SERVE

Gently coat the cherry tomatoes in the olive oil and season with salt. Garnish each one with flowers and herbs. Place the garnished cherry tomatoes on a garden-inspired serving vessel. Stuff the pattypan squash with the ratatouille filling, place the top on the squash to finish, and arrange with the tomato. Brush the daylily with lemon gel and top with Orange Gem marigold leaves to finish the trio.

TASTE THE GARDEN

flatbread with beeswax fudge and garden juice

THE INGREDIENTS CHANGE THROUGHOUT the year for this dish, based on what's in the garden at that particular time, but the presentation remains consistent. We bring to the table a beautiful earthenware jug that looks like a bouquet of flowers. In it is a cucumber juice that's flavoured with everything in the garden that's ripe at that time. In the spring that might mean spears of asparagus, geranium and very green elements, maybe some chamomile. As we go through the season, more summery ingredients show up—basil, mint, dill, maybe bronze fennel or green tomato. In autumn and winter, we transition to a warm tea made with root vegetables, pine needles and dried mushrooms. This recipe is a base, but the idea is it should be a welcome to the season, so make up your own version using whatever is the most ripe and luscious at that moment.

SERVES 4

Garden Juice

4 English cucumbers, juiced (about 4 cups of juice)

½ cup lightly packed fresh dill fronds

½ cup lightly packed fresh lemon verbena leaves

½ cup lightly packed fresh mint leaves

2 lemongrass stalks, tough outer leaves and stems discarded, roughly chopped

1 tablespoon fresh lemon juice

1 teaspoon kosher salt

Beeswax Fudge

1 cup nutritional yeast

6 tablespoons water

1 cup (12 g) shaved beeswax

7 tablespoons vegetable oil

½ tablespoon kosher salt

1 batch Flatbread (page 70)

Garnishes

Pansies

Bouquet of herbs made from lemon verbena, flowering basil, geranium flowers, lavender, lemongrass

Bee pollen

FOR THE GARDEN JUICE

Place the cucumber juice, dill, lemon verbena, mint and lemongrass in a high-speed blender and blend for 1 minute to coarsely chop and bruise the herbs and aromatics. Pour the mixture into a container, cover and store in the refrigerator until ready to use, at least 1 hour, to allow the flavours to infuse.

Just before serving, strain the juice through a fine-mesh sieve into a pouring jug. Season with the fresh lemon juice and salt.

FOR THE BEESWAX FUDGE

Fill a medium bowl with ice. Half-fill a medium saucepan with water and bring to a simmer. In a medium bowl, stir together the nutritional yeast and water to make a paste. In a separate medium bowl, melt the beeswax over the pot of simmering water. When melted, slowly whisk in the vegetable oil until combined.

Nestle the bowl of nutritional yeast paste in the ice and, while whisking, quickly drizzle the beeswax mixture into the yeast paste. The beeswax will solidify as it cools, so it's important to incorporate it quickly and evenly. (It's helpful to do this with two people, one holding the bowl of ice and whisking while the other pours the beeswax.) Season with the salt. The fudge should have the texture of smooth peanut butter. Transfer to a squeeze bottle or piping bag fitted with a small plain tip.

TO SERVE

Break the flatbread into 4 equal pieces and dot some of the beeswax fudge on top of each. Garnish with flowers and dust with bee pollen. Place the bouquet of herbs into the pouring jug. Pour the garden juice into glasses and and leave the jug at the table to enjoy the fragrance and beauty of the herbs.

EGGPLANT PURÉE

with pickled eggplant, yogurt and marjoram

IN THIS RECIPE WE TAKE a single ingredient and blow it up in a bunch of different ways. We have a couple varieties of eggplant in the garden, so we wanted to tell the story of that vegetable. At the restaurant we use very lightly cooked baby white eggplant and confit eggplant that's barely cooked in oil. The pickled eggplant is shaved almost like potato chips and pan-fried in vegetable oil before we marinate it and layer it almost like a lasagna. To finish, we make a simple eggplant purée that's garnished with olive oil, thick yogurt and sumac. Staghorn sumac grows all over southern Ontario, but you rarely see it on menus. It adds a nice tart citrusy element that rounds out the dish beautifully.

SERVES 6

Pickled Eggplant

1 Japanese or Italian eggplant

2 tablespoons vegetable oil

1 teaspoon chopped fresh thyme

1 teaspoon chopped fresh rosemary

½ teaspoon kosher salt

1 tablespoon minced garlic

2 tablespoons red wine vinegar

Confit Eggplant

1 Italian eggplant

4 cups vegetable oil, or as needed

6 sprigs fresh thyme

4 garlic cloves, crushed

Eggplant Purée

4 Italian eggplants

¼ cup vegetable oil, more for brushing the eggplant

2 teaspoons kosher salt, divided

1½ cups sliced white onion

¼ cup sliced garlic

4 sprigs fresh thyme

1 tablespoon fresh marjoram leaves

3 cups whipping (35%) cream

1 cup Vegetable Stock (page 285)

Garnishes

Plain natural full-fat yogurt

Extra-virgin olive oil

Fresh marjoram leaves

Sumac powder

FOR THE PICKLED EGGPLANT

Using a sharp knife, meat slicer or mandoline, slice the eggplant into ⅛-inch-thick rounds. Heat the vegetable oil in a large frying pan or cast-iron skillet over high heat. When the oil is hot, working in batches, place the eggplant slices in the pan and sear quickly on both sides until golden brown. Remove from the pan and lay the eggplant slices in a medium deep casserole dish or bowl. Evenly sprinkle the eggplant with some chopped thyme, rosemary, salt and a scant layer of minced garlic. Lightly drizzle with red wine vinegar. Repeat until all the eggplant slices are seared and stacked with the aromatics sprinkled between each layer. The numbers of layers will depend on the size of your eggplant and the size of your container. Cover and marinate in the refrigerator for at least 2 hours or up to 3 days. These pickles get even better with age.

FOR THE CONFIT EGGPLANT

Preheat the oven to 325°F (160°C).

Cut the eggplant into 1-inch-thick rounds. Place the slices in a medium saucepan, roasting pan or Dutch oven and add enough vegetable oil to completely submerge the eggplant. Add the thyme and garlic. Cover the pan with a lid and bake for 30 minutes or until the eggplant is tender. Allow the eggplant to cool in the flavoured oil. When cool, remove the eggplant from the oil and transfer to a cutting board. Cut the eggplant with a small cookie cutter or knife into bite-size pieces. Return the eggplant to the cooking oil. Heat gently when ready to serve.

RECIPE CONTINUES . . .

FOR THE EGGPLANT PURÉE

Increase the oven temperature to 400°F (200°C). Line a baking sheet with parchment paper.

Cut the eggplants in half lengthwise. Using a paring knife, score the flesh. Brush with vegetable oil and season with 1 teaspoon of the salt. Place the eggplant halves cut side down on the prepared baking sheet and roast for 30 minutes or until the flesh is tender. Remove from the oven and allow to cool slightly. Using a spoon, scoop out the cooked flesh and reserve the flesh and juices in a medium bowl. Discard the skins.

In a medium saucepan over medium-low heat, gently cook the onions and garlic in the vegetable oil until tender, being careful not to get any colour on the vegetables, about 4 minutes. Add the eggplant flesh and cooking juices, the remaining 1 teaspoon salt, the thyme, marjoram, cream and vegetable stock. Simmer for 15 minutes. Remove from the heat and allow to cool slightly. Remove the thyme sprigs and discard. Strain the liquid into another container, reserving it for adjusting the consistency of the purée.

In a high-speed blender, purée the vegetables, adding enough of the liquid in a slow, steady stream while blending to achieve a smooth, velvety consistency. When processed, adjust the seasoning with more salt if required. Strain through a fine-mesh sieve back into the saucepan and heat gently.

TO SERVE

Drain the warmed confit eggplant on paper towel to absorb excess oil, season with salt and transfer to warm shallow bowls. Spoon on some of the yogurt, drizzle with olive oil and sprinkle the marjoram leaves to garnish. Add the pickled eggplant and some warm eggplant purée and dust with sumac.

WATERMELON GAZPACHO

with rosewater jelly and sour begonia flowers

I LOVE CHILLED SOUPS IN the summer. They're so fresh with lots of bright flavour, and the options are endless because they can be made with fruits or vegetables or even seafood and some meat broths. This gazpacho is an all-around fantastic and refreshing chilled soup for the summer months.

I created this recipe when I grew tired of making a typical gazpacho and wanted to do something different. We were receiving some incredible watermelons from a local farm at the time, and I decided to do something with them in a soup form. I didn't want it to be dessert, though, so I started out with elements of savoury that would work well with the sweetness and freshness of summer melon. Building on a base of shallot, celery, fennel and sweet peppers with tomato, hints of ginger and fresh herbs gives the finished soup substance and viscosity.

This fresh and delicious purée would also make a great base for a cocktail or a sorbet.

SERVES 4

Rosewater Jelly

1½ gelatin leaves

½ cup rosewater

1 tablespoon water

½ teaspoon sugar

⅛ teaspoon kosher salt

Watermelon Gazpacho

½ cup lightly packed fresh basil leaves

½ cup lightly packed fresh cilantro leaves

½ cup lightly packed fresh mint leaves

1 tablespoon olive oil

1 cup diced red bell peppers

½ cup sliced celery

½ cup sliced shallots

½ cup sliced fennel

1 teaspoon minced peeled fresh ginger

1 teaspoon sliced fresh jalapeño pepper or jalapeño Tabasco sauce

4 cups diced watermelon

2 cups ripe heirloom tomatoes

¼ cup rice wine vinegar

¼ teaspoon kosher salt

1 tablespoon fresh lime juice

Garnishes

20 pieces of watermelon cut into any geometric shapes

Begonia flowers, fresh mint, coriander or shiso leaves

FOR THE ROSEWATER JELLY

In a medium bowl, bloom the gelatin leaves by submerging them in cold water until soft, about 5 minutes. Lift the softened gelatin leaves from the bowl and squeeze out the water. Discard the water. In a small saucepan over low heat, bring the rosewater, water, sugar and salt to a simmer. Remove the saucepan from the heat and whisk in the bloomed gelatin until it is completely dissolved.

Pour the rosewater into a 1-cup container and refrigerate until the jelly is set, about 2 hours.

FOR THE WATERMELON GAZPACHO

Tie the basil, cilantro and mint into a sachet using cheesecloth and butcher's twine. In a medium

saucepan, heat the olive oil over low heat. Add the bell peppers, celery, shallots, fennel, ginger and jalapeño. Add the herb sachet and cook gently, stirring occasionally, until the vegetables are tender and translucent, about 5 minutes. Add the watermelon, tomatoes, rice wine vinegar and salt. Stir to mix the flavours, then remove from the heat. Using a fork, crush the tomatoes and melon in the saucepan to release some of their juices. Ensure the herb sachet is submerged in the juices. Allow to cool and marinate in the saucepan for up to 1 hour.

When cooled, remove the herb sachet and squeeze as much liquid as possible back into the saucepan. Discard the herb sachet. Strain the liquid through a fine-mesh sieve into another container,

RECIPE CONTINUES . . .

reserving it for adjusting the consistency of the soup. In a high-speed blender, purée the watermelon and cooked vegetables. If needed, add enough of the liquid in a slow, steady stream while blending to achieve a smooth, velvety soup consistency. While blending, add the lime juice. Strain through a fine-mesh sieve into a chilled soup terrine or other container until ready to serve. Allow the gazpacho to chill in the refrigerator for up to an hour after straining. Be sure to serve chilled.

TO SERVE

Place the watermelon pieces in a chilled soup bowl. Top with a spoonful of rosewater jelly, and garnish with begonia leaves and flowers. Pour the gazpacho into the bowl at the table to complete.

GOLDEN VEGETABLE SOUP
with olive oil and basil blossoms

AT THE HEIGHT OF SUMMER, when so many golden vegetables—golden beets, golden tomatoes, yellow pattypan squash and golden potatoes—are at their peak and super ripe and tasty, this simple chilled soup is a great way to get a real taste of the season. Garnish this with a few basil flowers or leaves, some good-quality cold-pressed canola or extra-virgin olive oil and a little bit of sea salt and you're ready to go. This soup is equally delicious served hot.

SERVES 6

Golden Vegetable Soup

½ cup olive oil

1 cup roughly sliced shallots

1 tablespoon roughly sliced garlic

½ teaspoon minced peeled fresh ginger

1 cup roughly chopped orange bell pepper

1 teaspoon kosher salt

1 teaspoon freshly ground white pepper

½ cup lightly packed fresh basil leaves

½ cup lightly packed fresh flat-leaf parsley

½ cup dry white wine

4 cups roughly chopped orange tomatoes

2 cups roughly chopped peeled English cucumber

Green jalapeño Tabasco sauce

Garnishes

6 boiled and peeled new potatoes, cut into bite-size pieces

3 boiled and peeled golden beets, cut into bite-size pieces

6 blanched pattypan squash, cut into bite-size pieces

6 ground cherries, pitted

12 blanched and peeled golden cherry tomatoes (see page 97)

Basil flowers or leaves

Extra-virgin olive oil, to drizzle

Sea salt

FOR THE GOLDEN VEGETABLE SOUP

In a medium saucepan, heat the olive oil over medium-low heat. Add the shallots, garlic, ginger and bell pepper and gently cook without browning, stirring often, until tender, about 5 minutes. Season with the salt and pepper. Tie the basil and parsley into a sachet using cheesecloth and butcher's twine. Add the white wine and herb sachet to the saucepan and reduce the wine by two-thirds. Stir in the tomatoes and cucumber and cook for another 5 minutes. Remove from the heat and allow to cool.

Remove the herb sachet and squeeze as much liquid as possible back into the saucepan. Discard the herb sachet. Strain the liquid into another container, reserving it for adjusting the consistency of the soup.

In a high-speed blender, purée the vegetables, adding enough of the liquid in a slow, steady stream while blending to achieve a smooth, velvety consistency. When processed, adjust the seasoning with a splash of jalapeño Tabasco sauce and more salt, if required. Strain through a fine-mesh sieve into a medium bowl and chill over ice. The soup can be stored, covered, in the refrigerator for up to 4 days.

TO SERVE

Pour the soup into chilled soup bowls. Gently place the prepared potatoes, beets, squash, ground cherries and golden cherry tomatoes into the soup. Finish with basil flowers or leaves, a drizzle of olive oil and a sprinkle of sea salt.

TASTE SUMMER

ripe tomatoes with tomato water, sun-dried tomato bun and basil

WITH THIS DISH, I WANTED to showcase the many varieties of our beautiful tomatoes in their glory by not doing too much to them and just letting them speak for themselves. Two things elevate this dish and make it elegant and interesting for the diner. First, we remove the tomato skins, and that takes away the fibrous chew and it becomes a whole other experience of eating tomato. Second, we make a tomato water with roughly chopped tomatoes seasoned with a bit of basil, garlic and salt and hung in layers of cheesecloth so the only thing that drips out is this beautiful clear liquid that is the essence of the tomato, the blood of the tomato.

This dish works beautifully as a salad on its own, but we wanted to take it up even further. So we took a focaccia recipe and transformed it into a tomato bread. We use the tomato water and some milk as the liquid. We sun-dry tomatoes to concentrate their flavour, purée them and fold them into the dough, so you have this warm, intensely flavoured tomato bread. This is my taste of summer.

At Langdon Hall, we aim for zero waste, using as much as we can from the products we use. Instead of composting the tomato skins, we dry them and use them in broths or in powders like the tomato salt in this recipe, which adds a nice punch of concentrated tomato flavour. In your home kitchen, making this tomato salt may be tricky because of the small amount of skins yielded. This recipe will turn out just fine with kosher salt in its place.

SERVES 4

Tomato Water
3 pounds (1.4 kg) ripe heirloom tomatoes, 6 cups roughly chopped

½ cup lightly packed fresh basil leaves

½ teaspoon sliced garlic

1 teaspoon kosher salt

Peeled Cherry Tomatoes
3 pounds (1.4 kg) cherry tomatoes of varying colour and size

1 tablespoon tomato water (recipe above)

Tomato Salt (optional; or ½ tablespoon kosher salt)
½ cup tomato skins (reserved from peeled cherry tomatoes)

1 tablespoon kosher salt

Tomato Buns
½ cup oil packed sun-dried tomatoes, drained

1 cup tomato water (recipe at left)

½ teaspoon active dry yeast

1 tablespoon sugar

1 tablespoon water

2¾ cups all-purpose flour

1½ tablespoons whole milk

4 tablespoons extra-virgin olive oil, divided

½ tablespoon tomato salt (recipe at left or kosher salt)

Garnishes
Purple basil leaves

Tomato salt (recipe at left)

Extra-virgin olive oil

½ cup tomato water (recipe at left)

FOR THE TOMATO WATER

Place a colander over a large bowl and line the colander with 3 layers of cheesecloth cut large enough to encase the tomato mixture once chopped.

In a high-speed blender and working in batches, roughly chop the tomatoes and basil with the garlic and salt. Pour the tomato mixture into the prepared colander. Bring the cheesecloth corners together and tie with butcher's twine to create a sack. Place the bowl in the refrigerator overnight to allow the tomato water to drip into the bowl. Do not squeeze the sack or the tomato water will be cloudy; allow the water to extract naturally with gravity.

The next day, pour the accumulated tomato water into a jar or container fitted with a lid. Store in the refrigerator for up to 3 days.

FOR THE PEELED CHERRY TOMATOES

Fill a medium bowl with ice water. Bring a medium saucepan of salted water to a boil over high heat. Using a paring knife, carefully score the cherry tomatoes at the stem. Group the tomatoes according to size and blanch in batches. Blanch the tomatoes in the boiling water for 10 seconds, or until you see the skin split, and start to peel away where you scored. Using a slotted spoon or spider, immediately remove the tomatoes from the boiling water and plunge them into the ice water to cool rapidly. When cool, remove the tomatoes from the ice water and peel away the skin. Reserve the skins. In a small bowl, toss the peeled cherry tomatoes with 1 tablespoon of the tomato water.

FOR THE TOMATO SALT

Set a dehydrator to 115°F (46°C).

Dry the reserved tomato skins well on paper towel. Lay them in a single layer on the dehydrator tray. Do not overlap the skins. Dehydrate for 4 to 8 hours, until the skins are completely dry and brittle. Transfer to a blender or spice grinder, add the salt and process to a fine powder. Pass the powder through a fine-mesh sieve and store in an airtight container in a dry area for up to 3 weeks.

FOR THE TOMATO BUNS

In a high-speed blender, purée the sun-dried tomatoes with 1 cup of the tomato water, about 2 minutes. Press through a fine-mesh sieve into a small bowl to remove any remaining stems or seeds.

In the bowl of a stand mixer, stir together the yeast, sugar and water. Cover with a damp kitchen towel and let ferment for 10 minutes in a warm area of the kitchen. Add the tomato mixture, flour, milk, and 2 tablespoons of the olive oil. Attach the dough hook and mix on medium speed for 30 seconds. Add the tomato salt or kosher salt. Mix on medium speed for another 3 minutes or until the dough comes together. Coat a medium bowl with some of the remaining 2 tablespoons olive oil and transfer the dough to the bowl. Cover with plastic wrap and proof in a warm area of the kitchen (or in a proofer) for 1 hour or until the dough has doubled in size.

Line a baking sheet with parchment paper. With oiled hands, portion the dough into 1-ounce (28 g) pieces. Roll them between your hands into balls about the size of a golf ball and arrange 3 inches apart on the prepared baking sheet. Proof for another 45 minutes covered lightly with a damp kitchen towel. The dough will double in size. When you press the dough with a finger, the indent will spring back.

Meanwhile, preheat the oven to 325°F (160°C). Bake the buns until baked through but not browned, 6 to 8 minutes. Ideally, serve warm.

TO SERVE

Arrange the prepared cherry tomatoes on a coupe plate or shallow bowl with the warmed tomato bun on the side. Garnish them with the fresh basil leaves and season with the tomato salt. Drizzle with extra-virgin olive oil and additional tomato water just before serving.

WINE PAIRING

This recipe represents the garden at its peak, so you want a wine that has fruit but is still bright and exuberant and speaking to the same flavours that are in the dish. You also need to have some acidity, though, to balance the strong tomato component. A wine with lower acidity is going to come across as having an almost oily texture in your mouth. I'd head to the south of Italy for this. I think Falanghina would be amazing. It has that bright melon note that's begging to go with this dish and also a herbal note, but it's still ripe. Vermentino would also work well. It still has that bright melon note and ripe fruit perfume and minerality, but it doesn't have quite the same ripeness of fruit.

For best results, do not store tomatoes in the refrigerator. If you pick the tomatoes yourself or get them from the farmers' market day of, that is the best time to prepare them for this dish.

Tomato water is unbelievable, and there are so many things you can do with it. You can reduce it down to concentrate it, use it in cocktails or vinaigrettes, make it into a granita—it's almost as versatile as a vegetable stock. Have fun with it!

After making the tomato water, don't let those chopped tomatoes and basil go to waste. Simply add them to a medium saucepan along with ½ cup of olive oil and stew over low heat for 20 minutes. You'll have a quick and easy tomato sauce for pasta or another use.

FOIE GRAS PARFAIT
with summer peach and brioche

THIS IS QUITE POSSIBLY ONE of my favourite combinations with foie gras. I've done this for years, having developed the recipe at Auberge du Pommier in Toronto back in 2004 while I was the chef there. It is a modern version of a torchon that takes on the texture of a parfait and offers a very clean and delicate fresh flavour. We marinate the foie gras with Crème de Pêche, a French peach liqueur, and make a peach purée flavoured with sugar, a bit of lemon juice and fresh lavender. The marriage of perfectly ripe Niagara peach with just-picked lavender from the garden and the foie gras on toasted brioche is a little bite of magic.

SERVES 6 TO 8

Foie Gras

1 Grade A lobe duck foie gras (1½ to 2 pounds/675 to 900 g)

2 to 4 quarts whole milk

2 teaspoons kosher salt

¼ teaspoon pink curing salt

¼ cup Crème de Pêche or other peach liqueur

6 gelatin leaves

1 cup whipping (35%) cream

Peach Purée

8 cups sliced ripe unpeeled peaches (about 12 medium peaches)

2 tablespoons fresh lemon juice

½ cup sugar

½ tablespoon fresh lavender leaves or flowers

1 teaspoon kosher salt

Brioche Batons

Four ½-inch-thick slices of brioche

¼ cup unsalted butter

Kosher salt

Garnishes

Chickweed

Lavender flowers

Star flowers

FOR THE FOIE GRAS
Place the foie gras in an airtight container and cover with the milk. Seal the container and soak in the refrigerator for up to 12 hours to help draw out some of the blood in the veins. When ready to clean the foie gras, drain the milk and rinse the foie gras well under cold running water. Pat dry, cover and let sit at room temperature for 1 hour or until it is soft all the way through before starting to devein it.

Set a sous vide water bath to 132.8°F (56°C).

Lay the foie gras smooth side down on a large sheet of parchment paper. Find the natural seam between the small and large lobes, then pull the lobes apart and disconnect the attaching vein. The same way you would butterfly a piece of meat, starting with the large lobe, cut a shallow slice along the centre of the lobe from one end to the other and gently spread the liver away from the central cluster of veins in the thickest part of the lobe. The veins spread from there like the branches of a tree, getting thinner and

smaller toward the thinnest part of the lobe. Follow the veins carefully by gently spreading the liver away from the veins. You can use a toothpick or butter knife to get under the veins to lift them right out of the lobe. Do the same with the small lobe. By the end, the lobes should be flat and free of any visible veins. This is a tedious job, but with the more veins you can remove, the final product will be smoother and better in colour and flavour.

Season the foie gras with the kosher salt, curing salt and Crème de Pêche evenly across the entire surface of foie gras. Using a large palette knife or pastry scraper, transfer the foie gras to a sous vide bag, ensuring all the liquor is added to the bag. Vacuum-seal on full pressure and cook in the water bath for 30 minutes.

Meanwhile, in a small bowl, bloom the gelatin leaves by submerging them in cold water until soft, about 5 minutes. Remove the softened gelatin leaves from the bowl and squeeze out the water. Add the

RECIPE CONTINUES . . .

gelatin to a small saucepan with the cream. Warm the cream over low heat, whisking to dissolve the gelatin completely. Remove from the heat.

Once the foie gras is cooked, empty the foie gras and its rendered fat into a medium bowl. The 132.8°F (56°C) temperature is perfect for emulsifying, so work quickly. Using a slotted spoon, transfer the solid pieces of foie gras to a high-speed blender and pulse to emulsify. Add the warm cream mixture and continue to blend on low to medium speed. In a steady stream, slowly pour in the warm foie gras fat. You'll notice the mixture thicken. Increase the speed of the blender as the emulsification progresses. The mixture should be the colour of café au lait and be smooth and shiny, almost like ice cream. Once blended, pass the mixture through a fine-mesh sieve into a small deep sheet pan, terrine mould or shallow casserole dish lined with plastic wrap. Cover and refrigerate for 4 to 8 hours, depending on the volume of your mould, until the parfait is well chilled and set firmly. If using a mould or tray, set the parfait about ¼ inch thick. The same thickness would apply to the slice if using a terrine mould.

Remove the parfait from the refrigerator and, using the plastic wrap, slide the parfait onto a cool flat surface. Using a sharp knife or 3-inch round cutter dipped in hot water, cut out 6 to 8 portions of the parfait and transfer to chilled plates using an offset palette knife. (Dipping the knife or cutter in hot water will help keep the cuts smooth and clean.) Let the parfait come to room temperature before serving.

FOR THE PEACH PURÉE

In a medium bowl, combine the sliced peaches with the lemon juice, sugar, lavender and salt. Cover and allow the peaches to macerate at room temperature for 2 hours or until the natural juices, sugar and lemon have made a tasty peach syrup. Strain through a fine-mesh sieve into another container, reserving the juice for adjusting the consistency of the purée. In a high-speed blender, purée the peaches, adding enough of the peach juice in a slow, steady stream while blending to achieve a smooth, velvety consistency. When processed, strain through a fine-mesh sieve into a small bowl or squeeze bottle.

FOR THE BRIOCHE BATONS

Remove the crusts and cut six to eight 2-inch × ½-inch × ½-inch rectangles from the brioche. In a medium frying pan over medium heat, melt the butter until frothing and starting to brown. Fry the brioche in the butter until golden brown, turning to fry evenly on all sides, about 30 seconds per side. Season with a pinch of salt and transfer to paper towel to absorb excess butter.

TO SERVE

Arrange the flower garnishes carefully around the edge of the foie gras parfait, showing off the beauty of the herbs and flowers. Dot some of the peach purée onto the plate and complete with warm fried brioche.

SNOW CRAB AND HERB BLOSSOMS

with pansies, crab bone and herb blossom cream

ATLANTIC SNOW CRAB IS ONE of my very favourite ingredients, and this recipe was developed to showcase the delicacy and sweetness of it while also capturing something of the playfulness of the cuisine at Langdon Hall. The sauce is made from the shells of the crab that we've infused with different floral aspects: flowering thyme and flowering fennel. We balance all that with a little Champagne vinegar and some lemon juice. To bring in even more of the garden aspect, we prettied it up with some pansies that not only are beautiful but also provide a very gentle, almost sour or sunflower seed flavour that contrasts nicely with the sweetness of the crab.

SERVES 4

Crab

2 live crabs (2 pounds/900 g each) or 3 pounds (1.4 kg) cooked snow crab legs

6 quarts Traditional Court Bouillon (page 290; optional if using cooked crab)

2 tablespoons unsalted butter

1 cup Vegetable and White Wine Nage (page 285)

Crab Bone and Herb Blossom Cream

2 cups roughly chopped or broken crab shells

1 tablespoon vegetable oil

¼ cup thinly sliced shallots

¼ cup thinly sliced fennel

½ tablespoon sliced garlic

2 fresh bay leaves

1 teaspoon kosher salt

½ cup dry white wine

¼ cup brandy

3 cups whipping (35%) cream

¼ cup mixed fresh herb flowers, such as thyme, fennel or dill, coriander or basil

½ tablespoon fresh lemon juice

1 teaspoon Champagne or white wine vinegar

Garnish

Pansies or violas

FOR THE CRAB

To cook live crab, separate the legs from the body and remove and discard the innards. Rinse out the body shells and reserve for the sauce. In a large pot, bring the court bouillon to a boil over high heat. When the broth is boiling, plunge the crab legs into it, reduce the heat to low and simmer for 10 minutes. Meanwhile, fill a large bowl with ice water.

Remove the pot from the heat. Using tongs, transfer the crab legs to the ice water to cool rapidly. When cool, remove the legs from the water. With kitchen shears or fine scissors, cut along the length of the shell to expose the meat, being careful not to damage the flesh. Remove the meat from the shell. Remove and discard the long, thin cartilage that runs down the centre of the leg meat. Store the prepared crab meat, covered, in the refrigerator for up to 3 days or until ready to use. Reserve the shells for the sauce. Bring the meat to room temperature before serving.

FOR THE CRAB BONE AND HERB BLOSSOM CREAM

Preheat the oven to 350°F (180°C).

Spread the crab shells evenly on a baking sheet lined with parchment paper and roast until golden and fragrant, about 25 minutes.

In a medium saucepan, heat the vegetable oil over medium-low heat. Add the shallots, fennel, garlic and bay leaves, season with salt, and cook gently without browning, stirring occasionally, until the vegetables are tender, about 6 minutes. Add the roasted crab shells and white wine, increase the heat to medium-high and reduce the wine until almost dry. Add the brandy and reduce until it is almost all evaporated, about 2 minutes. Add the cream and bring to a simmer. Reduce the heat to low and simmer for 8 minutes. Remove from the heat and stir in the herb flowers. Let the sauce steep for another 15 minutes.

Strain the sauce through a fine-mesh sieve into a small saucepan. Discard the shells and vegetables.

RECIPE CONTINUES . . .

Whisk in the lemon juice and Champagne vinegar. Keep warm.

TO SERVE

In a medium frying pan, melt the butter over medium heat. Add the vegetable and white wine nage and bring to a simmer. Add the crab meat, reduce the heat to low and baste the meat. Remove from the heat, cover the pan and allow the crab to slowly warm and absorb the liquid, about 90 seconds. Using a slotted spoon, transfer the crab to paper towel to dab excess liquid and then transfer to warm shallow bowls. Garnish the crab with the pansies.

Using an immersion blender, froth the crab bone and herb blossom cream to create a bubbly sauce. Finish the dish with some of the tasty bubbles.

JB'S TIP

Adding the herb flowers really brings the sauce to life. We are fortunate to have access to an abundance of flowering herbs in our garden. Simply using the chopped leaves of the plant will still produce a tasty herbaceous sauce.

KING CRAB

with orchard apple and wood sorrel

CRAB WITH APPLES MIGHT SEEM an unusual pairing, but this recipe is rooted in the theory of pairing sweet and sour with rich, fatty protein combinations. Think pork with apples or duck with cherries. Atlantic crab is so fatty and juicy—you can see the fat packed on it—you need something to cut that mouth-coating richness. The crab is also naturally sweet, so the sweet fruitiness of the apple works wonderfully to complement that, and the green apple–like sourness that the sorrel gives the dish brings in an amazing sweet-and-sour angle. Ultimately, this recipe is about focusing on three ingredients—apple, sorrel and crab—and letting them all shine on their own.

SERVES 4

½ pound (225 g) cleaned king crab meat, chilled

Apple Gel
4 cups Honeycrisp apple juice (4 or 5 large apples)
1 tablespoon honey
1 tablespoon apple cider vinegar
½ teaspoon kosher salt
1¼ teaspoons (3.9 g) agar powder

Apple Sorrel Purée
2 cups peeled and sliced Honeycrisp apple
½ tablespoon honey
½ tablespoon apple cider vinegar
½ teaspoon kosher salt
1 cup lightly packed fresh green sorrel leaves
1 cup lightly packed fresh baby spinach leaves
Pinch of xanthan gum

Pickled Apple
1 Honeycrisp apple, unpeeled
1 tablespoon honey
1 teaspoon fresh lemon juice
½ teaspoon apple cider vinegar
¼ teaspoon kosher salt

Garnishes
Apple or crabapple blossoms
Wood sorrel or other variety sorrel leaves

FOR THE APPLE GEL

In a medium saucepan over medium heat, reduce the apple juice by half. Add the honey, apple cider vinegar and salt. Whisk in the agar powder and bring to a boil. Pour into a small bowl, cover and refrigerate for 2 hours or until a firm jelly is set.

Remove the jelly from the bowl and cut into rough pieces. Transfer the jelly pieces to a blender and blend until smooth. Strain through a fine-mesh sieve into a small bowl or a squeeze bottle. Store, covered, in the refrigerator for up to 4 days.

FOR THE APPLE SORREL PURÉE

In a medium saucepan, combine the apples, honey, apple cider vinegar and salt. Cover and cook over low heat, stirring occasionally, until the apple is broken down to a mash and the liquid is reduced down to a glaze, about 30 minutes Transfer to a high-speed blender and add the sorrel and spinach leaves and xanthan gum. Blend on high speed for 2 minutes.

Strain through a fine-mesh sieve into a medium bowl and cool rapidly over ice while whisking. This will help maintain the green colour.

FOR THE PICKLED APPLE

Using a sharp knife or mandoline, slice the apple lengthwise into thin rounds, shaving until you reach the core. Turn and shave the other side. Discard the core.

In a medium bowl, whisk together the honey, lemon juice, apple cider vinegar and salt to make a dressing. Add the apple slices and toss gently to coat.

TO SERVE

Break or cut the crab meat into bite-size pieces and arrange on plates. Place the pickled apple slices on the crab and add a few small dots of the apple gel on top. Garnish with the apple blossom flowers and sorrel leaves. Add a tablespoon of the apple sorrel purée to each plate.

SABLEFISH

with onion soubise, Pernod cream and bronze fennel

THIS DISH WAS INSPIRED BY a walk in the garden with a special guest while we discussed my approach to creating dishes inspired by the property. We stood and discussed the distinctiveness of the bronze fennel plant and its intense flavour profile. I picked some during our walk, and an hour later served this dish to him in the dining room.

We're playing here with the idea of a classic fish velouté. You're basically making a delicious fish cream sauce flavoured with Pernod that you gently poach the fish in. Then, to soften the intensity of the sauce, we do a thick white onion purée that brings a velvety texture and adds some savoury to balance the anise flavour. We top it all with bronze fennel and borage flowers, which have a flavour similar to oyster, so it all has an oceany, licoricey subtleness.

SERVES 4

Pernod Cream

1 tablespoon unsalted butter

4 cups thinly sliced shallots

½ cup thinly sliced garlic

¼ cup lightly packed fresh tarragon leaves

1 teaspoon coriander seeds

6 star anise

2 fresh bay leaves

1 cup dry white wine

1 cup Pernod

1 cup Fish Stock (page 287)

6 cups whipping (35%) cream

½ teaspoon kosher salt

1 tablespoon fresh lemon juice

Onion Soubise

2 tablespoons unsalted butter

4 cups thinly sliced white onions

½ teaspoon kosher salt

2 cups whipping (35%) cream

Sablefish

1 fresh skinless wild sablefish fillet (½ pound/225 g), cut into 4 portions

Garnishes

Bronze fennel fronds

Fennel flowers

Borage flowers

FOR THE PERNOD CREAM

In a medium saucepan over medium-low heat, melt the butter until it bubbles. Add the shallots, garlic, tarragon leaves, coriander seeds, star anise and bay leaves and cook, stirring frequently, until the shallots are tender and translucent but not browning, 4 to 6 minutes. Increase the heat to medium-high and add the white wine. Reduce the wine until almost completely evaporated. Add the Pernod and reduce until almost completely evaporated, stirring occasionally. Add the fish stock and reduce the stock by two-thirds. Add the cream and bring to a simmer. Reduce the heat to medium-low and simmer gently, stirring occasionally, for 10 minutes to infuse all the flavours into the cream. Season with salt.

Strain the sauce through a fine-mesh sieve into a clean small saucepan. Discard the solids. Reduce

further to a sauce consistency. Taste and add salt, if needed. Whisk in the lemon juice. Keep warm.

FOR THE ONION SOUBISE

In a medium saucepan, melt the butter over medium-low heat. Add the onions and gently cook without browning, stirring often, until tender, about 5 minutes. Season with the salt. Add the cream, bring to a simmer and cook, stirring occasionally, for 10 minutes to ensure the onions are fully cooked and softened.

Strain the cream into another container, reserving it for adjusting the consistency of the purée. In a high-speed blender, purée the onions, adding enough of the cream in a slow, steady stream while blending to achieve a smooth, velvety consistency. Once processed, adjust the seasoning with more salt, if needed. Strain through a fine-mesh sieve into a clean saucepan.

TO SERVE

Bring the Pernod cream to a simmer. Lower the sablefish portions into the Pernod cream and gently poach them for 2 minutes. Remove the pan from the heat and leave the sablefish in the cream for 2 more minutes. Meanwhile, spoon a tablespoon of onion soubise onto each warm plate. Using a slotted spoon, remove the sablefish from the Pernod cream and place it beside the onion soubise. Spoon the warm Pernod cream over the sablefish to glaze and sauce the plate. Garnish with bronze fennel fronds, fennel flowers and borage flowers.

SEA SCALLOPS

with white beet purée and beetroot cream

BEETS AND SCALLOPS AREN'T A traditional pairing, but at the time we came up with this dish we had three or four different types of beets coming in from the garden and the dill was in full flower. At the same time, beautiful live scallops were coming to us from a First Nations fishery in British Columbia. We were going to create a beautiful beet dish anyway, so I figured why not work in the scallops? And you know what? It works.

We use different variations of beet here. There are poached beets and white beet purée and beets that have been roasted in salt and then dehydrated, resulting in a sun-dried texture. All these different textures work incredibly well alongside the caramelized crust of the scallop and the soft, delicate, barely cooked flesh. This dish is about celebrating the beet, but adding a bit of the ocean to it—which is why the wine pairing is something you wouldn't normally see with shellfish.

SERVES 6

Chewy Beets

3 cups kosher salt

2 large purple beets

1 cup purple beet juice (from 3 peeled medium beets)

½ cup sugar

½ cup blackberry juice

¼ cup white wine vinegar

White Beet Purée

2 cups peeled and sliced white beets

2 cups whipping (35%) cream

1 teaspoon kosher salt

Beetroot Cream

1 tablespoon unsalted butter

2 cups thinly sliced shallots

½ cup thinly sliced garlic

½ cup thinly sliced celery

⅓ cup thinly sliced fennel

Reserved scallop side muscles (see at right)

½ tablespoon fresh thyme leaves

1 tablespoon fresh dill flowers or chopped dill

1 fresh bay leaf

2 star anise

1 teaspoon coriander seeds

1 cup dry white wine

1 cup thinly sliced purple beet

½ cup Fish Stock (page 287)

2½ cups whipping (35%) cream

1 teaspoon kosher salt

1 tablespoon fresh lemon juice

Poached Beets

8 cups water, divided

8 cups white wine vinegar, divided

2 cups sugar, divided

2 tablespoons kosher salt, divided

12 baby purple beets, scrubbed

12 baby golden beets, scrubbed

Scallops

18 large (U-10) fresh dry sea scallops, side muscle removed for the beetroot cream, at room temperature

1 teaspoon kosher salt

2 tablespoons vegetable oil, divided

2 tablespoons unsalted butter, divided

2 garlic cloves, crushed, divided

2 sprigs fresh thyme, divided

1 tablespoon fresh lemon juice

Garnish

Baby beet greens

FOR THE CHEWY BEETS

Set a dehydrator to 115°F (46°C). Preheat the oven to 350°F (180°C).

Make a bed of the salt in a small baking sheet or ovenproof medium frying pan. Place the beets on the salt and bake for 40 minutes or until tender. Allow to cool on the salt to room temperature.

Meanwhile, in a small saucepan, bring the beet juice, sugar, blackberry juice and white wine vinegar

to a simmer and reduce by 1½ cups to a glaze. Remove from the heat and allow to cool.

Peel the beets, cut each one into 3 slices and then cut each slice crosswise into 1-inch pieces, giving you 4 to 6 pieces per slice. Lay the pieces of beet on the dehydrator tray. Dehydrate for 8 hours brushing at the beginning of each hour with the beet glaze. In the end they will be lacquered and dehydrated to the texture of chewy candy.

FOR THE WHITE BEET PURÉE

In a medium saucepan, simmer the beets in the cream over medium-low heat, stirring often, until tender, about 15 minutes. Strain into another container, reserving the cream for adjusting the consistency of the purée. In a high-speed blender, purée the beets, adding enough of the cream in a slow, steady stream while blending to achieve a smooth, velvety consistency. Once processed, adjust the seasoning with the salt. Strain through a fine-mesh sieve into a small saucepan. Warm gently and keep covered.

FOR THE BEETROOT CREAM

In a medium saucepan over medium-low heat, melt the butter until it bubbles. Add the shallots, garlic, celery, fennel and reserved scallop side muscles and cook, stirring frequently, until the vegetables are starting to soften, about 8 minutes. Add the thyme, dill, bay leaf, star anise and coriander seeds and continue to cook gently for 3 minutes to flavour the vegetables with the herbs and spices.

Increase the heat to medium-high and add the white wine. Reduce the wine until almost completely evaporated. Add the beets and fish stock and reduce the stock by two-thirds. Add the cream and bring to a simmer. Reduce the heat to medium-low and simmer gently, stirring occasionally, for 10 minutes to infuse all the flavours into the cream.

Strain the sauce through a fine-mesh sieve into a clean saucepan. Discard the solids. Taste and add salt, if needed. Whisk in the lemon juice.

FOR THE POACHED BEETS

Evenly divide the water, white wine vinegar, sugar and salt between 2 medium saucepans. Add the purple beets to one pan and the golden beets to the other. Simmer over medium-low heat until tender, about 20 minutes. Remove from the heat and allow the beets to cool in the poaching liquid.

Remove the beets from one of the saucepans, reserving the poaching liquid. Using a kitchen towel, carefully rub the skin off the beets, being careful not to damage the flesh. Return the beets to their warm liquid. Repeat with the second pan of beets.

FOR THE SCALLOPS

Dry the scallops on paper towel and season them with the salt. Cook the scallops in 2 batches; crowding them will result in steaming and poor caramelization. Heat 1 tablespoon of the vegetable oil in a large cast-iron skillet or frying pan over medium-high heat. When the oil is hot, carefully add half of the scallops and cook without moving until the bottom is caramelized and the flesh is opaque halfway up the scallop, 1 to 2 minutes. Remove the pan from the heat and add 1 tablespoon of the butter, 1 crushed garlic clove and 1 sprig of the thyme. Allow the butter to melt and start foaming, then baste the scallops with the hot butter to just barely cook the top. This should take no longer than 1 minute. Using an offset or fish spatula, transfer the scallops to paper towel, drizzle lemon juice over the top, and keep somewhere warm. Wipe the pan clean and repeat with the remaining scallops.

TO SERVE

Spoon a line of the white beet purée down the centre of each warm plate. Remove the beets from the poaching liquid and dry with paper towel. Arrange the poached beets, chewy beets and beet greens around the plate and finish with the seared scallops. Using an immersion blender or whisk, froth the beetroot cream, skim the froth with a spoon and spoon onto the plate.

WINE PAIRING

Beets are a really fun pairing. You want a wine that's fresh and youthful, with a little bit of sweet fruit note to it and little to no tannins, something fun and juicy to drink that's delicate and fresh. And that is the definitive Beaujolais. It's going to have floral notes and a sweet fruit component, not confected, but with plenty of fresh strawberries. You don't want one that's had carbonic maceration, and you don't want to get into that pear-drop, banana-y character—stay away from that—just all fruit and floral and maybe a tiny little bit of spice is fine. I don't pair red wine with seafood just to go against the grain, but when it works, it really works!

On the Importance of

BRINING

PEOPLE OFTEN ASK, "Why does your chicken taste so much better, and why does your pork taste so juicy and good?" and the big "secret" is that we brine it. By brining, you add a little spice, a little herbaceousness, and a little salt and pepper, so when you actually cook it, not only does the brine help the structure of the protein, it imparts flavour.

With brining, before you even cook something, you're seasoning it and adding those flavours that you typically would while you're cooking. If you're roasting chicken, say, and adding salt and pepper and throwing some garlic and thyme in a pan, you're flavouring the outside of the protein, but if you give it an opportunity to sit in a brine with those same ingredients for eight or twenty-four hours, that flavour goes right into the flesh, and the mouthfeel and taste are so much better. It's elevated to extraordinary.

I approach making a brine the same way I do making stocks and jus for sauce. I always tend to do a neutral base and then from that I can do all sorts of derivatives. That way I can take it in a different direction each time. I think of brines as almost like a mother sauce. For the most part, the solution is usually around the ratio of 4 cups of water to ¼ cup of salt to a tablespoon of sugar, but really, no two brines are the same. A brine can be filled with Asian ingredients, like lemongrass, star anise and coriander seed. Whatever you put in sends the dish in that direction.

My background and cooking is French inspired, so I'm always going to add garlic, thyme, shallot and bay leaf, but as we develop the garden and greenhouses and grow things that are not necessarily local, we're playing a lot more with those citrus elements.

If you really want to blow the socks off when using a brine like this, you add all those flavour elements into the roasting pan to reinforce the flavour, and if you're going to baste the meat with butter, it picks up all those flavour nuances from the brine, creating a flavour bomb experience sure to be remembered.

PORK BELLY

with mustard greens and honey mustard sauce

WE CAME UP WITH THIS recipe one day when we'd just received a delivery of beautiful pork from Murray's Farm. We also had all sorts of different varieties of mustard in the garden. Some had gone to flower while others were just leaves and buds that hadn't flowered yet, but because they were so young and so fresh, their spiciness worked beautifully against the fattiness of the pork. Although the mustard sauce is powerful, it's not super intense against the fattiness of the pork, so it acts as a kind of mellowing agent and gives the dish its lovely, perfect balance.

The oven method is just as delicious but it will be harder to achieve a clean and precise cut of the belly when portioning.

SERVES 4

Pork Belly and Brine

8 cups water

¼ cup kosher salt

¼ cup curing salt (I use Insta Cure #2)

¼ cup sugar

2 tablespoons coriander seeds

1 tablespoon fennel seeds

1 tablespoon mustard seeds

1 tablespoon black peppercorns

¼ cup fresh thyme leaves

2 fresh bay leaves

3 garlic cloves, crushed

½ cup sliced carrots

½ cup sliced white onion

1 fresh boneless skin-on pork belly (1½ pounds/675 g)

1 tablespoon vegetable oil, for searing

1 cup thickly sliced white onion (for oven method)

1 cup thickly sliced carrots (for oven method)

Honey (optional)

Honey Mustard Sauce

¼ cup honey

¼ cup grainy mustard

½ tablespoon freshly ground grains of paradise

½ teaspoon fresh thyme leaves

½ teaspoon kosher salt

½ teaspoon pure maple syrup

Garnishes

Brassica and mustard greens

Brassica flowers

Cold-pressed canola oil

Kosher salt

FOR THE PORK BELLY

In a medium saucepan, bring the water, kosher salt, curing salt and sugar to a boil. When the water is boiling, remove from the heat and add the coriander seeds, fennel seeds, mustard seeds, black peppercorns, thyme, bay leaves, garlic, carrots and onion. Allow the brine to cool to room temperature.

Place the pork belly in a deep container large enough to hold the pork fully submerged in the brine. Add the brine, cover and refrigerate for 24 hours.

Remove the pork belly from the brine and pat dry with paper towel. Discard the brine.

SOUS VIDE METHOD

Set a sous vide water bath to 156°F (69°C). Vacuum-seal on full pressure the pork and cook in the water bath for 5 hours. Remove from the water bath and chill in an ice bath. Once chilled, press the bag between 2 baking sheets with heavy weight on top and refrigerate overnight. The goal is to have the skin and pork belly as flat as possible.

Preheat the oven to 340°F (170°C).

Remove the pork belly from the vacuum bag, pat dry and trim off any excess fat. Season the skin side with kosher salt. In an ovenproof frying pan or cast-iron skillet large enough to hold the belly flat, heat the vegetable oil over medium-high heat. When the oil is hot, place the pork belly skin side down in the pan and sear the skin, pressing the belly in the pan to ensure an even sear. It will take about 60 seconds to get a good crust started on the skin. Place foil over the pork and place another ovenproof

RECIPE CONTINUES . . .

pan on top of the foil to gently press the pork belly flat. Transfer the pan to the oven and cook gently until the pork is warmed through and the skin is golden brown and crispy, about 20 minutes. Remove the top skillet and foil and transfer the belly skin side down to a cutting board.

OVEN METHOD

Preheat the oven to 325°F (160°C).

On a rimmed baking sheet or in a casserole dish large enough to hold the pork belly, spread the onion and carrots. Lay the brined pork belly skin side up on the vegetables. Rub the skin with vegetable oil and sprinkle with kosher salt. Add ½ cup water to the pan and cook, uncovered, for 2 hours. Remove from the oven and baste with the rendered fat and cooking juices. If the pan looks dry, add another ½ cup water. Continue cooking for an additional 1½ hours, basting every 20 minutes. Increase the oven temperature to 400°F (200°C) and cook for another 30 to 40 minutes,

basting every 10 minutes to ensure the skin is crispy and glazed. In the last 30 to 40 minutes you can also brush some honey onto the skin to help the caramelization. Once the skin is crisp and the pork is fork-tender, transfer to a cutting board and rest at room temperature for 15 minutes before carving.

FOR THE HONEY MUSTARD SAUCE

In a small bowl, stir together the honey, grainy mustard, grains of paradise, thyme, salt and maple syrup. Cover and refrigerate until ready to use.

TO SERVE

With a sharp knife, slice down through the pork belly from the flesh side finishing through the skin. You will get a cleaner cut this way. In a small bowl, toss the brassica greens and flowers with a very small amount of the canola oil and kosher salt. Place the sliced pork on the plates, garnish with the seasoned leaves and flowers, and add a spoonful of the honey mustard sauce.

BABY GEM LETTUCE
with heritage hen egg gribiche and garden pickles

A GOOD SALAD HAS TO start with great produce. In the case of Langdon Hall, we are fortunate enough to be able to step out into our garden, pull up lettuce, pull up radishes, collect some herbs that are growing just beside them, bring it all in, wash it and put together this fantastic dish. When you take all of that freshness and incorporate something with more texture and flavour—in this case an egg salad with mayonnaise, lots of fresh herbs, new garden pickles and a little mustard—it becomes the perfect salad. You've got something creamy and velvety going along with something fresh, acidic and crisp, with great hits of flavour popping up all over.

SERVES 4

Radish Pickle
½ cup sliced breakfast radish
½ cup white wine vinegar
¼ cup water
2 tablespoons sugar
¾ teaspoon kosher salt
1 teaspoon coriander seeds
2 star anise

Baby Onion Pickle
½ cup red or white small pearl onions, sliced in half lengthwise
½ cup white wine vinegar
¼ cup water
2 tablespoons sugar
1 teaspoon coriander seeds
¾ teaspoon kosher salt
½ teaspoon fresh thyme leaves
1 fresh bay leaf

Baby Carrot Pickle
½ cup sliced baby carrots
½ cup white wine vinegar
¼ cup water
2 tablespoons sugar
¾ teaspoon kosher salt
1 teaspoon coriander seeds
½ teaspoon mustard seeds

Gribiche
6 large heritage or regular eggs, simmered for 10 minutes and peeled
½ cup Mayonnaise (page 280)
1 tablespoon lemon zest
2 teaspoons fresh lemon juice
1 tablespoon chopped fresh flat-leaf parsley
1 tablespoon chopped fresh tarragon
1 tablespoon chopped chives

2 tablespoons chopped cornichons
1 tablespoon drained, rinsed and chopped capers
1 tablespoon minced shallot
1 tablespoon grainy mustard
½ teaspoon kosher salt
1 teaspoon freshly ground black pepper

Baby Gem Lettuce
2 heads Baby Gem lettuce, cut in half lengthwise and rinsed
2 tablespoons Shallot Vinaigrette (page 282)
Freshly ground grains of paradise
Kosher salt

Garnishes
20 cornichons, finely diced
16 whole fresh baby radishes
20 thin slices of fresh baby radish

FOR THE RADISH PICKLES
Place the sliced radish in a 2-cup mason jar. In a small saucepan, combine the white wine vinegar, water, sugar, salt, coriander seeds and star anise. Bring to a simmer over medium heat, then pour the pickling liquid into the jar to cover the radishes. Allow to cool, seal the jar with the lid and refrigerate for 48 hours before using.

FOR THE BABY ONION PICKLES
Place the halved onions in a 2-cup mason jar. In a small saucepan, combine the white wine vinegar, water, sugar, coriander seeds, salt, thyme and bay leaf. Bring to a simmer over medium heat, then pour the pickling liquid into the jar to cover the onions. Allow to cool, seal the jar with the lid and refrigerate for 48 hours before using.

RECIPE CONTINUES . . .

FOR THE BABY CARROT PICKLES

Place the sliced carrots in a 2-cup mason jar. In a small saucepan, combine the white wine vinegar, water, sugar, salt, coriander seeds and mustard seeds. Bring to a simmer over medium heat, then pour the pickling liquid into the jar to cover the radishes. Allow to cool, seal the jar with the lid and refrigerate for 48 hours before using.

FOR THE GRIBICHE

Chop the eggs into ¼-inch rough dice. Place the chopped eggs in a medium bowl and add the mayonnaise, lemon zest and juice, parsley, tarragon, chives, cornichons, capers, shallot and mustard. Mix well with a spoon or rubber spatula. Season with the salt and pepper. Cover and refrigerate until ready to use. This will keep well in the fridge for up to 3 days.

TO SERVE

Arrange the halved Gem lettuce cut side up in a shallow bowl or on a plate. Spoon a little of the shallot vinaigrette over the lettuce and season with grains of paradise and a pinch of salt. Top the lettuce with a couple tablespoons of the gribiche. Garnish each salad with the radish, onion, and carrot pickles and diced cornichons. Finish the dish with fresh whole and sliced baby radishes.

JB'S TIP

If you have some good-quality store-bought or family-recipe pickles on hand—carrot, onion or radish—feel free to use them instead, although making your own is easy and the results are superior.

BUTTER LETTUCE
with chardonnay vinegar jelly and egg yolk jam

WE GROW A LOT OF lettuces in the garden and have many great farms in the area that provide us with hydroponic and organic lettuce varieties, but the challenge is always, how do we take something as common as a salad and elevate it to something memorable and special? For this recipe, we decided to take whole heads of butter lettuce, cut them in half and then, instead of filling them with all sorts of vinaigrette, dress them with cubes of seasoned Chardonnay vinegar jelly. Similarly, instead of oil, we took an egg yolk jam and dotted that through, so a vinaigrette's oily, fatty texture comes from the jam and its acidity comes from the jelly. The whole thing is strewn with flowers and herbs—bronze fennel, citrusy marigold, peppery arugula flowers, wild mint flowers, anise hyssop and basil flowers—so it's very fresh and very floral with different layers of flavour and surprise with every bite. We've listed the kinds we use, but feel free to mix it up with whatever's most readily available.

SERVES 4

Chardonnay Vinegar Jelly
5 gelatin leaves
½ cup Chardonnay vinegar
¼ cup water
2 tablespoons honey
1 teaspoon kosher salt

Egg Yolk Jam
6 egg yolks
½ teaspoon kosher salt

For serving
2 small heads butter lettuce, outer leaves removed, washed and split in half
1 teaspoon kosher salt

Garnishes
Lime Leaf Powder (page 283)
Arugula flowers
Marigold leaves and flowers

Rose petals
Pansies
Anise hyssop
Bronze fennel
Chervil
Mint leaves and flowers
Basil leaves and flowers

FOR THE CHARDONNAY VINEGAR JELLY
In a medium bowl, bloom the gelatin leaves by submerging them in cold water until soft, about 5 minutes. Lift the softened gelatin leaves from the bowl and squeeze out the water. Discard the water.

In a small saucepan, warm the Chardonnay vinegar, water, honey and salt over medium heat. Whisk in the bloomed gelatin until completely dissolved. Pour into a small container lined with plastic wrap and cool to room temperature. Cover and refrigerate until the jelly is set, about 2 hours.

Remove the jelly from the container and cut into ½-inch cubes. Store, covered, in the refrigerator until ready to use.

FOR THE EGG YOLK JAM
Set a sous vide water bath to 158°F (70°C). Carefully place the egg yolks in a sous vide bag and vacuum-seal on full pressure. Cook in the water bath for 35 minutes. Once cooked, chill in an ice bath. Transfer to a food processor, add the salt and blend until smooth. Transfer to a piping bag or squeeze bottle and store in the refrigerator until ready to use. (If you don't have access to a sous vide circulator, soft-poaching the egg yolks in good-quality olive oil would be fantastic.)

TO SERVE
Dot the centre of each plate with some of the egg yolk jam to secure the lettuce to the plate. Place the lettuce cut side up on the jam to secure. Dot some of the egg yolk jam in and around the lettuce leaves, adding cubes of Chardonnay vinegar jelly as you go. Dust the plate with a small amount of lime leaf powder and cover the salad generously with the flowers and herbs. Season with salt.

BERRIES 'N CREAM

with sweet cicely and raspberry vinegar jelly

MY FAVOURITE TIME TO MAKE this berry dish is at the peak of the season when we're enjoying the super-ripe berries that are coming in from around the property and nearby farms: blueberries, wild strawberries, lingonberries, blackberries, raspberries, ground cherries, currants. The more the merrier. The base is top-quality, really fresh 35% to 45% cream flavoured with a hint of citrus, and we garnish the dish with sweet cicely to add a subtle licorice flavour. If there's no cicely handy, feel free to use fennel tops, mint or tarragon or go without any herbs at all. The berries are the star here. To best bring out the distinctive character of each type of berry, we macerate some, leave others fresh, and bring in a complex touch of acidity by combining vinegar and raspberry juice to make a sharp berry jelly.

SERVES 4

Citrus Cream

1 lemongrass stalk, tough outer
  leaves and stems discarded,
  roughly chopped
1 tablespoon lemon zest
1 teaspoon lime zest
2 cups whipping (35%) cream
Pinch of kosher salt

Raspberry Vinegar Jelly

2 cups fresh raspberries
1 tablespoon sugar
¼ teaspoon kosher salt
2 tablespoons white balsamic vinegar
2 gelatin leaves

Fresh Cleaned Berries

1 cup hulled strawberries
1 cup pitted sweet cherries

½ cup blueberries
½ cup mulberries
½ cup red and black currants
½ cup pitted ground cherries
1 teaspoon sugar

Garnishes

Sweet cicely
Anise hyssop
Mint leaves

FOR THE CITRUS CREAM

In a 4-cup mason jar or other container, combine the chopped lemongrass and lemon and lime zests. Pour the cream over the aromatics, cover with the lid and leave to infuse with the citrus flavours overnight in the refrigerator.

The next day, when you're just about ready to use it, strain the cream through a fine-mesh sieve into a pouring jug and stir in the salt to season.

FOR THE RASPBERRY VINEGAR JELLY

In a medium bowl, crush the raspberries with the sugar, salt and white balsamic vinegar with the back of a fork. Cover the bowl with plastic wrap and leave to macerate for 1 hour at room temperature.

Strain the macerated raspberry mixture through a fine-mesh sieve into a small saucepan and discard the crushed raspberries. You should have about 1 cup of juice.

In a medium bowl, bloom the gelatin leaves by submerging them in cold water until soft, about

5 minutes. Lift the softened gelatin leaves from the bowl and squeeze out the water. Discard the water.

Gently bring the raspberry juice to a simmer over low heat. Remove the juice from the heat and whisk in the bloomed gelatin until completely dissolved. Line a square 4-cup container with plastic wrap, leaving an overhang. Pour in the raspberry juice and refrigerate until the jelly is set, at least 2 hours.

When ready to serve, flip the jelly out onto a cutting board, remove the plastic wrap and cut into ½-inch cubes.

TO SERVE

Divide the citrus cream among shallow serving bowls. Slice some of the larger berries in half or into thin slices and leave the others whole. Mix the berries in a large bowl. Sprinkle with the sugar and gently mix the berries until the sugar dissolves into their juices. Spoon the berries into the bowls with some of their juices. Garnish with the sweet cicely, anise hyssop, mint and raspberry jelly cubes.

SWEET CORN
with chanterelle mushrooms and chickweed

CORN IS A GREAT INGREDIENT: it's abundant, it's home-grown and it's delicious. Its natural sweet flavour works really well with everything from earthy elements to proteins to shellfish and fish. In this recipe we're letting it shine on its own with just wild chanterelles. This started out as a garnish for a rabbit dish, then for a chicken dish, and then for a crab dish, but I love it just on its own, a showcase for something from the farm and the forest.

SERVES 4

Corn Purée

1 tablespoon unsalted butter

2 cups fresh sweet corn kernels (about 4 sweet corn cobs)

2 cups whipping (35%) cream

1 teaspoon kosher salt

Chanterelle Mushrooms

1 tablespoon vegetable oil

5 ounces (140 g) button chanterelle mushrooms (2 cups)

2 garlic cloves, crushed

½ tablespoon fresh thyme leaves

Kosher salt

2 cups fresh sweet corn kernels (about 4 sweet corn cobs)

2 tablespoons unsalted butter

1 tablespoon minced shallot

1 cup Madeira

Garnishes

Chickweed

Cornflowers or bachelor's buttons

Thyme or oregano flowers

FOR THE CORN PURÉE

Melt the butter in a medium saucepan over low heat. Add the corn kernels and cook gently, stirring occasionally, until tender, about 5 minutes. Add the cream and salt. Partially cover with a lid, allowing the steam to escape, and cook at a low simmer for 10 minutes.

When the corn is cooked, strain the cream into another container, reserving it for adjusting the consistency of the purée. In a high-speed blender, purée the corn, adding just enough of the cream in a slow, steady stream while blending to achieve a smooth, thick purée similar to a velvety pudding consistency. When processed, adjust the seasoning with salt, if needed. Strain through a fine-mesh sieve back into the saucepan. Keep covered. Heat gently before serving.

FOR THE CHANTERELLE MUSHROOMS

In a medium frying pan, heat the vegetable oil over medium heat. Add the mushrooms, garlic and thyme. Season with the salt and fry, stirring frequently to prevent browning, for 1 minute. Stir in the corn. Reduce the heat to low, stir in the butter and shallots and cook for 1 minute, until the butter is foaming and starting to brown. Add the Madeira and reduce until the wine is evaporated completely. Using a slotted spoon, transfer the corn and mushrooms to paper towel to absorb excess fat.

TO SERVE

Place 2 tablespoons of warm corn purée just off-centre on each plate. Generously spoon the mushroom and corn mixture beside the corn purée. Garnish with chickweed, cornflowers and thyme flowers.

ZUCCHINI

with homemade ricotta, red currants and garden herbs

I LOVE THE CHALLENGE OF TAKING a familiar ingredient and doing a deep dive on it to see how much we can get out of it. Zucchini is a vegetable that can be used in so many different ways. It's great raw, in a soup or deep-fried, and the leaves and the flowers are incredible, but it doesn't really have a lot of flavour on its own, so you really have to bump it up. In this recipe, the lemon verbena leaves and the sour red fruit complement the roasted zucchini beautifully. Add creamy ricotta and the toasted crunch of hazelnuts and you have an ideal summer snack.

SERVES 4

Ricotta Cheese
2 cups whole milk
1 cup whipping (35%) cream
¼ cup white vinegar
2 tablespoons fresh lemon juice
1 tablespoon kosher salt

Roasted Zucchini
2 medium yellow zucchini
1 tablespoon kosher salt
2 tablespoons vegetable oil
½ tablespoon minced garlic
½ cup Shallot Vinaigrette (page 282)

Garnishes
Red currants
Crushed peeled and toasted
    hazelnuts
Lemon verbena leaves
Zucchini flowers
Chives
Shaved raw zucchini

FOR THE RICOTTA CHEESE
Place a colander or fine-mesh sieve over a large bowl and line it with 3 layers of cheesecloth. In a medium saucepan over medium heat, bring the milk and cream to just under a simmer. Stir in the vinegar, lemon juice and salt and continue to simmer for 1 minute. You should see a clear separation of the liquid (whey) and solids (curd). Remove from the heat and let cool to room temperature.

Pour the whey and curds through the cheesecloth. Transfer to the refrigerator and let the whey strain out of the cheese overnight.

The next day, spoon the ricotta out of the colander into a small bowl and season with more lemon juice and salt, if desired. Store in a covered container in the refrigerator for up to 3 days.

FOR THE ZUCCHINI
Preheat the oven to 350°F (180°C).

With a sharp knife, cut the zucchini in half lengthwise. Lay the zucchini halves cut side up on a cutting board and, using a paring knife, lightly score the flesh in a crisscross pattern. Season the scored side of the zucchini with the salt. In a large cast-iron skillet, heat the vegetable oil over medium-high heat until the oil starts to smoke lightly. Carefully lay the zucchini cut side down in the pan and fry until the flesh is golden brown and lightly caramelized, 1 to 2 minutes. Turn the zucchini over and spread the minced garlic on them evenly to coat. Transfer to the oven and bake until the zucchini is cooked and tender, about 4 minutes. Transfer the zucchini to a plate to cool.

TO SERVE
Place a zucchini half in the centre of each plate, then drizzle with some of the shallot vinaigrette. Spread a generous amount of ricotta evenly over the surface of the zucchini. Sprinkle a few currants over the ricotta, letting them fall naturally into the crevices of the cheese. Sprinkle with the hazelnuts and scatter the lemon verbena, zucchini flowers and chives from one end to the other. In a small bowl, toss the shaved zucchini with a little salt and shallot vinaigrette and arrange on top to finish the dish.

SUMMER HERB GARDEN RISOTTO

with sweet peas and fine herbs

THERE IS SOMETHING SPECIAL AND exciting about a perfect risotto. When you look at this spoon of rice it doesn't look complicated, and it's not, but when you take the time to compile the best ingredients, follow the basic rules of rice cookery and use the right technique, it truly becomes something incredible. Risotto is also a blank canvas for flavours. In this case, for spring or summer, we focus on freshness by starting with a very tasty, well-balanced herbal vegetable nage to cook your rice in and then finishing it with a purée of sweet peas. We stir in butter and good-quality Parmigiano-Reggiano or pecorino at the end to give it a tiny bit of acidity and sharpness, so you wind up with a luxurious taste of the garden in risotto form.

SERVES 4

Summer Herb Garden Risotto

6 to 7 cups Vegetable and White Wine Nage (from 1 batch, page 285)

2 tablespoons extra-virgin olive oil, more for serving

½ cup minced shallots

1 cup arborio or carnaroli rice

½ teaspoon kosher salt

½ cup English Pea Purée (page 51)

½ tablespoon unsalted butter

½ cup grated Parmigiano-Reggiano, more for serving

FOR THE SUMMER HERB GARDEN RISOTTO

In a medium saucepan, bring the vegetable and white wine nage to a boil over medium-high heat. When the nage is boiling, reduce the heat to a low simmer.

Heat the olive oil in a medium saucepan or casserole dish over medium-low heat. Add the shallots and cook gently, stirring occasionally, until tender and translucent, 4 to 6 minutes. Add the rice, stir to coat with the oil and shallots, and cook, stirring frequently, for 2 minutes. Increase the heat to medium and add 1 cup of the hot nage and the salt. Cook, stirring constantly and keeping the rice at a gentle simmer, until all the liquid is absorbed. Repeat adding enough hot nage to just cover and moisten the rice, stirring until each addition is absorbed before adding more, until the risotto is creamy and the rice al dente, 16 to 20 minutes. Remove from the heat and stir in the sweet pea purée, butter and Parmigiano-Reggiano. Season with more salt, if needed.

TO SERVE

Ladle the risotto into warm shallow bowls and top with extra grated Parmigiano-Reggiano and olive oil.

JB'S TIPS

This is a good opportunity to make a delicious herb stock using your stems. People often just toss their herb stems in the compost, but they have a lot of flavour, so why not make a delicious stock that you can freeze and pull out whenever you want a nice fresh pop of summery herb-garden flavour.

This is also a great opportunity to get the most out of your Parmesan. We save the rinds of Parmigiano-Reggiano and add them to the stock to give the risotto another dimension of cheese flavour.

ROSEMARY COUNTRY LOAF

OUR MUCH-LOVED THIRTY-YEAR-OLD ROSEMARY BUSH was the inspiration for this recipe. It's a very special plant that lives in a great big stone pot, spending its summers soaking up the sun in the garden and wintering in a place of pride in the greenhouse. The needles are slick with a delicious natural sap, and when it flowers, we harvest the beautiful sweet purple blossoms to add a special touch to all kinds of dishes.

In this rustic country loaf the rosemary is the star, offering a herbaceous, savoury note to the soft, clean flavour of the bread. The thin crust makes this loaf the perfect choice for a sandwich or served modestly with a plate of cheese.

MAKES 1 LOAF

Country Loaf

1 cup water, at room temperature

2 tablespoons chopped fresh rosemary

1¼ teaspoons kosher salt

2 cups all-purpose flour

⅓ cup light rye flour

¼ teaspoon active dry yeast

FOR THE DOUGH

In the bowl of a stand mixer, combine the water, rosemary and salt. Spoon the all-purpose flour and rye flour evenly over the water and sprinkle the yeast on top. Attach the dough hook and, on low speed, mix all the ingredients together until combined. Turn the mixer to medium speed and mix for 5 minutes or until the dough forms a smooth ball and pulls away from the side of the bowl. Transfer the dough to an oiled medium bowl, cover with a damp kitchen towel and proof at room temperature until it doubles in size, 45 minutes to 1 hour.

Turn the dough out onto a work surface and form into a ball. Allow to rest for 10 minutes. Shape into an oval loaf. Place on a baking sheet lined with parchment paper, cover with a damp kitchen towel and proof for another 45 minutes to 1 hour. The dough will almost double in size, and when you press it with a finger, the indent will spring back.

BAKE THE BREAD

While the dough proofs the final time, preheat the oven to 450°F (230°C) with a cast-iron pan on the bottom rack.

When the dough is proofed, add 2 cups of ice cubes to the cast-iron pan to create steam. Immediately score the loaf and place on the middle or top rack of the oven. Reduce the oven temperature to 375°F (190°C) and bake for 20 minutes. At the 15-minute mark, remove the cast-iron pan to develop the crust. The bread will be a golden brown colour and sound hollow when fully baked. Cool on a rack to room temperature. This bread is best enjoyed the day it is baked. Bag or wrap the bread in cotton cloth and keep for up to 2 days in a cool place.

JB'S TIPS

This country loaf is a wonderful base recipe to learn from. Play around with the herb component: thyme, dill or chives all work really well. For that matter, it is just as great with no herbs at all. However you decide to go, I think the best way to serve it is warm with a little good-quality extra-virgin olive oil for dipping, or with fresh Cultured Butter (page 21) and flaky sea salt on the side.

Keep in mind that all ovens are different; you might have to make minimal adjustments to the temperatures and bake time as you learn this recipe.

LILAC BLOSSOM PANNA COTTA
with raspberry consommé jelly, raspberry yogurt sponge cake and lilac blossoms

LILAC GROWS ALL OVER THE property here, and the smell when it first blooms as we're rolling into spring is just phenomenal. Flavour-wise, the flower pollen and nectar are quite delicate but potent, and they really do well in this recipe with the cream.

If you don't have access to ripe lilac blossoms, dried lavender is an excellent, widely available substitute. Instead of the flower elements you could take the panna cotta in a citrus direction, adding a bit of zest and straining it out before the panna cotta sets. Steeping a floral tea such as chamomile, jasmine or garden flower blend in the cream would also work beautifully in this recipe.

SERVES 4

Lilac Blossom Panna Cotta
¾ cup whipping (35%) cream
½ cup lilac blossoms
1¼ gelatin leaves
2 tablespoons sugar
⅓ cup whole milk, cold
1 teaspoon lilac water or bitters
⅛ teaspoon fresh lemon juice

Raspberry Consommé
2 cups fresh or frozen raspberries

3 tablespoons sugar
⅛ teaspoon kosher salt

Raspberry Consommé Jelly
1¼ gelatin leaves
½ cup raspberry consommé (recipe at left)

Raspberry Purée (makes about ½ to ⅔ cup)
1 cup ripe raspberries

Raspberry Yogurt Sponge Cake
¼ cup plain natural full-fat yogurt
⅓ cup raspberry purée (recipe at left)
¼ cup sugar
2 tablespoons egg white powder
2 tablespoons all-purpose flour
⅛ teaspoon kosher salt

Garnishes
Raspberries, torn into small pieces
Lilac flowers

FOR THE LILAC BLOSSOM PANNA COTTA

In a small saucepan, heat the cream to a simmer over medium-low heat. Remove from the heat, add the lilac blossoms and steep for 30 minutes.

In a small bowl, bloom the gelatin leaves by submerging them in cold water until soft, about 5 minutes. Lift the softened gelatin leaves from the bowl and squeeze out the water. Discard the water.

Strain the cream through a fine-mesh sieve and return it to the saucepan. Discard the lilac blossoms. Add the sugar to the steeped cream and bring back to a simmer. Remove from the heat and whisk in the bloomed gelatin until completely dissolved. Stir in the cold milk, lilac water and lemon juice, then strain the mixture through a fine-mesh sieve into a bowl with a pouring spout or a jug. Pour into 4 small serving bowls. Cover with plastic wrap and chill in the refrigerator overnight.

FOR THE RASPBERRY CONSOMMÉ

In a small bowl, mix the raspberries with the sugar and salt. Cover with a kitchen towel and let stand in a warm space for 6 hours.

Using a small mesh strainer lined with cheesecloth or a coffee filter, strain the juice into another small bowl. Allow the juice to naturally drip—do not press the fruit or the consommé will be cloudy.

FOR THE RASPBERRY CONSOMMÉ JELLY

In a medium bowl, bloom the gelatin leaves by submerging them in cold water until soft, about 5 minutes. Lift the softened gelatin leaves from the bowl and squeeze out the water. Discard the water.

In a small saucepan, warm the raspberry consommé over medium heat. Do not boil. Whisk in the bloomed gelatin until completely dissolved. Pour into a small container, cover and refrigerate until set, about 2 hours. Store in the refrigerator until ready to use.

RECIPE CONTINUES . . .

FOR THE RASPBERRY PURÉE

In a high-speed blender, purée the raspberries. Press the purée through a fine-mesh sieve into a small bowl to remove any seeds. Transfer to a mason jar with a lid or other covered container and keep in the refrigerator until ready to use or up to 3 days.

FOR THE RASPBERRY YOGURT SPONGE CAKE

Add the yogurt to a blender and top with the raspberry purée. (Layer these first to help incorporate the ingredients more easily.) Add the sugar, egg white powder, flour and salt. Blend on low speed until combined. Strain through a fine-mesh sieve. Pour the batter into a 1-litre siphon canister, filling it halfway. Secure the lid and charge with 2 cartridges of CO_2, shaking well after each charge. Leave in the refrigerator overnight.

Poke several holes around the sides and bottom of six 12-ounce paper coffee cups using a paring knife to allow some of the steam to escape. Siphon the aerated cake batter into the cups, filling them about halfway. Place one cup at a time in the microwave and cook at 70 percent power for 50 seconds or until the sponge cake is nearly fully baked—moist but no longer in a liquid state. Take the cup out of the microwave and place it upside down on the countertop. The residual steam will finish the cooking. Repeat with the remaining cups. Allow to cool completely. Remove the cake from the cups and tear into small bite-size pieces. There will be leftover batter and cake.

TO SERVE

On the set panna cotta, arrange pieces of the raspberry yogurt sponge cake. Using a spoon, place a scoop of the raspberry consommé jelly beside the sponge cake. Garnish with the torn raspberry pieces and lilac blossoms.

BLACKBERRY BOMBE

with vanilla mousse and vanilla shortbread

THIS IS ONE OF THOSE dishes that is all about taking one particular ingredient and blowing it up in a variety of different ways to really showcase it. We start with a white chocolate mousse and glaze it in blackberry juice, then we garnish it with wild and farmed blackberries and add a blackberry ganache. For a pop of colour and sweet herbaceousness we add a bit of Queen Anne's lace, a type of wild carrot. It has a lovely fruity carrot flavour and is so abundant here, and tasty, we take every opportunity to introduce guests to a little bit of the wild plants on the property, but at home you could easily garnish this with mint or basil or anise hyssop.

SERVES 6

Vanilla Shortbread

⅔ cup unsalted butter, at room temperature

½ cup icing sugar

1 teaspoon kosher salt

½ vanilla bean, split in half lengthwise and seeds scraped

1 egg yolk

1 cup all-purpose flour

Blackberry Purée

3 pounds (1.4 kg) fresh blackberries

Blackberry Jam

2 tablespoons sugar

⅛ teaspoon apple pectin powder

1 cup blackberry purée (recipe above)

Blackberry Chantilly

6.2 ounces (175 g) white chocolate, chopped

½ cup whipping (35%) cream

½ cup blackberry purée (recipe at left)

Vanilla Anglaise

½ cup whipping (35%) cream

½ cup whole milk, divided

½ vanilla bean, split in half lengthwise and seeds scraped

½ cup sugar

4 large egg yolks

Vanilla Mousse

5 gelatin leaves

1 cup whipping (35%) cream

Blackberry Glaze

2½ gelatin leaves

½ cup sugar

2 teaspoons pectin NH

1½ cups blackberry purée (recipe at left)

⅔ cup water

Garnishes

Fresh wild blackberries

Queen Anne's lace

FOR THE VANILLA SHORTBREAD

In the bowl of a stand mixer fitted with the paddle attachment, combine the butter, icing sugar, salt and vanilla bean seeds. Beat on medium speed until well combined. Add the egg yolk and beat to combine. Add the flour and mix on low speed just until incorporated. Scrape the dough out of the bowl, flatten it into a disc, wrap in plastic wrap and chill for 1 hour in the refrigerator.

Preheat the oven to 325°F (160°C). Line a baking sheet with parchment paper or a silicone mat.

On a lightly floured surface, using a floured rolling pin, roll out the dough to ⅛-inch thickness.

Prick the dough all over with a fork. Cut 6 circles with a round cutter to fit the base of a 2¾-inch (7 cm) bombe mould. Transfer to the prepared baking sheet and bake until golden, about 8 minutes. Transfer to a rack and let cool.

FOR THE BLACKBERRY PURÉE

In a high-speed blender, purée the blackberries. Press the purée through a fine-mesh sieve into a medium bowl to remove any seeds. Transfer to a container or large mason jar with a lid, cover and keep in the refrigerator until ready to use.

RECIPE CONTINUES . . .

FOR THE BLACKBERRY JAM

In a small saucepan, mix together the sugar and apple pectin. Add the blackberry purée and stir well. Cook over medium heat, stirring occasionally, until the mixture reaches 212°F (100°C). Working quickly because the jam will firm up quickly, pour into mini (1 tablespoon) semi sphere silicone moulds. Freeze until solid, about 2 hours. Transfer the remaining blackberry jam to a piping bag fitted with a small plain tip and refrigerate until ready to use.

FOR THE BLACKBERRY CHANTILLY

Place the white chocolate in a small bowl. In a small saucepan, bring the cream to a simmer over medium heat. Pour it over the white chocolate and stir gently with a rubber spatula until the chocolate has melted completely and the mixture is smooth. Cool the mixture to room temperature. Using a rubber spatula, fold the blackberry purée into the white chocolate mixture. Cover and refrigerate overnight.

When ready to serve, whip to medium peaks and transfer to a piping bag fitted with a small plain tip.

FOR THE VANILLA ANGLAISE

In a medium saucepan, combine the cream, ¼ cup of the milk and the vanilla bean and seeds. Bring to a simmer over medium heat. In a small bowl, whisk together the sugar, egg yolks and the remaining ¼ cup milk. When the cream mixture is simmering, slowly pour it into the egg mixture while whisking continuously. Return the mixture to the saucepan and gently stir with a rubber spatula while heating to 180°F (82°C). Strain through a fine-mesh sieve into a medium bowl. Cool to room temperature before making the vanilla mousse.

FOR THE VANILLA MOUSSE

In a small bowl, bloom the gelatin leaves by submerging them in cold water until soft, about 5 minutes. Remove the softened gelatin leaves from the bowl and squeeze out the water. Discard the water.

In a small saucepan, warm half of the vanilla anglaise. Add the bloomed gelatin and stir until completely dissolved. Strain the warmed vanilla anglaise through a fine-mesh sieve into the remaining vanilla anglaise. (Straining again will ensure any solids are removed.) Stir to combine.

In a separate medium bowl, whip the cream to medium peaks, then fold the whipped cream into the vanilla anglaise mixture using a whisk. Transfer the mixture to a piping bag (no tip required) and pipe into six 5-ounce semi sphere silicone moulds (use about ⅓ cup per mould). Allow the mousse to partially set in the fridge for about 15 minutes. The mousse will have the texture of a soft ice-cream parfait. Pop the frozen blackberry jam from the moulds and gently push the jam, curved side down, into the vanilla mousse until the base of the jam is level with the top of the mousse. Do not submerge the jam. Gently place a vanilla shortbread cookie on top and gently press the cookie until it is level with the base of the mould. Freeze overnight.

FOR THE BLACKBERRY GLAZE

In a small bowl, bloom the gelatin leaves by submerging them in cold water until soft, about 5 minutes. Remove the softened gelatin leaves from the bowl and squeeze out the water. Discard the water.

In a small saucepan, mix together the sugar and pectin NH. Add the blackberry purée and water, mixing with a whisk. Bring to a boil over medium heat, stirring occasionally, until the temperature reaches just above a simmer (210°F/99°C). Remove from the heat, add the bloomed gelatin and stir until the gelatin has dissolved completely. Strain the glaze through a fine-mesh sieve into a clean small saucepan. Allow the glaze to cool to 86°F (30°C).

When the glaze has cooled, pop the frozen bombes out of their moulds and place them on a rack set on a baking sheet to collect excess glaze. Slowly pour the glaze over the frozen bombes to coat. Transfer the tray of bombes to the refrigerator for 5 minutes to set the glaze. Reheat the glaze to ensure it is 86°F (30°C) and repeat the process. Allow the excess glaze to drip off the bombes for a minute, then use a palette knife to move the bombes to a plate or a baking sheet lined with parchment paper and refrigerate until ready to serve.

TO SERVE

Use a palette knife to transfer the bombes to chilled plates. Pipe alternating dots of blackberry jam and blackberry Chantilly around the edge of each bombe. Decorate with blackberries and Queen Anne's lace.

GOAT MILK SORBET

with olive oil, grains of paradise, basil and sea salt

THIS IS AN EXAMPLE OF a dish that came about from being so closely connected to the local farmers. Farmer Murray came into the kitchen one day and said, "I've got a friend who has this beautiful fresh goat milk. Is that something you could use?" And we said, "Absolutely!" It was beautiful milk, so we decided to have some fun with it and made it into this sorbet. It's incredible: soft and delicate with big goat milk flavour. It put me in mind of tearing into a piece of young goat cheese or just-made burrata.

At the same time, the garden was filled with all these basil plants that were flowering. We typically use those little flowers here and there, but for this dish I wanted to really celebrate this amazing milk and those flowers. The timing was perfect, and the result is something profoundly delicious that truly speaks to the season and how special the taste-of-place experience is at Langdon Hall.

SERVES 4

Goat Milk Sorbet
½ cup sugar
⅓ cup water
⅓ cup dextrose
3 tablespoons glucose syrup
⅛ teaspoon sorbet stabilizer
1 cup plain goat milk yogurt

Garnishes
Freshly ground grains of paradise
Sea salt
Small basil leaves and flowers
Extra-virgin olive oil

FOR THE GOAT MILK SORBET

In a small saucepan, combine the sugar, water, dextrose and glucose syrup. Heat over medium-low heat, stirring occasionally. When the sugars have dissolved, after about 3 minutes, whisk in the sorbet stabilizer and bring to a simmer over medium heat. When simmering, remove from the heat and whisk in the goat milk yogurt. Allow the mixture to cool. Strain through a fine-mesh sieve into an ice-cream maker and process according to the manufacturer's instructions until the ice cream has a soft-serve consistency. Scrape into a chilled airtight container and freeze until hard, about 4 hours. Keep frozen until ready to use.

TO SERVE

Scoop the sorbet onto chilled plates or bowls. Sprinkle with a few grains of freshly ground grains of paradise and sea salt. Top with small basil leaves and flowers. Drizzle the extra-virgin olive oil around the sorbet and serve immediately.

JB'S TIP

This dish really brings home how, when you show an interest and you're passionate about what you do, when you treat farmers and your colleagues with respect, and they see how much you appreciate the hard work they do, they look out for you. By appreciating the hard work of individuals and being kind, sometimes things just fall into your lap.

CITRUS SEMIFREDDO

with lemon curd and coconut lime yogurt

THERE ARE SO MANY DIFFERENT ways to enjoy frozen desserts—they don't always have to just be about ice cream—and this is one of my favourites. We take all the citrusy ingredients from the garden—lemon verbena, lime leaves—and enhance them with zest from lemons, limes and oranges. The garnishes—coconut lime yogurt, lemon curd, lemon candy and tiny daisies—are there to balance the dish and keep it fresh while maintaining focus on the citrus.

SERVES 8

Citrus Curd

½ cup sugar

⅓ cup cornstarch

½ teaspoon kosher salt

¼ cup fresh orange juice

2 tablespoons fresh lemon juice

2 tablespoons fresh lime juice

2 large eggs

Citrus Semifreddo

1 cup whole milk

20 lemon verbena leaves

8 lime leaves

2 tablespoons lemon zest

2 tablespoons orange zest

2 teaspoons lime zest

4 large egg yolks

½ cup sugar

4 ounces (120 g) chopped white chocolate (about ⅔ cup)

3 tablespoons + 1 teaspoon orange liqueur (I use Orangella)

¼ teaspoon kosher salt

1 cup whipping (35%) cream

Lemon Curd

½ cup sugar

⅓ cup cornstarch

½ teaspoon kosher salt

½ cup fresh lemon juice

2 large eggs

Coconut Lime Yogurt

⅔ cup coconut milk yogurt

1 teaspoon lime zest

1 tablespoon fresh lime juice

¼ cup icing sugar

Lemon Candy

Zest curls from 1 lemon (using a julienne zester)

½ cup water

1 cup sugar

Garnishes

Small yellow daisies

Small white daisies

FOR THE CITRUS CURD

In a small saucepan, mix together the sugar, cornstarch and salt. In a small bowl, whisk together the orange juice, lemon juice, lime juice and eggs, then whisk into the cornstarch mixture. Cook over low heat, stirring constantly with a rubber spatula, until the mixture has thickened. This will take only a few minutes once the mixture is hot. Strain the curd through a fine-mesh sieve. Pour into 8 mini semi sphere silicone moulds (use about 1 tablespoon per mould). Freeze the curd until firm, about 2 hours.

FOR THE CITRUS SEMIFREDDO

In a medium bowl, combine the milk, lemon verbena, lime leaves, lemon zest, orange zest and lime zest. Cover and steep at room temperature for 1 hour.

Strain half of the milk through a fine-mesh sieve into a small saucepan and bring it to a simmer over low heat.

In a small bowl, whisk together the egg yolks and sugar. Strain in the remaining half of the milk through a fine-mesh sieve and stir together. Slowly pour the simmering milk into the egg mixture while whisking. Return the mixture to the saucepan and gently whisk while heating to 180°F (82°C). Remove from the heat and add the white chocolate, orange liqueur and salt. Whisk until the chocolate is melted. Strain through a fine-mesh sieve into a medium bowl and cool to room temperature.

In a separate medium bowl, whip the cream to soft peaks, then gently fold the whipped cream into the citrus mixture using a whisk. Scrape the mixture

RECIPE CONTINUES . . .

into a piping bag (no tip required) and pipe into eight 5-ounce semi sphere silicone moulds (use about ½ cup per mould). Allow the semifreddo to partially set in the freezer for about 15 minutes. Pop the frozen citrus curd from the moulds and gently push the curd, curved side down, into the centre of the semifreddo. The bottom of the curd should be covered by the semifreddo mixture. Freeze until set, about 8 hours.

FOR THE LEMON CURD

In a small saucepan, mix together the sugar, cornstarch and salt. In a small bowl, whisk together the lemon juice and eggs, then whisk into the cornstarch mixture. Cook over low heat, stirring constantly with a rubber spatula, until the mixture has thickened. This will take only a few minutes once the mixture is hot. Strain the curd through a fine-mesh sieve and allow to cool. Using a funnel, scrape the curd into a squeeze bottle or piping bag fitted with a small plain tip.

FOR THE COCONUT LIME YOGURT

In a small bowl, stir together the coconut yogurt, lime zest, lime juice and icing sugar. Using a funnel, pour the curd into a squeeze bottle or piping bag fitted with a small plain tip.

FOR THE LEMON CANDY

In a small saucepan, bring about an inch of water and the lemon zest to a simmer over medium heat to blanch. Do not boil. Drain the water and repeat four more times to cook the lemon and remove the bitterness from the zest. After the final blanch, rinse the lemon.

In the same saucepan, bring ½ cup water and the sugar to a boil over high heat, then add the lemon zest and cook for 4 minutes. Strain the zest out of the syrup. Save the lemon syrup for another use. Spread the zest on a baking sheet lined with parchment paper and allow to dry at room temperature.

TO SERVE

Place the citrus semifreddo in the centre of a chilled bowl. Allow to sit for about 10 minutes before serving to soften slightly. Pipe alternating dots of the coconut lime yogurt and lemon curd around the edge of the semifreddo. Place lemon candy curls on some of the dots. Alternate yellow and white daisies around the base of the semifreddo to finish.

HEIRLOOM ROSE AND BERRY TRIFLE
with rosewater jelly, raspberry yogurt sponge cake, Chambord Chantilly and raspberries

I WAS WALKING THROUGH THE garden one day nibbling rose petals off the bush—we have a lot of heirloom roses on the property—and I was struck by how intensely perfumed and flavoured they were. We use the rosehips in the autumn to make jams and jellies and things, but it got me thinking about making a dish that really focused on the flavour of the rose in summer, and I thought this dessert was a great way to do that. We start with a fluffy, light-flavoured berry cake, partner it with some foraged berries and jelly made from rosewater, and dust the whole thing with a powder of dehydrated roses, so it's almost as if you're sitting among rose bushes while you're eating it.

The roses we have on the property are sweet and tender and smell like roses on steroids. If you don't have access to fragrant, unsprayed roses, just use more of the macerated raspberries in place of the petals.

SERVES 4

Berry Rose Powder
1 tablespoon fresh rose petals
½ cup thinly sliced strawberries
½ cup raspberries, cut in half

Raspberry Purée (makes ½ to ⅔ cup)
1 cup ripe raspberries

Raspberry Yogurt Sponge Cake
¼ cup plain natural full-fat yogurt
⅓ cup raspberry purée (recipe above)
¼ cup sugar

2 tablespoons egg white powder
2 tablespoons all-purpose flour
⅛ teaspoon kosher salt

Chambord Chantilly
3 ounces (85 g) white chocolate, chopped
6 tablespoons Chambord liqueur
1 cup whipping (35%) cream

Rosewater Jelly
1½ gelatin leaves
½ cup rosewater

1 tablespoon water
½ teaspoon sugar
⅛ teaspoon kosher salt

Macerated Raspberries
1 cup fresh raspberries
1 teaspoon sugar
½ teaspoon fresh lemon juice

Garnish
Fresh rose petals

FOR THE BERRY ROSE POWDER
Set a dehydrator to 115°F (46°C).

Lay the rose petals, strawberries and raspberries on the dehydrator tray. Do not overlap. Dehydrate for 4 to 8 hours, until the petals and berries are completely dry and brittle. Transfer to a high-speed blender or spice grinder and process to a fine powder. Pass the powder through a fine-mesh sieve and store in an airtight container in a dry area for up to 3 days with a silica pack.

FOR THE RASPBERRY PURÉE
In a high-speed blender, purée the raspberries. Press the purée through a fine-mesh sieve into a small bowl

to remove any seeds. Transfer to a mason jar with a lid or other covered container and keep in the refrigerator until ready to use or up to 3 days.

FOR THE RASPBERRY YOGURT SPONGE CAKE
Add the yogurt to a blender and top with the raspberry purée. (Layer these first to help incorporate the ingredients more easily.) Add the sugar, egg white powder, flour and salt. Blend on low speed until combined. Strain through a fine-mesh sieve. Pour the batter into a 1-litre siphon canister, filling it halfway. Secure the lid and charge with 2 cartridges of CO_2, shaking well after each charge. Leave in the refrigerator overnight.

RECIPE CONTINUES . . .

Poke several holes around the sides and bottom of six 12-ounce paper coffee cups using a paring knife to allow some of the steam to escape. Siphon the aerated cake batter into the cups, filling them about halfway. Place one cup at a time in the microwave and cook at 70 percent power for 50 seconds or until the sponge cake is nearly fully baked—moist but no longer in a liquid state. Take the cup out of the microwave and place it upside down on the countertop. The residual steam will finish the cooking. Repeat with the remaining cups. Allow to cool completely. Remove the cakes from the cups and tear into bite-size pieces. There will be leftover batter and cake.

FOR THE CHAMBORD CHANTILLY

Place the chopped white chocolate in a medium bowl. In a small saucepan, bring the Chambord liqueur to a boil over medium heat and reduce by half. Remove from the heat and allow to cool.

In a separate small saucepan, bring the cream to a simmer over medium heat. Pour it over the white chocolate and stir gently with a rubber spatula until the chocolate has melted completely and the mixture is smooth. Stir in the reduced Chambord. Transfer to a container with a lid and chill in the refrigerator overnight.

The next day, transfer the mixture to a bowl and whip to medium soft peaks. Refrigerate until ready to use.

FOR THE ROSEWATER JELLY

In a medium bowl, bloom the gelatin leaves by submerging them in cold water until soft, about 5 minutes. Lift the softened gelatin leaves from the bowl and squeeze out the water. Discard the water.

In a small saucepan over low heat, bring the rosewater, water, sugar and salt to a simmer. Remove the saucepan from the heat and whisk in the bloomed gelatin until it is completely dissolved. Pour into a small container and cool to room temperature. Cover and refrigerate until the jelly is set, about 2 hours.

FOR THE MACERATED RASPBERRIES

Just before serving, in a small bowl, gently mix together the raspberries, sugar and lemon juice.

TO SERVE

Place a few pieces of the raspberry yogurt cake close together on plates. Spoon the macerated raspberries and some of their juices over the cake. Top with a spoon of rosewater jelly. Completely cover the raspberries and cake with the Chambord Chantilly. Dust the berry rose powder over the Chantilly. Spoon some more of the rosewater jelly onto the Chantilly. Garnish with fresh fragrant rose petals.

FIRST
FROST

A FAMILY, FROLICKING IN the gold and ochre leaves that last night's wind storm scattered across the great lawn, pauses to take a selfie. A bellman hustles over and offers to snap the shot for them. Delighted, the trio hand over the phone and embrace in the fresh, clear morning air. Click.

Autumn at Langdon Hall returns each year like an old friend, and the Carolinian forest surrounding the property puts on its finest display to welcome her arrival. Huge sugar maples show off their best burnt-orange and red, black walnuts shine chrome yellow, and the kousa dogwood, dazzling in shades of magenta, offers up ripe berries ready for jamming.

Climbing hydrangea forms a great gold arch up and across a wide trellis. Wander beneath it and open the gate it frames to discover one of the season's most magnificent displays. In a cozy corner behind the cloister building, a pair of sensational trees are putting on a show.

As the first buttery-yellow leaves of the katsura trees fall from their pink stems, they release a sweet, intoxicating aroma. "Cotton candy," a visiting five-year-old exclaims, inhaling deeply, while her little brother, trying to stuff a handful of leaves in his mouth, declares, "Birthday cake." A chemical compound called maltol—it's often used in perfumes and incense, but also appears naturally in things like baked bread, smoked pork and roasted barley—is responsible for the tree's heady, sweet aroma. Curiously, not everyone can smell it, but for those who can, it defines the season.

As the crisp days open more and there's more space in the canopy, the artistry of the garden, something that at first appears organic, starts to reveal the guiding hand of its ingenious design. The way the deciduous trees are trimmed to the same level at their bottoms, creating a line of sight that offers glimpses of the understorey beyond. The staggered way some species are planted, one Scotch pine here, two butternut hickory there, not only encourages air to flow but creates movement that draws the eye—and people—deeper into the woods and allows more colours, more species, more forest to be appreciated.

While guests relish in a spot of forest bathing, Langdon Hall's beloved honeybees are gearing up for one of the busiest times of the year, and the hives literally buzz with activity. Having produced so much honey for the kitchen—eighty-nine pounds, a bumper crop this year—they now turn their focus to looking after themselves as they prepare for the long winter ahead.

Self-care for bees doesn't include a trip to the spa for a Vichy scrub and Swedish massage, but Langdon Hall does its best to pamper the VIBs nonetheless. Thoughtfully, the gardening team has planted plenty of yarrow and goldenrod, both fall-blooming plants that are heavy with pollen and nectar at this time of year, close to the hives so the weary creatures won't have to travel far to stock up in the shortening days.

Not far from the hives, the gardeners have just broken out the antique apple press and are filling the barrel with dozens of shiny, perfectly ripe specimens. The ancient orchard doesn't produce in the same quantity as it did in its youth, but the fruit that comes is precious. Some will be saved for the pastry chefs, some will be turned into jelly to garnish roast duck or roast pork, and the rest might become syrup the bartenders can experiment with in cocktails.

While the bees may be winding down, tomatoes are on their last legs and asparagus is just a fond memory, there are plenty of ingredients in the garden that delight in the arrival of the first frost. All of the brassicas—cabbage, Brussels sprouts, turnips, kales—benefit from that first snap of cold that sends them into overdrive. To prevent freezing, they draw sugar up from their roots and send it to the leaves, making them sweeter, more tender and even more vibrant. Similarly, leeks, carrots and parsnips all hunker down and sweeten up in the cold.

Inside the warm kitchen, the brigade gets busy fermenting, pickling and drying all the lovely seeds they're harvesting: coriander, fennel, basil, mustard, arugula. "I think the more engaged and involved we get in the seasons on the property in the garden and the forest, the more excited we get about pushing even further in preservation and using every single part of the plant," Jason says. The last of the stone fruit is now ready for preserving. Sour cherry compote is ready to adorn a rich cheesecake; Niagara peaches, the best in the world, get cooked into a sharp chutney that will set off a slice of roast pork crowned with crackling; and the plums are puréed with mustard to spread on a grilled chicken sandwich.

Laden with produce, a trio of cooks haul heaping trayloads of squash, somehow managing to keep their crisp white jackets and monogrammed aprons immaculate, into the kitchen and lay their bounty out on a table. It is time for the annual squash tasting, and the cooks will soon get busy roasting up their harvest.

"Every year the bounty of squashes taste a little bit different depending on where they were growing and how the soil was treated and the climate of that particular season," Jason explains. "We might find one that's especially buttery and chocolaty and rich, so we'll use it with the pigeon. Another might be really juicy and nutty and full of flavour, so we'll do a soup with that one. Or we combine them in ways to achieve exactly the flavour we're looking for."

As the table continues to fill with gourds—dainty Golden Nuggets; cylindrical striped delicates; tapered butternuts; teardrop-shaped red kuris; massive, prehistoric-looking Blue Hubbards; vibrant vermillion Cinderellas—the scene begins to resemble a Caravaggio still life. One by one people come along and survey the arrangement and one by one they reach for their cameras to document the scene. Click.

AUTUMN SQUASH SOUP
with sweetbreads, chestnuts and orchard apple

SOUPS TELL STORIES AND are a comfort food that warms the soul. A soup talks all about the season, and while that's true of most cuisine, it's even more pronounced in a soup. You look at this one and automatically you're drawn to autumn. The flavours displayed here are just an explosion of that season—squash, apple, cinnamon and sage.

SERVES 4

Pickled Apple Pearls

1 Honeycrisp apple

½ cup Calvados

½ cup apple juice

¼ cup apple cider vinegar

¼ cup sugar

Sweetbreads

½ pound (225 g) fresh veal
    sweetbreads

1 tablespoon unsalted butter

½ cup thinly sliced white onion

½ cup thinly sliced celery

½ cup peeled and thinly sliced
    carrot

1 teaspoon sliced garlic

½ cup loosely packed fresh flat-leaf
    parsley

½ tablespoon fresh thyme leaves

1 teaspoon fresh rosemary leaves

2 fresh bay leaves

2 whole cloves

½ teaspoon black peppercorns

½ cup dry white wine

6 cups Chicken Stock (page 286)

1 tablespoon kosher salt

Squash Soup

1 tablespoon unsalted butter

½ cup thinly sliced white onion

½ cup peeled and thinly sliced
    carrot

¼ cup sliced garlic

3 cups peeled and roughly chopped
    butternut squash
    (14 ounces/400 g squash)

1 (1 inch) cinnamon stick

3 star anise

½ tablespoon fresh thyme leaves

¼ teaspoon black peppercorns

½ cup dry white wine

¼ tablespoon kosher salt

4 cups Vegetable Stock (page 285)
    or Chicken Stock (page 286)

½ teaspoon pure maple syrup

Chestnut Purée

½ tablespoon unsalted butter

¼ cup sliced shallots

½ teaspoon minced garlic

1 cup peeled and blanched
    chestnuts

1 teaspoon fresh thyme leaves

½ cup Madeira

½ cup Chicken Stock (page 286)

¼ cup whipping (35%) cream

Kosher salt

Apple Jelly

1 cup apple juice

1 tablespoon apple cider vinegar

2 tablespoons sugar

1 teaspoon kosher salt

3 gelatin leaves

Glazed Chestnuts and Sweetbreads

Poached sweetbreads (recipe at left)

1 teaspoon vegetable oil

½ teaspoon kosher salt

½ teaspoon freshly ground black
    pepper

12 chestnuts, peeled

1 tablespoon unsalted butter

1 garlic clove, crushed

1 sprig fresh thyme

½ cup Madeira

Garnish

Sage leaves and flowers

FOR THE PICKLED APPLE PEARLS

Peel the apple. Using a small melon baller (½ inch in diameter), scoop out as many perfect balls as you can. You will need 3 to 5 balls per serving; place the apple balls in a 2-cup mason jar. Save the rest for another use.

In a small saucepan, combine the Calvados, apple juice, apple cider vinegar and sugar. Bring to a simmer over medium heat and simmer gently for

5 minutes. Pour the pickling liquid into the mason jar to cover the apple balls. Allow to cool, then cover with the lid and refrigerate for at least 48 hours before using.

FOR THE SWEETBREADS

Soak the sweetbreads in ice water for 8 hours, changing the water two or three times.

In a medium saucepan, melt the butter over medium heat until it bubbles. Add the onion, celery, carrots and garlic and cook gently, stirring frequently, until the vegetables are tender and translucent, 4 to 5 minutes. Add the parsley, thyme, rosemary, bay leaves, cloves and black peppercorns and mix well. Add the sweetbreads and turn to coat in the vegetables, herbs and spices. Pour in the white wine and reduce until almost dry, about 5 minutes. Add the chicken stock and salt, bring to a simmer, then reduce the heat to low and continue to simmer gently for 5 minutes. Remove from the heat and allow the sweetbreads to cool slightly in the stock, about 8 minutes.

Remove the sweetbreads from the stock and dry with paper towel. Using a small paring knife, cut away any fat and pull away as much membrane and connective tissue as you can, being careful not to break up the sweetbreads. Return the sweetbreads to the stock, cover and store in the refrigerator overnight.

FOR THE SQUASH SOUP

In a medium saucepan, melt the butter over low heat. Add the onion, carrots and garlic and cook gently, stirring occasionally, until tender, about 5 minutes. Add the squash and continue cooking for another 5 minutes.

Tie the cinnamon, star anise, thyme and black peppercorns into a sachet using cheesecloth and butcher's twine. Add to the saucepan. Increase the heat to medium-high and add the white wine. Reduce the wine until almost completely evaporated, then add the salt and vegetable stock. Reduce the heat to a low simmer and cook gently for 15 minutes to infuse all the flavours into the stock and to cook the vegetables thoroughly. Remove from the heat. Remove the spice sachet and squeeze any liquid into the saucepan. Discard the sachet.

In batches, transfer the soup to a high-speed blender and purée to a smooth, velvety consistency. When processed, strain through a fine-mesh sieve into a clean medium saucepan. Heat gently, stir in the maple syrup, cover and keep warm.

FOR THE CHESTNUT PURÉE

In a small saucepan, melt the butter over low heat. Add the shallots and garlic and cook gently, stirring occasionally, until tender, about 2 minutes. Add the chestnuts, thyme and Madeira, increase the heat to medium and reduce the liquid to one-third. Add the

chicken stock and simmer until reduced by half. Add the cream and continue to simmer, stirring occasionally, for 3 minutes. Transfer to a high-speed blender and purée to a smooth, thick, creamy consistency. Once processed, season with salt. Strain through a fine-mesh sieve and transfer to a squeeze bottle or small container and refrigerate until ready to use. Allow the purée to come to room temperature before using.

FOR THE APPLE JELLY

In a small saucepan, gently bring the apple juice, apple cider vinegar, sugar and salt to a simmer over low heat.

Meanwhile, in a medium bowl, bloom the gelatin leaves by submerging them in cold water until soft, about 5 minutes. Lift the softened gelatin leaves from the bowl and squeeze out the water. Discard the water. Remove the apple liquid from the heat and whisk in the bloomed gelatin until it is completely dissolved. Line a small 2- to 4-cup container with plastic wrap, leaving a generous overhang. Pour in the apple liquid, cover and refrigerate until the jelly is set, about 2 hours. When set, flip the jelly onto a cutting board, remove the plastic wrap and cut into ½-inch cubes. Keep chilled.

FOR THE GLAZED CHESTNUTS AND SWEETBREADS

When ready to serve, remove the sweetbreads from the stock and pat dry with paper towel. Discard the stock. Carefully pull roughly 1-inch pieces of the sweetbread from the cluster or simply cut into 1-inch cubes.

Heat the vegetable oil in a large sauté pan over medium-high heat. Add the sweetbreads and season with salt and pepper. Fry the sweetbreads, occasionally rolling around in the oil, until golden brown, about 90 seconds per side. Add the chestnuts, butter, garlic and thyme and stir while the butter melts and bubbles, 2 minutes. Once the butter has lightly browned, add the Madeira. Bring to a boil and reduce to a glaze while basting the sweetbreads and chestnuts, about 2 minutes. Remove from the heat and keep warm.

TO SERVE

In coupe bowls, scatter the glazed chestnuts and sweetbreads. Garnish with the cubed apple jelly and pickled apple pearls and dot the bowls with the chestnut purée. Finish garnishing with the sage leaves and flowers and complete by pouring in the autumn squash soup at the table.

WINE PAIRING

I love a Viognier with this soup, though if you want to splash out, a Condrieu from the Rhone valley with a little bit of oak aging would also be great. Viognier has a lovely exotic note and a spiciness that works so well with the sweet lusciousness of this soup and its autumn spices. You don't want something linear. The soup fills your mouth, so you want something that has that same richness and weight on the palate. A lot of time, pairings go sideways because people don't think about how the wine works as it's going over your palate. It has to match weights, or there has to be a reason why you want to cut through fat. This dish needs something that balances out and can hold its own against everything that's going on. Viognier is not over the top, but it's lush. It's a wine you can appreciate so much on the bouquet. It has richness and decadence to it and a perfumed florality but without making you think you've walked through a perfume display. The soup is so well balanced already, and the Viognier is just adding more of what the soup is already about.

BEETROOT JELLY AND GOAT CHEESE MACARON

CANAPÉS AND AMUSE-BOUCHES ARE THAT first bite that sets the tone for the rest of the meal. This one is meant to be something playful that starts a conversation and lets diners know they can expect delicious garden ingredients prepared in ways that are out of the ordinary.

Beets and goat cheese are a classic combination, but what's unexpected here is that we take savoury ingredients and prepare them the way we would for the end of a meal, only we serve them at the beginning. The goat cheese is whipped to a nice smooth paste and then sandwiched between macaron shells. We pair the macaron with a beetroot jelly that is almost like a pâte de fruit, but on the savoury side, and top it all off with a borscht-flavoured jam. Top it all off with a beetroot gel, dill and dill flowers.

MAKES UP TO 25 MACARONS

Macarons (makes fifty 1½-inch macaron shells)

1½ cups almond flour

1 cup + 1 tablespoon icing sugar

½ cup large egg whites (about 4 egg whites), divided

¾ cup granulated sugar

3 tablespoons water

Beetroot Gel

1¼ cups red beet juice (from 4 peeled medium beets)

⅓ cup fresh orange juice

2 tablespoons white wine vinegar

½ tablespoon (4.7 grams) agar powder

½ cup lightly packed fresh dill leaves

Garden Borscht Jelly

1 teaspoon olive oil

½ cup thinly sliced white onion

¼ cup thinly sliced leeks (white part only)

2 tablespoons thinly sliced celery

2 tablespoons thinly sliced peeled carrot

1 teaspoon thinly sliced garlic

½ teaspoon minced peeled fresh ginger

1 lemongrass stalk, tough outer leaves and stems discarded, roughly chopped

½ teaspoon kosher salt

1 cup thinly sliced peeled red beets

1 fresh bay leaf

2 tablespoons lightly packed fresh tarragon leaves

2 tablespoons lightly packed fresh dill leaves

2 tablespoons lightly packed fresh flat-leaf parsley

1 tablespoon orange zest

2 cups beet juice (from 6 peeled medium beets)

¼ cup red wine vinegar

2 tablespoons rice wine vinegar

1 tablespoon fresh orange juice

6 gelatin leaves

1 tablespoon dill pollen

Goat Cheese Filling

1 cup soft aged goat cheese, rind removed

1 cup soft fresh goat cheese

½ cup whipping (35%) cream

Garnish

Dill leaves and flowers

FOR THE MACARON SHELLS

Position the racks in the upper and lower thirds of the oven. Preheat the oven to 240°F (115°C). Line 2 baking sheets with parchment paper or silicone mats, and prepare 2 piping bags with ¼-inch plain tips. Set up a stand mixer fitted with the whisk attachment.

In a medium bowl, sift the almond flour and icing sugar. Mix in ¼ cup of the egg whites and stir to make a firm paste.

In a small saucepan, combine the granulated sugar and water and cook over high heat until the syrup reaches 245°F (118°C), about 3 minutes. Meanwhile, in the stand mixer, whip the remaining ¼ cup egg whites on medium speed until frothy. While whipping, slowly add the hot syrup to the egg whites and continue to whip until medium peaks form.

Fold the meringue into the almond paste in 3 additions, folding in the final addition delicately to

RECIPE CONTINUES . . .

protect the air in the meringue batter. Transfer the batter to the piping bags and pipe 1½-inch rounds onto the prepared baking sheets, about 1 inch apart. Allow to rest at room temperature until a skin forms, about 20 minutes. If you touch a macaron with a dry finger, it should not come away wet. Bake for 18 to 24 minutes, turning the baking sheets every 6 minutes to ensure even baking. The macarons are done when they have a firm shiny shell, are still slightly chewy in the centre and release cleanly from the parchment paper or silicone mat. Cool completely on the baking sheets and store in an airtight container in a dry area.

FOR THE BEETROOT GEL

In a medium saucepan, combine the beet juice, orange juice and white wine vinegar. Whisk in the agar powder and bring to a boil over medium heat. Remove from the heat, add the dill and allow to infuse for 2 minutes. Strain through a fine-mesh sieve into a medium bowl and refrigerate for 2 hours or until the jelly is firmly set.

Remove the jelly from the bowl and cut into rough pieces. Transfer the jelly pieces to a blender and blend until smooth. Strain through a fine-mesh strainer (to remove any small lumps) into a small bowl or squeeze bottle. Store, covered, in the refrigerator.

FOR THE GARDEN BORSCHT JELLY

In a medium saucepan, heat the olive oil over medium heat. Add the onion, leek, celery, carrot, garlic, ginger and lemongrass. Reduce the heat and cook, stirring often, over medium-low heat until the vegetables are tender, about 5 minutes. Add the salt, sliced beets, bay leaf, tarragon, dill, parsley and orange zest and continue to cook for 2 more minutes. Add the beet juice, red wine vinegar, rice wine vinegar and orange juice. Reduce the heat to low and simmer, stirring occasionally, for 10 minutes.

Meanwhile, in a medium bowl, bloom the gelatin leaves by submerging them in cold water until soft,

about 5 minutes. Remove the softened gelatin leaves from the bowl and squeeze out the water. Discard the water.

Strain the borscht through a fine-mesh sieve into a clean saucepan, pressing as much liquid out of the vegetables as possible. Discard the vegetables. Add the bloomed gelatin to the borscht and whisk until it is completely dissolved. Allow to cool to room temperature.

Line a deep baking pan or similar container with plastic wrap. Pour the borscht into the prepared pan to roughly 1-inch thickness. Transfer the baking pan to the refrigerator and chill until set, at least 2 hours.

When ready to serve, turn the borscht jelly out onto a cutting board and remove the plastic wrap.

FOR THE GOAT CHEESE FILLING

Place the aged goat cheese, fresh goat cheese and cream in a medium bowl. Half-fill a medium saucepan with water and bring to a simmer. Place the bowl of cheese over the simmering water and stir as the steam warms the bottom of the bowl and gently melts the cheese. Keep stirring until smooth. Pass through a fine-mesh sieve into a medium bowl. Set the bowl inside a larger bowl of ice and cool while stirring. When the filling is completely cool, use a rubber spatula to transfer it to a piping bag fitted with a plain medium or large icing tip.

TO SERVE

Pipe some goat cheese filling onto the flat side of one of the macaron shells. The amount of filling should be equivalent to the size of the macaron. Top with a second macaron shell, flat side down, and gently press to push the filling to the edge of the macaron. Place the macaron on a small plate, dot the top with beetroot gel and garnish with dill leaves and flowers. Cut the borscht jelly into 1-inch cubes and in a small bowl, toss with the dill pollen to coat. Garnish the plate with the borscht jelly cubes.

JUNIPER-SMOKED TROUT
with evergreen aïoli and young spruce tips

I'VE ALWAYS BEEN DRAWN TO the many different kinds of fir and spruce and pine that grow in the Carolinian forest that surrounds us, and I love trying to capture the flavour of that forest and find ways to use it to connect dishes to the property. We have lots of juniper bushes here, and it's great to be able to just take some of that off the bush, light it on fire and put it in a baking dish with a trout fillet, cover it and let it gently smoke in a warm oven. The juniper smoke is incredible with the fish. To bring in even more of that coniferous flavour, we incorporate juniper berries and a forest mayonnaise flavoured with white pine needles, giving off all kinds of delicious fresh evergreen flavours. The white pine brings notes of citrus, horseradish and mustard.

SERVES 4

Pine Oil

2 cups white pine needles

2 cups vegetable oil

Evergreen Aïoli (makes extra)

2 egg yolks

½ tablespoon Dijon mustard

1 teaspoon white wine vinegar

2 cups pine oil (recipe above)

1 teaspoon fresh lemon juice

1 teaspoon kosher salt

Smoked Trout

½ cup kosher salt

¼ cup sugar

6 juniper berries

2 fillets (12 ounces/340 g each) skin-on rainbow trout

2 cups roughly chopped young juniper branches or apple or white birch chips

Garnish

Young spruce tips

FOR THE PINE OIL

Set a sous vide water bath to 194°F (90°C). In a sous vide bag, combine the white pine needles and vegetable oil. Vacuum-seal on full pressure and cook in the water bath for 1 hour. Remove the bag from the water bath, place in the refrigerator and let infuse overnight.

The next day, strain through a fine-mesh sieve lined with cheesecloth into a 2-cup mason jar. Cover with the lid and set aside until ready to use.

FOR THE EVERGREEN AÏOLI

In a medium bowl, whisk together the egg yolks, mustard and white wine vinegar to form a paste. While whisking, slowly drizzle in the pine oil to emulsify. Season with the lemon juice and salt. If the aïoli becomes too thick, thin it with a few drops of room-temperature water.

FOR THE SMOKED TROUT

Combine the salt, sugar and juniper berries in a high-speed blender. Blend on high speed for 1 minute to combine the ingredients well. Lightly season both sides of the trout fillets with the cure mixture. It is important that the fillets are not overly seasoned with the cure. It will stay on the fish throughout the entire process, so adding too much will over-season the fillets. Depending on the size of the fillets, you may have extra cure mixture. Place the fillets skin side down on a wire rack and refrigerate for 3 hours to cure lightly and dry slightly.

Prepare a smoker or barbecue with juniper branches or apple or white birch wood. If using a smoker, once the fire has burned down to a low temperature, place the wire rack with the fish in the smoker with the fish on the opposite side of the coals. (If using a barbecue, turn on one side, leaving

RECIPE CONTINUES . . .

the other cold. Place the juniper or wood chips in a small roasting pan lined with foil, light them with a torch and allow them to burn to a low temperature, then blow out the flame to allow the wood to smoulder and smoke. Place the fish on the cold side of the barbecue. Place some of the juniper branches or wood chips near the coals to generate more smoke. Keep in mind that you are not generating more heat here, only smoke to release the aromas of juniper. Close the lid.) Smoke for no more than 10 to 20 minutes, depending on the size of the smoker or barbecue. Maintain the heat at 200 to 220°F (100 to 105°C) so the fish does not overcook. When the fish is ready, it should be cooked rare to medium-rare doneness and still be moist and juicy with a sweet smokiness.

Allow the fish to cool to room temperature. Peel the skin away from the flesh. Using a sharp knife, cut the fillet into 4 portions.

TO SERVE

The trout can be enjoyed cold, at room temperature or gently heated in the oven. Serve with the evergreen aïoli and garnish with soft young spruce tips.

JB'S TIP

Don't be intimidated by the evergreen aïoli. But, if you really don't want to make it, this smoked trout would be equally delicious with a simple garlic aïoli or a mayonnaise spruced up with some maple syrup and chopped juniper berries or some fresh herbs and chopped capers. Alternatively, any tartar sauce-type condiment will work fine.

TROUT TOAST

with toasted brioche, crème fraîche, sunflower and pickled shallots

I LOVE TOAST. YOU CAN serve anything on toast. I created this recipe for the Wilks' Bar menu, where we take our inspiration from traditional pub and bar food but try to make it different, fresh and memorable. This is basically a play on a tartine, but instead of a thick piece of sourdough with rillettes or a salad on it, we've taken brioche, gently fried it in butter and then topped it with some lightly cured trout that we hit with just enough fruitwood smoke to cook it. Then we dress it with some sunflower petals, sunflower seeds and crème fraîche. This would make an elegant canapé or accompaniment to a light lunch.

We have an amazing trout source in Ontario thanks to Sean Brady at Kolapore Springs Fish Hatchery. Sean produces beautiful, very fresh products that come right from the water to our kitchen, so we really want to treat them with the respect they deserve. Sometimes trout gets a bad rap because it's not overly expensive and it's a local lake fish, but it's delicious and very versatile and something I always like to have on the menus.

SERVES 4

Pickled Shallots

½ cup thinly sliced shallots

1 cup white balsamic vinegar

1 teaspoon sugar

¼ teaspoon kosher salt

1 teaspoon coriander seeds

½ teaspoon mustard seeds

1 teaspoon fresh thyme leaves

1 fresh bay leaf

Smoked Trout

1 cup sugar

½ cup kosher salt

1 tablespoon lemon zest

1 tablespoon chopped fresh dill

5 star anise

1 teaspoon coriander seeds

1 teaspoon fennel seeds

1 teaspoon juniper berries

¼ teaspoon white peppercorns

1 skin-on rainbow trout fillet
   (12 ounces/340 g)

2 cups apple or white birch chips

Toasted Brioche

Three 1-inch slices of brioche, crust
   removed

¼ cup unsalted butter, softened

Garnishes

Crème Fraîche (page 281)

Toasted sunflower seeds

Small sunflower or yellow daisy
   petals

FOR THE PICKLED SHALLOTS

Place the shallots in a 2-cup mason jar. In a small saucepan, combine the white balsamic vinegar, sugar, salt, coriander seeds, mustard seeds, thyme and bay leaf. Bring to a simmer over medium heat and simmer for 2 minutes. Pour the pickling liquid into the jar to cover the shallots. Allow to cool, seal the jar with the lid and refrigerate for at least 48 hours before using.

TO CURE THE TROUT

In a medium bowl, combine the sugar and salt. In a food processor, combine the lemon zest, dill, star anise, coriander seeds, fennel seeds, juniper berries and white peppercorns. Pulse to roughly chop. Add the

spice mixture to the bowl of sugar and salt and stir well.

Spread one-third of the cure mixture in a baking sheet or casserole dish large enough to hold the trout flat. Lay the trout fillet skin side down on the cure mixture, ensuring that all the skin is in contact with the cure. Pour the remaining mixture over the trout to cover it completely. Press gently to firmly pack the mixture around the fish. Cover the dish with plastic wrap and place in the refrigerator to cure for 3 hours.

Remove the trout from the cure mixture, rinse under cold running water and pat dry with paper towel. The fish is now ready to smoke. Place it skin side down on a small wire rack.

RECIPE CONTINUES . . .

TO SMOKE THE TROUT

Prepare a smoker or barbecue with apple or white birch wood. If using a smoker, once the fire has burned down to a low temperature, place the wire rack with the fish in the smoker with the fish on the opposite side of the coals. (For a gas barbecue, turn on one side, leaving the other cold. Place the wood chips in a small roasting pan lined with foil, light them and allow them to burn down to a low flame and reduced temperature, then blow out the flame to allow the coals to smoulder and smoke. Place the fish on the cold side of the barbecue and close the lid.) Once the fire has burned down so the temperature is low, place the trout in the smoker with indirect heat, allowing the fish to cook slowly and take on the flavour of the smoke. Smoke for no more than 5 to 10 minutes, depending on the size of the smoker and heat buildup. Maintain the heat at 350°F (180°C) so the fish does not overcook. When the fish is ready, it should be cooked medium-rare to medium doneness and still be moist and juicy with a light smokiness.

Remove the trout from the smoker or barbecue. With the tip of a knife or fork, gently flake the fish off the skin.

FOR THE TOASTED BRIOCHE

Cut 4 rectangles about 4 inches in length and 1 inch wide by 1 inch thick from the brioche. In a medium frying pan over medium heat, melt the butter until bubbling. Fry the brioche in the butter until golden brown, turning to fry evenly on all sides, about 30 seconds per side. Transfer to paper towel to absorb excess butter.

TO SERVE

Transfer the crème fraîche to a squeeze bottle. Place pieces of trout on the toasted brioche. Add a few dots of crème fraîche to the top of the fish. Garnish with sunflower seeds, flower petals and some pickled shallots.

SALISH MUSSELS

with yeast butter, chickweed and samphire powder

SOMETHING SPECIAL HAPPENS WHEN YOU put mussels in a pot filled with aromatics and some liquid to create steam that gives them life—or takes their life, I guess—and then pull them out as soon as they've opened up. It's always a good idea to take that leftover cooking liquid, now infused with the natural juices of the opened mussels, and reduce it down to concentrate the flavours. In this recipe we add yeast flakes and butter to that reduction to make a delicious glaze to coat the mussels with. Chickweed from the garden adds a fresh sweet corn flavour, and we bring in a bit of the ocean with dehydrated seaweed that lends an almost matcha element.

SERVES 4

Samphire Powder

4 cups loosely packed samphire (sea asparagus)

Salish Mussels

20 live mussels

1 teaspoon vegetable oil

¼ cup sliced shallots

2 garlic cloves, sliced

6 sprigs fresh thyme

2 sprigs fresh tarragon

1 cup dry white wine

Yeast Butter

½ cup reserved mussel cooking liquid

1 cup cold unsalted butter, cubed

¼ cup nutritional yeast

1 teaspoon fresh lemon juice

½ teaspoon kosher salt

Garnish

Chickweed

FOR THE SAMPHIRE POWDER

Set a dehydrator to 120°F (50°C).

Rinse the samphire and dry well with paper towel. Lay the samphire in a single layer on the dehydrator tray and dehydrate for about 8 hours or until completely dry and brittle. Transfer to a high-speed blender and process on high speed to a fine powder. Reserve in a small bowl for dusting.

FOR THE SALISH MUSSELS

Wash the mussels well in cold water and, if needed, clean and debeard them. Heat the vegetable oil in a medium saucepan over low heat. Add the shallots and garlic and gently cook without browning, stirring occasionally, until soft and translucent, about 5 minutes.

Increase the heat to medium and add the mussels, thyme and tarragon. Stir well. Add the white wine, increase the heat to high and bring the wine to a boil. Cover with a lid and cook the mussels for

1 minute or until they have opened. Remove the pot from the heat and, using a slotted spoon or spider, transfer the mussels to a large bowl. Discard any mussels that did not open. Strain the cooking liquid through a fine-mesh sieve into a small saucepan and reserve for the yeast butter. Working over the bowl to catch any liquid, remove the mussel meat from the shells. Reserve the mussels in a small bowl and discard the shells. Reserve the liquid that has collected in the large bowl.

FOR THE YEAST BUTTER

Warm the mussel cooking liquid over medium-low heat until simmering and reduce by half, about 5 minutes. Reduce the heat to low. Once the sauce stops simmering, whisk in the cubed butter, a few pieces at a time, until melted. Keep the temperature under a simmer. Whisk in the nutritional yeast and season with the lemon juice and salt and keep, covered, in a warm place.

RECIPE CONTINUES . . .

TO SERVE

To warm the mussels, gently heat the remaining reserved cooking liquid in a large sauté pan until just simmering. Add the mussels, remove the pan from the heat, and allow the mussels to warm through. Spoon 1 tablespoon of the yeast butter onto each plate. Place the mussels on top and spoon more of the yeast butter over them to coat. Dust with the samphire powder and garnish with the chickweed.

JB'S TIPS

I love mussels and I tend to use them a lot as an accompaniment to something else, like in a sauce for fish or vegetables, because of how great their flavour is, but of course they're also fantastic all on their own. I'm not picky: I can go east coast or west coast. The Salish and the honey mussels from British Columbia are much bigger, and their meat is lusciously plump and full. The east coast mussels from Prince Edward Island are a smaller variety but equally delicious.

Well-stocked grocery stores will often carry seaweed powder or matcha powder, and that can be used in a pinch if you don't have time to make your own. If you don't have access to fresh chickweed, you can use pea shoots, chervil, parsley, tarragon or chives.

SEAFOOD CHOWDER

with humpback shrimp, oysters and potato leek purée

THIS IS A MODERN SPIN on clam or seafood chowder that we've elevated by using poached oysters and humpback shrimp. I like to use a mix of both east and west coast oysters because they're so different. The colder waters of the east coast give the oysters a crisp, briny flavour, almost like algae, whereas you get a cucumber-like freshness and creamy texture from west coast oysters. For this chowder, we have used west coast shrimp and east coast oysters.

We cook the oysters just briefly with the leeks in the final seconds, and depending on the size of the shrimp, we either add them to the leeks or, if they're tiny, we just serve them raw on a warm plate. When we pour the hot purée over them, that's enough to cook them just a little bit, but fresh shrimp are so delicate and sweet that even if they're not fully cooked, they're amazingly delicious.

SERVES 4

Leek and Potato Purée

2 tablespoons unsalted butter, divided

1 cup sliced leeks (white part only)

½ cup sliced shallots

¼ cup sliced garlic

1 fresh bay leaf

1 teaspoon fresh thyme leaves

½ teaspoon white peppercorns

2 cups peeled and sliced Yukon Gold potatoes

1 cup Fish Stock (page 287)

1 teaspoon kosher salt

4 cups whipping (35%) cream

1 tablespoon fresh lemon juice

Almond Brioche Crumb

½ cup day-old brioche cut into ½-inch dice

½ tablespoon brown sugar

6 garlic cloves

2 cups vegetable oil, for deep-frying

Kosher salt

1 cup Marcona almonds, roughly chopped

½ teaspoon freshly cracked black pepper

Seafood

8 fresh medium Malpeque oysters

1 tablespoon unsalted butter

1 cup leeks (white part only) sliced ½ inch thick

½ cup Fish Stock (page 287), Vegetable Stock (page 285) or Vegetable and White Wine Nage (page 285)

12 fresh humpback or spot shrimp, peeled and deveined

1 teaspoon kosher salt

Garnish

Fresh tarragon leaves

FOR THE LEEK AND POTATO PURÉE

Melt 1 tablespoon of the butter in a medium saucepan over low heat. Add the leeks, shallots and garlic and cook gently, stirring occasionally, until tender, about 5 minutes.

Tie the bay leaf, thyme and white peppercorns into a sachet using cheesecloth and butcher's twine. Add the sachet to the saucepan along with the potatoes and cook gently, stirring occasionally, for 5 minutes. Add the fish stock, season with the salt and bring to a simmer. Continue to cook for 5 minutes. Add the cream and cook, partially covered, on a low simmer until the potatoes are tender, about 15 minutes longer.

Remove the sachet and squeeze as much liquid as possible back into the saucepan. Discard the sachet. Strain the cream into a medium bowl, reserving it for adjusting the consistency of the chowder. In a high-speed blender, purée the vegetables, adding enough of the cream in a slow, steady stream while blending to achieve a smooth, velvety consistency. Once processed, add the lemon juice and adjust the seasoning with salt, if needed. Strain through a fine-mesh sieve back into the saucepan and keep covered. Heat gently when ready to serve.

FOR THE ALMOND BRIOCHE CRUMB

Preheat the oven to 300°F (150°C).

Place the diced brioche on a baking sheet lined with parchment paper and toast the bread, stirring occasionally, until completely dry and golden, 20 to 30 minutes. Allow to cool to room temperature. Transfer the toasted brioche and the brown sugar to a high-speed blender. Blend on high speed to a fine powder.

Slice the garlic as thinly as possible using a mandoline or sharp knife.

In a small saucepan, heat the vegetable oil over medium heat to 250°F (120°C). In small batches, so the garlic chips don't stick together or clump, deep-fry the garlic slices until they are light golden and crispy all the way through, about 2 minutes. Be careful not to burn the garlic or it will taste bitter. Using a slotted spoon, transfer the chips to paper towel to drain. Season with a pinch of salt.

Place the almonds and fried garlic in a high-speed blender and pulse 6 times to mix. Make sure to use a spatula to scrape down the sides of the blender as this mixture will become tacky. Add the brioche powder and continue to blend until fully incorporated and crumbly. The mixture should have the consistency of wet coarse sand. Season with salt and pepper.

FOR THE SEAFOOD

Shuck the oysters, reserving the juices. In a small frying pan, melt the butter over medium heat. Add the leeks, reduce the heat to low, and cook gently until the leeks are almost cooked through, 2 to 3 minutes. Add the fish stock, bring to a simmer and cook until the leeks are glazed and tender. Add the oysters and shrimp to the pan and swirl to coat in the hot liquid. Remove from the heat and season with the salt. Allow the oysters and shrimp to warm through from the residual heat of the pan, being careful not to overcook the seafood.

TO SERVE

Arrange 2 oysters, 3 shrimp and a few leeks in each warmed bowl. Bring the leek and potato purée to a simmer over medium heat, whisk in the remaining butter and oyster juice, then pour over the seafood. Sprinkle with the almond brioche crumb and garnish with fresh tarragon leaves.

LOBSTER
with celery and cilantro

I HAVE FOND MEMORIES OF spending summers on the shore in Amherst, Nova Scotia, at my grandparents'. One thing that was always a must during those visits was a lobster boil. We'd go with my grandfather down to the docks and wait for the lobster fishermen to come in. Then we'd select our lobsters, bring them home and have lobster races on the kitchen floor. Eventually we'd end up outside at the picnic table beside a big pot of boiling water. As soon as those lobsters came out of the water, we'd start cracking shells.

What I wanted to do with this recipe is keep it true to my training by respecting the animal and not wasting any part of it. We serve the lobster with its own cooking stock made into jellies and also use the elements of a court bouillon as the garnish: celery with the leaves, celery root, fresh cilantro, coriander seeds and cilantro flowers. Court bouillon is the best way to cook shellfish when serving it chilled or in a salad. It flavours the sweet flesh and adds hints of herbal notes and acidity.

SERVES 4

Cilantro Oil

1 cup lightly packed fresh cilantro leaves

½ cup lightly packed baby spinach leaves

1 tablespoon crushed coriander seeds (preferably fresh green)

1½ cups vegetable oil

Cilantro Aïoli

2 egg yolks

1 tablespoon white wine vinegar

1 teaspoon Dijon mustard

1½ cups cilantro oil (recipe above)

1 teaspoon kosher salt

Poached Lobster

4 quarts Traditional Court Bouillon (page 290)

2 live lobsters (about 1½ pounds/675 g each) or cooked tail and claw meat from 2 lobsters

Lobster Broth Jelly

Shells and bodies of 2 lobsters

1 tablespoon vegetable oil

1 cup sliced shallots

1 cup roughly chopped fennel

½ cup sliced garlic

1 lemongrass stalk, tough outer leaves and stems discarded, roughly chopped

4 star anise

2 teaspoons coriander seeds

½ tablespoon fresh thyme leaves

1 fresh bay leaf

1 cup lightly packed fresh tarragon leaves

1 cup lightly packed fresh cilantro leaves

1 cup lightly packed fresh flat-leaf parsley leaves

2 cups brandy

8 cups reserved lobster court bouillon

5 gelatin leaves

Baked Celery Root

1 celery root, cleaned

1 tablespoon vegetable oil

1 tablespoon kosher salt

Celery Root Cream

Reserved cooked celery root skin and scraps (from baked celery root above)

2 cups whipping (35%) cream

Pinch of celery salt

Poached Celery

2 stalks celery, peeled and sliced on the diagonal into 12 (2-inch) pieces

Glazed Celery

1 cup ice wine

1 cup Vegetable Stock (page 285)

1 tablespoon white balsamic vinegar

½ teaspoon kosher salt

Garnishes

Celery salt

Celery heart leaves

Cilantro leaves and flowers

Fresh coriander seeds

RECIPE CONTINUES . . .

FOR THE CILANTRO OIL

Fill a medium bowl with ice water. Bring a medium saucepan of salted water to a boil over high heat. Drop the cilantro and spinach leaves into the boiling water and blanch for 20 seconds. Drain the leaves and plunge them into the ice water, stirring to cool rapidly. When cooled, remove from the ice water and squeeze as much liquid as possible from the leaves. In a high-speed blender, combine the blanched herbs with the crushed coriander seeds and vegetable oil. Blend for 3 minutes or until you've achieved a smooth, green purée. Pour the purée into a medium jar, cover and store in the refrigerator for 2 hours.

Strain the oil through a fine-mesh sieve or several layers of cheesecloth. You will be left with a bright green cilantro-flavoured oil. The oil can be made the day before and stored in the refrigerator in a sealed container.

FOR THE CILANTRO AÏOLI

In a medium bowl, whisk together the egg yolks, white wine vinegar and mustard to mix well. While whisking, add the cilantro oil in a slow, steady stream, allowing it to emulsify into the yolk mixture. The aïoli will thicken to the texture of a silky mayonnaise. If it becomes too thick, thin it with a few drops of room-temperature water. Mix in the salt. Transfer to a squeeze bottle or small container with a lid and refrigerate for up to 5 days.

FOR THE POACHED LOBSTER

Fill a large bowl with ice water. In a large pot, bring the court bouillon to a boil over medium-high heat. When the court bouillon is boiling, plunge the lobsters head first into the court bouillon and cover with a lid. Bring back to a gentle boil, remove the lid and continue cooking for 4 minutes. Using a pair of tongs, remove the lobsters and place them on a baking sheet. Keep the court bouillon at a simmer. With a kitchen towel, twist the tails off the lobsters and plunge them into the ice water to stop the cooking. Remove the arms with claws attached and return them to the simmering court bouillon to continue cooking for an additional 3 minutes. Transfer the claws to the ice water. Reserve the bodies for the lobster broth jelly.

When the tails and claws are cool, carefully remove the meat and store, covered, in the refrigerator. Slice the tails in half lengthwise and clean out the vein that runs the length of the tail. Keep the shells for the lobster broth jelly. Reserve 8 cups of the court bouillon and let cool for the lobster broth jelly. The remaining court bouillon can be frozen for another use.

FOR THE LOBSTER BROTH JELLY

Using kitchen shears, cut the lobster bodies into 6 pieces. Add them to the reserved shells.

In a medium saucepan, heat the vegetable oil over medium-high heat. Add the lobster shells and bodies and pan-roast for 5 minutes, stirring occasionally to cook evenly while being careful not to scorch them. When nicely roasted, reduce the heat to medium-low and add the shallots, fennel, garlic and lemongrass; stir to mix. Add the star anise, coriander seeds, thyme, bay leaf, tarragon, cilantro and parsley. Continue to stir and cook gently until the vegetables are tender, about 5 minutes. Add the brandy, increase the heat to medium and cook until the liquid is almost completely evaporated. Add the reserved court bouillon and bring to a simmer, then reduce the heat to low and simmer, uncovered, for 1 hour or until the liquid is reduced to 2 cups. Strain the lobster broth through a fine-mesh sieve into a small saucepan. Discard the solids. Return the broth to a simmer.

In a medium bowl, bloom the gelatin leaves by submerging them in cold water until soft, about 5 minutes. Lift the softened gelatin leaves from the bowl and squeeze out the water. Discard the water. Remove the lobster broth from the heat and whisk in the bloomed gelatin until it is completely dissolved.

Line a small container with plastic wrap, leaving a generous overhang. Pour in the lobster broth and allow to cool slightly. Cover and refrigerate until the jelly is set, about 2 hours. When set, flip the jelly out onto a cutting board, remove the plastic wrap and cut into 1-inch cubes. Keep chilled.

FOR THE BAKED CELERY ROOT

Preheat the oven to 300°F (150°C).

Rub the celery root liberally with the vegetable oil and salt, then wrap in 2 layers of foil. Place the foil-wrapped celery root on a baking sheet and bake until tender all the way through when poked with a long knife or skewer, about 1½ hours. Cooking time will depend on the root size and density. Allow the wrapped celery root to cool for 10 to 15 minutes or until you can comfortably touch it with your hands.

Remove the celery root from the foil, cut away the outer skin and dice the flesh into ¼-inch cubes. Transfer to a medium bowl, cover and keep in the refrigerator until ready to use. Reserve the skin and other scraps for the celery root cream.

FOR THE CELERY ROOT CREAM

In a small saucepan, gently bring the celery root scraps and cream to a simmer over medium-low heat. Season with celery salt and simmer for 5 minutes. Strain the cream into another container, reserving it for adjusting the consistency of the purée. In a high-speed blender, purée the celery root, adding enough of the cream in a slow, steady stream while blending to achieve a smooth, velvety consistency. Once processed, adjust the seasoning with celery salt, if needed. Strain through a fine-mesh sieve into a small bowl and let cool. Transfer to a squeeze bottle and keep in the refrigerator until ready to use.

FOR THE POACHED CELERY

Fill a medium bowl with ice water. Bring a small saucepan of salted water to a boil and boil the celery for 2 minutes. Drain the celery and plunge into the ice water. This will stop the cooking and preserve its bright green colour. When cool, remove from the ice water and dry on paper towel. Transfer to the bowl with the baked celery root.

FOR THE GLAZED CELERY

In a small saucepan, bring the ice wine, vegetable stock and white balsamic vinegar to a gentle simmer over medium heat and simmer the liquid until it is reduced to a glaze.

When ready to serve, toss a tablespoon of the ice wine glaze with the poached celery and baked celery root to coat. Season with salt.

TO SERVE

Toss the lobster to lightly coat with the remaining ice wine glaze. Season with celery salt, if needed. Place 1 tail half and 1 claw on each plate. Arrange the cubes of lobster broth jelly and pieces of glazed celery and celery root around the lobster. Dot the plate with cilantro aïoli and celery root cream. Decorate with celery heart leaves, cilantro leaves and flowers, and fresh coriander seeds.

JB'S TIP
If you don't live on the shore and can't meet the fishers at the dock, you can still buy live lobster at most grocers and markets. A good tip to remember when buying fresh lobsters is that a lively, active lobster is a good indication it's fresh.

BABY BEETS
with goat milk yogurt and dill

WE ALWAYS HAVE UP TO half a dozen varieties of beets in our garden, so there's almost always some kind of beet production going on in the kitchen, from pickling to salt-roasted to dehydrating for our chewy beets (page 110). This dish is a simple play on the idea of beet and goat cheese or beet and yogurt. It takes a familiar combination and reimagines it in a fun, fresh way. This is the humble beet at its best.

SERVES 4

Baby Beets
10 purple baby beets
8 cups water
1 cup red wine vinegar
1 cup sugar
2 tablespoons kosher salt
6 sprigs fresh dill
2 fresh bay leaves

Goat Milk Yogurt
1 cup reserved purple beet cooking
    liquid (see at left)
1 cup plain goat milk yogurt

Garnishes
Flaky sea salt
Fresh young beet greens
Dill fronds

FOR THE BABY BEETS
Wash the beets and place them in a medium saucepan. Add the water, red wine vinegar, sugar, salt, dill and bay leaves. Bring to a simmer over medium heat and simmer for 1 hour or until fork-tender. Remove from the heat and allow to cool in the cooking liquid.

When cool enough to handle, using a slotted spoon, transfer the beets to a medium bowl. Strain the cooking liquid into a separate medium bowl. Using a kitchen towel, rub the skin off the beets, being careful not to damage the flesh. Cut the beets in half. Add the beets to the cooking liquid and set aside until ready to serve.

FOR THE GOAT MILK YOGURT
Strain 1 cup of the beet cooking liquid through a fine-mesh sieve into a medium bowl. Whisk in the goat milk yogurt.

TO SERVE
Arrange the beets cut side down on plates. Season with flaky sea salt. Garnish with the beet greens and dill fronds. Pour the goat milk yogurt to flood the plate.

AUTUMN FRUITS
with tomato water, melon and berries

THIS RECIPE SHOWCASES THE PURE, true essence of the season and what's available in the garden. When it comes to tomatoes and late-harvest berries, I focus on just keeping them as natural as possible. They are so delicious just on their own they don't need any intervention. Mother Nature has taken care of all the hard work. This dish is built around a simple tomato water that's flavoured with basil and a hint of garlic. Then we add sweet cherry tomatoes bursting with flavour and some fruit that's at the peak of ripeness. We garnish the whole thing with a really nice oil, peppery nasturtium, bolted radish seed pods and seasonal flowers, so you get this complex and interesting experience of the autumn flavours in the garden.

SERVES 4

Tomato Water

6 cups ripe heirloom tomatoes, cut into chunks or quarters (3 pounds/1.4 kg)

½ cup lightly packed fresh basil leaves

¼ teaspoon sliced garlic

1 teaspoon kosher salt

Cherry Tomatoes and Melon

1 ripe cantaloupe melon

1 ripe honeydew melon

12 ripe cherry tomatoes

½ teaspoon kosher salt

1 tablespoon extra-virgin olive oil

1 tablespoon white balsamic vinegar

Garnishes

Wild raspberries

Black currants

Radish seed pods

Arugula flowers

Basil

Pansies

Marigolds

Nasturtium leaves

Purple basil

Watercress

Extra-virgin olive oil or cold-pressed canola oil, for drizzling

Pinch of kosher salt, for seasoning

FOR THE TOMATO WATER

Place a colander over a large bowl and line the colander with 3 layers of cheesecloth cut large enough to encase the tomato mixture once chopped.

In a high-speed blender and working in batches, roughly chop the tomatoes and basil with the garlic and salt. Pour the tomato mixture into the prepared colander. Bring the cheesecloth corners together and tie with butcher's twine to create a sack. Place the bowl in the refrigerator overnight to allow the tomato water to drip into the bowl. Do not squeeze the sack or the tomato water will be cloudy; allow the water to extract naturally with gravity.

The next day, pour the accumulated tomato water into a jar or container fitted with a lid. Store in the refrigerator for up to 3 days.

FOR THE CHERRY TOMATOES AND MELON

Peel the melons, cut in half and remove the seeds. Using a knife or 1-inch shaped cookie cutters, cut the melons into bite-size pieces and transfer to a small bowl.

Fill a small bowl with ice water. Bring a medium saucepan of salted water to a boil. Using a paring knife, carefully score the cherry tomatoes at the stem. Blanch the tomatoes in the boiling salted water for 10 to 20 seconds or until you see the skin split and start to peel away where you scored. Using a slotted spoon or spider, immediately remove the tomatoes from the boiling water and plunge them into the bowl of ice water to cool rapidly. When cool, remove from the ice water and peel away and discard the skin. Add the peeled cherry tomatoes to the bowl of prepared melon. Toss the cherry tomatoes and melon with the salt, olive oil and white balsamic vinegar.

TO SERVE

Place the cherry tomatoes, melon pieces, raspberries and currants in a circle in the middle of bowls. Pour the tomato water into the centre of the bowls. Garnish the melon and tomatoes with the herbs and flowers. Drizzle with the olive oil and season with salt.

ORCHARD APPLE

with fresh cheese, lemon balm and marigold

THIS RECIPE ILLUSTRATES HOW EASY it is to make your own cheese, but it also celebrates the beauty and elegance of a roasted piece of fruit and how much satisfaction you can get from it. We use this fresh cheese all over the place. Its clean flavour and creamy texture go beautifully with so many different things. It shows up with dessert, with breakfast, with fresh tomatoes, with salad, with fresh or roasted fruit. Try it with poached asparagus in the spring or smeared on a bagel with some smoked salmon any time. In this recipe, the apple is roasted in such a way that it basically becomes self-caramelizing. It's best roasted the same day it is served so it doesn't spend any time in the refrigerator once it is caramelized.

SERVES 4

Lemon Balm Oil
4 cups loosely packed fresh lemon
  balm leaves
1 cup vegetable oil

Chewy Apple
1 Honeycrisp apple
1 cup apple juice
2 tablespoons apple cider vinegar

Fresh Cheese
2 cups whole milk
½ cup whipping (35%) cream
2 tablespoons buttermilk
1 teaspoon (4 g) sheep rennet

Roasted Apple
2 Honeycrisp apples
1 tablespoon vegetable oil

1 tablespoon sugar
1 teaspoon fresh thyme leaves
2 tablespoons unsalted butter

Garnishes
Orange Gem marigold petals
Lemon balm leaves
Flaky sea salt
Lime Leaf Powder (page 283)

FOR THE LEMON BALM OIL
Fill a small bowl with ice water. Bring a small saucepan of salted water to a boil and blanch the lemon balm for 30 seconds. Drain the lemon balm and transfer it to the ice water to stop the cooking. Once cooled, squeeze out excess water so the lemon balm is as dry as possible. In a high-speed blender, blend the lemon balm with the vegetable oil for 3 minutes or until you've achieved a smooth green purée. Chill the purée in the refrigerator for 2 hours.

Strain the oil through a fine-mesh sieve lined with cheesecloth into a small bowl. You will be left with a bright green lemon balm–flavoured oil. This can be made the day before and stored in the fridge in a mason jar or other sealed container.

FOR THE CHEWY APPLE
Preheat the oven to 350°F (180°C). Set a dehydrator to 115°F (46°C).

Slice the apple crosswise into ½-inch-thick slices and remove the core with a small round cutter.

Transfer the apple slices to a baking sheet lined with parchment paper, cover with foil and bake until tender and cooked through, 15 to 20 minutes. Remove from the oven and allow to cool.

Meanwhile, in a small saucepan, bring the apple juice and apple cider vinegar to a simmer over medium-high heat and reduce until you are left with 1 to 2 tablespoons of syrupy glaze, 8 to 10 minutes. Remove from the heat and allow to cool.

Cut the cooled apple slices into 1-inch squares. Lay the apple sections on the dehydrator tray. Do not overlap the apple pieces.

Dehydrate for 6 hours. Every hour, brush the apples with the apple juice glaze. (Alternatively, you can dehydrate the apple in the oven set at the lowest setting. Dehydrating time will depend on the temperature.) When dehydrated, the apple will be lacquered and dehydrated to a chewy but still tender texture with intense flavour. Be careful not to over-dehydrate or the apple will become too chewy and sticky; you still want some tenderness to them.

RECIPE CONTINUES . . .

Store in a sealed container in the refrigerator until ready to use. Allow the chewy apples to come to room temperature before serving. The leftover glaze can be stored in a sealed container at room temperature and used to drizzle over the finished dish if desired.

FOR THE FRESH CHEESE

Half-fill a medium steamer pot with a perforated basket insert with water and bring to a simmer over medium-high heat. Reduce the temperature to maintain a light simmer.

In a medium saucepan over high heat, bring the whole milk, cream and buttermilk to just under a simmer (194°F/90°C). Add the rennet and stir for 10 seconds to dissolve. Pour the mixture into a 6-inch glass casserole dish and carefully set into the steamer basket over the simmering water. Cover with the lid and steam for 2 minutes. Remove from the heat, keep covered, and let sit in the pot for 1 hour, until the cheese has set and formed a firm curd like soft tofu.

Carefully remove the casserole dish from the pot and store, covered, in the refrigerator until ready to use or for up to 3 days. The cheese is best used the day of. Bring to room temperature before serving.

FOR THE ROASTED APPLE

Preheat the oven to 400°F (200°C).

Cut the apples in half stem to base. Using a melon baller or a small round cutter, remove the cores. Shave a very thin slice off each side of the apple so it sits flat.

Heat a large ovenproof frying pan over medium-high heat. Add the vegetable oil to the pan and place the apple halves cut side down in the pan. Cook until golden brown, 2 minutes. Sprinkle the sugar and thyme evenly between the apples and gently swirl the pan to coat the apples. Add the butter and continue to swirl as the butter melts, coating the apples in the sugar and butter. Transfer to the oven and bake for 4 to 6 minutes, until tender and cooked through. Remove from the oven and allow to cool.

TO SERVE

Transfer the roasted apples caramelized side up to plates and brush with any caramelized thyme from the frying pan. Spoon a portion of the fresh cheese beside the caramelized apple and garnish the dish with the chewy apples, Orange Gem marigold petals and lemon balm leaves. Season with flaky sea salt and lime leaf powder. Drizzle the lemon balm oil into the centre of each roasted apple and around the plate.

BARBECUED CAULIFLOWER
with gochujang sauce, roasted peanuts, cilantro and pineapple yogurt

SOMETHING MAGICAL HAPPENS WHEN YOU cook vegetables over a grill or smoking wood and white coals. It introduces a great umami flavour, taking the vegetable to the same level of sensory satisfaction as a Sunday roast or perfectly grilled piece of meat. Inspired by Korean barbecue, we take a whole cauliflower and slowly cook it over smoking charcoals, brushing it the whole time with the fermented chili paste known as gochujang. When done, it is sticky and gooey, with some caramelized parts and some spots that are still moist and juicy. Sweet fruit yogurt makes a lovely cooling accompaniment to the spicy sauce.

SERVES 4

Gochujang Sauce
2⅓ cups gochujang fermented hot chili paste
1⅓ cups rice wine vinegar
½ cup ketchup
½ cup soy sauce
½ cup water
½ cup mirin
¼ cup vegetable oil
1 cup packed brown sugar

2 teaspoons garlic powder
1 teaspoon onion powder
1 teaspoon kosher salt
1 cup unsalted butter, melted

Cauliflower
1 medium head of cauliflower, stem and leaves attached
1 tablespoon vegetable oil
½ tablespoon kosher salt

Pineapple Yogurt
1 cup plain full-fat or coconut milk yogurt
¼ cup minced fresh pineapple
1 teaspoon fresh lime juice

Garnishes
Salted roasted peanuts
Fresh cilantro leaves

FOR THE GOCHUJANG SAUCE
In a medium saucepan, combine the gochujang, rice wine vinegar, ketchup, soy sauce, water, mirin and vegetable oil. Add the brown sugar, garlic powder and onion powder and salt and whisk to combine. Over medium heat, bring to a simmer and reduce, stirring frequently, to a sauce consistency, about 15 minutes. Remove from the heat and whisk in the melted butter.

FOR THE CAULIFLOWER
Trim the leaves back to expose two-thirds of the head if the cauliflower is enclosed.

Preheat a gas barbecue on high heat until it reaches at least 400°F (200°C). Open the lid and turn one side of the barbecue off. If using wood embers or charcoal, slide the embers to one side.

Rub the cauliflower head, gently pulling the leaves away where needed, with the vegetable oil and salt and place it in the off side of the barbecue, leaves and stem down. Close the lid and cook for 10 minutes.

Turn the temperature down low and brush the cauliflower well with the gochujang sauce. If using charcoal, monitor the heat and add more charcoal or wood if needed. Continue grilling, brushing with sauce every 5 minutes or so, for 40≈minutes or until the cauliflower is fork-tender throughout and glazed in sauce. Remove from the barbecue and allow to cool slightly.

FOR THE PINEAPPLE YOGURT
Place the yogurt in a small bowl. Stir in the pineapple and lime juice.

TO SERVE
Remove any large leaves or stem from the cauliflower and discard. Carve the cauliflower into chunks or wedges and arrange on plates. Sprinkle with the peanuts and cilantro leaves. Spoon some pineapple yogurt on the side to complete the dish.

BEER-BATTERED FISH AND CHUBBY CHIPS

with brassica flowers

A STAPLE ON THE MENU since the inception of Wilks' Bar, our fish and chips still evolve each time the menu changes. In the past few years, I've aimed to do something a bit more modern. It's been really fun and we've come up with some delicious and innovative versions.

In this case, we're showcasing where the ocean meets the garden. At different times of the year, depending on what's in season, we might use halibut from the west coast or cod from Fogo Island. Both are equally fantastic in a fish and chips scenario. The fish is coated in a simple beer batter, and we always try to use a beer from local breweries. We've used all styles of beer, but I think an amber or pale ale is an all-around winner.

The chips themselves are super cool. We challenged ourselves to make the most delicious, crispiest, most flavour-filled fried potatoes that we could, and these are the result. We boil whole potatoes until they almost fall apart, then put them in the oven for a bit just to dry off. From there, we break them into natural, sort of rock-shaped pieces that we deep-fry. Because they've been boiled, nearly 20 percent of the oil goes into the potatoes, making them ultra-crisp outside and creamy inside. As soon as they come out of the oil we hit them with all these different flavour elements—garlic confit oil, salt, pepper, dehydrated Worcestershire powder, malt vinegar powder, chive powder, sumac powder—so you get this all-dressed crispy potato. You don't have to use all those flavourings at home, of course. Just salt and pepper and the chips will still be pretty special.

SERVES 4

12 cups vegetable oil, for deep-frying

Chubby Chips
2 large russet potatoes, peeled
4 sprigs fresh thyme
2 fresh bay leaves
1 garlic clove, crushed
1 teaspoon Garlic Confit oil (page 282)
½ teaspoon freshly ground white peppercorns
½ tablespoon kosher salt
1 teaspoon Worcestershire powder

1 teaspoon malt vinegar powder
1 teaspoon sumac powder
1 teaspoon chive powder

Beer Batter
1 cup all-purpose flour
2 tablespoons cornstarch
2 teaspoons baking powder
1 cup lager beer

Beer-Battered Fish
1 Atlantic cod fillet (1 pound/450 g), cut into 4 equal portions, at room temperature

3 teaspoons kosher salt, divided
2 cups all-purpose flour

Garnishes
Lemon Gel (page 284)
Bronze fennel fronds and flowers
Mustard flowers
Radish flowers
Worcestershire powder
Malt vinegar powder
Chive powder
Sumac powder

FOR THE CHUBBY CHIPS

In a medium saucepan, cover the potatoes with cold water. Add the thyme, bay leaves and garlic and bring to a boil over high heat, then reduce the heat to a simmer and continue to cook for 40 minutes or until the potatoes are almost soft enough to fall apart when pressed. Drain the potatoes and place on a rack on a small baking sheet to dry and cool for 20 minutes.

Preheat the oven to 350°F (180°C). Line a baking sheet with parchment paper.

Using the back of a spoon, press and break the potatoes into rough 1½-inch pieces. Arrange the potatoes on the prepared baking sheet and bake for 5 minutes to help remove some of the moisture. Remove from the oven and allow to cool to room temperature.

FOR THE BEER BATTER

Meanwhile, in a medium bowl, sift together the flour, cornstarch and baking powder. Slowly add the beer, whisking until the batter is smooth and free of lumps. Allow the batter to rest at room temperature for at least 30 minutes before using.

DEEP-FRY THE CHUBBY CHIPS

Line a medium bowl with paper towel. In a deep pot, heat the vegetable oil to 360°F (185°C). Working in batches, carefully place the potatoes in the hot oil and deep-fry until golden brown, about 4 minutes.

Using a slotted spoon or spider, remove the potatoes from the hot oil and place them in the prepared bowl to remove any excess oil. (Reserve the pot of oil for deep-frying the fish.) Remove the paper towel from the bowl and season the fried potatoes with a drizzle of the garlic confit oil, the white pepper and salt, then toss with the Worcestershire powder, malt vinegar powder, sumac powder and chive powder. Keep warm.

FOR THE BEER-BATTERED FISH

Lay the cod fillets on paper towel and pat dry. Season very lightly with 1 teaspoon of the salt. In a medium bowl, mix together the flour and the remaining 2 teaspoons salt. Dredge the cod in the flour mixture.

Heat the pot of vegetable oil to 350°F (180°C). Whisk the beer batter. Shake off excess flour from the cod and dip the fish into the beer batter to completely coat the fish. Carefully place the battered cod in the hot oil and deep-fry for 7 minutes, turning the cod over from time to time. When golden and crispy, remove the cod from the hot oil with a slotted spoon or spider and drain on a wire rack.

TO SERVE

Dab the cod with paper towel to remove excess oil and arrange on plates. Dot the fish with lemon gel and place the herb and flower garnishes organically on top of the fish. Place the chubby chips in a pile next to the fish and sprinkle again with the Worcestershire powder, malt vinegar powder, chive powder and sumac powder.

CARROT AND MUNG BEAN PORRIDGE
with carrot-top pesto, orange coriander bubbles and crème fraîche

ONE OF MY FAVOURITE APPROACHES to vegetarian cooking is to take a single ingredient and try to blow it up in as many ways as possible. Sometimes we'll cook something in its own juice to concentrate the flavour, add a dehydrated component and then introduce a crispy element. When you finally get to the point of tasting the finished dish, the idea is that the different textures, the crunch and the creaminess, with a little bit of acidity and freshness really creates something memorable. It takes the ordinary and transforms it to extraordinary.

This dish is an example of that approach. The base is mung beans cooked in the style of risotto, and then we bring in the carrot in a variety of forms: as a purée, a stock, cooked in their own juice, greens and flowers. The whole thing is seasoned with wild and regular ginger to enhance that intense carrot flavour and dressed with bubbles made from carrot juice, orange juice and coriander. This dish is really a huge homage to the carrot.

SERVES 4

Carrot Purée

2 cups carrot juice

1 tablespoon unsalted butter

1 teaspoon kosher salt

2 cups thinly sliced peeled carrots

Carrot-Top Pesto

4 cups loosely packed fresh carrot tops

½ cup chopped fresh chives

½ tablespoon kosher salt

1 teaspoon minced garlic

1 teaspoon minced Anaheim chili

¼ cup extra-virgin olive oil

¼ cup vegetable oil

¼ cup white balsamic vinegar

Carrot Porridge

1 cup split orange mung beans

3 tablespoons unsalted butter, divided

1 tablespoon minced shallot

1 teaspoon minced garlic

1 teaspoon minced peeled fresh ginger

1 teaspoon minced red serrano chili

2 teaspoons kosher salt

1 teaspoon freshly ground grains of paradise or black pepper

⅔ cup peeled orange carrot cut into ⅛-inch dice

⅔ cup peeled yellow carrot cut into ⅛-inch dice

3 cups carrot juice

½ cup carrot purée (recipe at left)

1 tablespoon fresh lemon juice

Orange Coriander Bubbles

3 fresh parsley stems

3 fresh bay leaves

2 tablespoons black cardamom pods

2 tablespoons coriander seeds

1 tablespoon fresh thyme leaves

8 tablespoons unsalted butter, divided

1 cup sliced shallots

1 tablespoon sliced peeled fresh ginger

1 teaspoon kosher salt

2 cups thinly sliced peeled carrots

1½ cups carrot juice

1 cup fresh orange juice

1 tablespoon fresh lemon juice

Garnishes

Crème Fraîche (page 281)

Perilla leaves

Cilantro leaves and flowers

RECIPE CONTINUES . . .

FOR THE CARROT PURÉE

Fill a medium bowl with ice water. In a medium saucepan, bring the carrot juice, butter and salt to a boil over high heat. Drop in the carrots, bring back to a simmer and cook until the carrots are tender, 10 to 15 minutes. Using a slotted spoon or spider, transfer the carrots to a high-speed blender, reserving the cooking liquid. Blend the carrots to a thick, velvety smooth purée like a thick soup. If the purée is too thick, thin it with a little of the carrot cooking liquid. Pass the purée through a fine-mesh sieve into a small bowl.

FOR THE CARROT-TOP PESTO

In a high-speed blender, combine the carrot tops, chives, salt, garlic, chili, olive oil, vegetable oil and white balsamic vinegar. Blend on high speed for 1 minute or until a smooth purée is achieved. Transfer to a small bowl or jar with a lid. Refrigerate until ready to use.

FOR THE CARROT PORRIDGE

Soak the mung beans in cold water for 30 minutes. Drain and rinse well.

In a medium saucepan, melt 2 tablespoons of the butter over medium heat. Add the shallot, garlic, ginger, chili, salt and grains of paradise and cook gently, stirring occasionally, for 2 minutes. Stir in the orange and yellow carrots and continue to cook over low heat until the vegetables are tender, about 10 minutes. Add the rinsed mung beans and enough of the carrot juice to cover the contents of the saucepan. Bring to a boil, then reduce the heat to a simmer and cook, stirring frequently to prevent scorching, until the mung beans are tender, about 10 minutes. The liquid will reduce down nicely. If the porridge absorbs too much of the liquid and becomes thick, add more carrot juice and butter to thin it slightly. When the mung beans are tender, stir in the carrot purée, lemon juice and the remaining 1 tablespoon butter. Add more salt, if needed.

FOR THE ORANGE CORIANDER BUBBLES

Tie the parsley, bay leaves, cardamom pods, coriander seeds and thyme and tie into a sachet with cheesecloth and butcher's twine.

In a medium saucepan, melt 2 tablespoons of the butter over low heat until bubbling. Add the sachet of herbs, shallots, ginger and salt and cook gently, stirring occasionally, until the vegetables are tender and translucent and the spices are aromatic, about 5 minutes. Add the carrots, increase the heat to medium-low and continue to cook, stirring occasionally, for another 5 minutes. Add the carrot juice, bring to a simmer and cook for 6 minutes longer or until the carrots are tender. Remove from the heat and cool slightly in the liquid.

Remove the sachet and squeeze out any liquid into the saucepan. Discard the sachet. Transfer the carrots and their cooking liquid to a high-speed blender and purée. When processed, season with salt, if needed. Strain through a fine-mesh sieve into a small saucepan. Keep covered.

TO SERVE

Stir the orange and lemon juice and remaining 6 tablespoons butter into the carrot bubbles. Heat gently, then froth the sauce with an immersion blender.

Spoon the carrot porridge into warm bowls. Drizzle with the carrot-top pesto. Dot crème fraîche around the porridge. Spoon the orange coriander bubbles on the porridge and garnish with the perilla leaves and cilantro leaves and flowers.

JB'S TIP

In the late summer, we harvest a lot of wild carrot seed (Queen Anne's lace). We preserve it simply by boiling it in vinegar and storing it in the refrigerator. This adds a nice carrot spice note to the pesto. But it's also delicious without.

VENISON HEART
with pickled mushrooms, spruce aïoli and fried rosemary

MY DAD'S SIDE OF THE family are big hunters, and the times I spent with them in Parry Sound were really important for me. That's where I learned to shoot a .22, went fishing for pike and pickerel and learned from my dad and grandfather how to fillet fish. It was there I got my first exposure to beaver, venison, moose, bear and duck. I've always had an interest in game because of that connection to family time spent in the bush, and I think those experiences are part of the reason I became a chef. When I was on *Iron Chef Canada* and I found out the secret ingredient was venison I got a bit anxious, because I knew if I didn't bring home the win, I was going to hear about it at the hunt camp! When venison is cooked with care and an understanding of how to prepare the lean meat, it can be something so savoury and delicious. It is important to not overcook or expose game to direct high heat as it will overcook quickly and the flavour will become very gamey and the texture dry.

SERVES 4

Pickled Mushrooms

1 cup mixed fresh mushrooms (chanterelle, enoki and oyster), trimmed

1 cup water

1 cup white wine vinegar

¼ cup sugar

1 fresh bay leaf

1 sprig fresh thyme

1 tablespoon coriander seeds

½ tablespoon mustard seeds

1 teaspoon juniper berries

¼ teaspoon kosher salt

Spruce Oil

2 cups young spruce tips

2 cups vegetable oil

Spruce Aïoli

2 egg yolks

1 tablespoon Dijon mustard

1 teaspoon white wine vinegar

½ teaspoon minced garlic

2 cups spruce oil (recipe at left)

1 teaspoon fresh lemon juice

1 teaspoon kosher salt

Venison Heart

1 to 2 venison hearts (about 1 pound/450 g total)

1 tablespoon kosher salt

½ teaspoon freshly ground black pepper

2 tablespoons vegetable oil

4 garlic cloves, crushed

4 sprigs fresh thyme

1 sprig fresh rosemary

4 juniper berries, roughly chopped

¼ cup unsalted butter

1 tablespoon seasoned duck fat (optional)

Garnishes

Fried rosemary sprig (from cooking the venison heart)

Creeping thyme

Roughly chopped juniper berries

Mushroom powder

FOR THE PICKLED MUSHROOMS

Place the mushrooms in a 2-cup mason jar. In a small saucepan, combine the water, white wine vinegar, sugar, bay leaf, thyme, coriander seeds, mustard seeds, juniper berries and salt. Bring to a simmer over medium heat and simmer for 2 minutes to allow the sugar to dissolve. Pour the pickling liquid into the jar to cover the mushrooms. Allow to cool, seal the jar with the lid and refrigerate for at least 48 hours before using.

FOR THE SPRUCE OIL

SOUS VIDE METHOD

Set a sous vide water bath to 194°F (90°C). Place the young spruce tips and vegetable oil in a sous vide bag. Vacuum-seal on full pressure and cook in the water bath for 1 hour. Remove the bag from the water bath, place in the refrigerator and let infuse overnight.

The next day, strain through a fine-mesh sieve lined with cheesecloth into a 2-cup mason jar. Cover with the lid and set aside until ready to use.

RECIPE CONTINUES . . .

Fill a small bowl with ice water. Bring a small saucepan of salted water to a boil. Add the spruce tips and blanch for 30 seconds. Drain the spruce tips and plunge them into the ice water to stop the cooking. When cooled, drain the spruce tips and squeeze out excess water so they are as dry as possible. In a high-speed blender, blend the spruce tips with the vegetable oil until you've achieved a smooth green purée, about 3 minutes. Pour the purée into a jar and store, covered, in the refrigerator for 2 hours.

Strain the oil through a fine-mesh sieve lined with cheesecloth into a 2-cup mason jar. Cover with the lid and refrigerate until ready to use.

FOR THE SPRUCE AÏOLI

In a medium bowl, whisk together the egg yolks, mustard, white wine vinegar and garlic to form a paste. While whisking, slowly drizzle in the spruce oil to emulsify. Season with the lemon juice and salt. If the mixture is too thick, thin it with a few drops of room-temperature water. Transfer to an airtight container or squeeze bottle and store in the refrigerator.

FOR THE VENISON HEART

Cut the top off the heart to remove the fat. Butterfly the heart and clean away any connective tissue. Cut the heart lengthwise into 4 equal portions. Season with the salt and pepper. Heat the vegetable oil in a large cast-iron skillet or frying pan over medium-high heat. Carefully add the venison heart steaks to the hot oil and cook until golden brown on the bottom, about 2 minutes. Flip the steaks and add the crushed garlic, thyme, rosemary, juniper berries, butter and duck fat (if using) to the pan. Continuously baste the heart with the aromatic butter while cooking for an additional minute. Remove from the pan to a cutting board or plate and allow it to rest for 4 minutes, keeping it warm. Reserve the aromatics and fat in the pan.

TO SERVE

Drain the pickled mushrooms on paper towel to remove excess liquid. Slice the venison heart steaks in half into two ½-inch slices. Heat the cooking fat and brush the venison with the flavoured fat. Lay the warm slices off-centre on each plate. Drain the fried rosemary sprig on paper towel, pick off the leaves and sprinkle over the heart. Dot the plate with the spruce aïoli. Scatter the mushrooms about the plate. Garnish with the creeping thyme and chopped juniper and dust the plate with mushroom powder.

JB'S TIPS

I get the deer heart most years during hunting season so always have an opportunity to make this dish or to create something new. We don't always leave the hunt successful, though, and in that case this recipe can be made with loin of venison, bison or beef. Butterfly the meat into steaks and prepare it the same way.

The spruce aïoli can be replaced with a simple garlic aïoli or a mayonnaise spruced up with some maple syrup and chopped juniper and rosemary. Alternatively, a Dijonnaise (1 tablespoon mayonnaise mixed with 1 tablespoon Dijon) or creamed horseradish will make a great accompaniment to this dish.

HERITAGE HEN MOUSSE
with mushrooms and roasted hen bone sauce

THIS RECIPE SHOWCASES SOME OF the earlier, more classical training I received in Europe. It is a warm cooked mousse made with chicken breast and emulsified with heavy cream and rich egg yolk. It is then poached gently and served in an earthy, fortified wine sauce flavoured with mushrooms and thyme. This is a good example of focusing on one special ingredient, the hen, and complementing it with different preparations using various parts of the bird, thereby intensifying the flavour of the final dish. The delicate mousse, with the creamy sauce made from the roasted bird bones, topped off with a crunchy toasted savoury bread crumb made with the hen skin, thyme leaves and buttery brioche—together this is a little bite of heaven.

SERVES 4

Chicken Skin Crumb

1 cup day-old brioche cut into ½-inch dice

Skin from 2 chicken breasts

Pinch of kosher salt

1 teaspoon fresh thyme leaves

Heritage Hen Mousse

1 boneless, skinless heritage hen breast (9 ounces/255 g)

2 large egg yolks

1 teaspoon kosher salt

½ cup whipping (35%) cream

Roasted Hen Bone Sauce

2 pounds (900 g) chicken wings, roughly chopped (4 cups)

1 tablespoon unsalted butter

1 cup thinly sliced shallots

3 ounces (85 g) hen-of-the-woods mushrooms, sliced (1 cup)

½ cup sliced garlic

2 fresh bay leaves

1 teaspoon black peppercorns

¼ cup fresh thyme leaves

¼ cup lightly packed fresh flat-leaf parsley

3 cups Madeira, divided

1 cup Chicken Stock (page 286)

1 cup Veal Jus (page 289)

6 cups whipping (35%) cream

Sautéed Mushrooms

6 ounces (170 g) lion's mane mushrooms

6 ounces (170 g) hen-of-the-woods mushroom

2 king oyster mushrooms

1 tablespoon vegetable oil

2 garlic cloves, crushed

½ tablespoon kosher salt

2 tablespoons unsalted butter

1½ tablespoons minced shallot

1 teaspoon fresh thyme leaves

FOR THE CHICKEN SKIN CRUMB

Preheat the oven to 300°F (150°C).

Spread the diced brioche on a baking sheet lined with parchment paper and toast the brioche until completely dry and golden, 20 to 30 minutes. Remove from the oven and allow to cool to room temperature.

Lay the chicken skins on a cutting board. Using the back of a knife, scrape the skin clean of any fat or muscle debris. Spread the chicken skin on a baking sheet lined with parchment paper, season with the salt and cover with another piece of parchment paper. Weight it down with a second baking sheet. Transfer to the oven and cook for 20 minutes, until the skin is golden brown and crispy. Periodically check for rendered fat and drain it off if necessary. Transfer the roasted skins to paper towel to absorb any excess fat and allow to cool to room temperature. In a high-speed blender, combine the roasted skins and toasted brioche and process to a fine crumb. Stir in the thyme and adjust seasoning with salt. Store in an airtight container with a silica pack.

FOR THE HERITAGE HEN MOUSSE

Finely chop the hen breast and place in a high-speed blender with the egg yolks and salt. Blend until finely puréed. Using a firm rubber spatula, press the purée through a fine-mesh sieve into medium bowl. Cover the bowl and chill in the refrigerator for 1 hour.

Place the bowl of chilled hen purée in a larger bowl of crushed ice to help keep the mousse chilled

RECIPE CONTINUES . . .

at all times. Add the cream to the hen purée in small amounts, folding it into the purée with a spatula until the mixture is completely cohesive.

Half-fill a medium saucepan with water and bring to a simmer over medium-high heat. Drop a teaspoon of the hen mousse into the water and poach for 1 minute. Remove with a slotted spoon and taste the mousse for seasoning. Add more salt to the uncooked mousse, if needed. Keep the water at a simmer.

Lay a 12-inch square of plastic wrap on a work surface. Spoon an even line of mousse along the bottom of the plastic, leaving a 2-inch or so border at each side. Roll the mousse up in the plastic to form a 1½ to 2 inch-thick log and tie the ends with butcher's twine like a sausage.

Add the wrapped mousse to the simmering water and poach for 3 minutes. Remove the pan from the heat and leave the mousse in the hot water for another 5 minutes. Transfer the cooked mousse to a bowl of ice water to cool completely. Remove the mousse from the ice water and refrigerate for at least 1 hour. Cut the plastic wrap at the ends and unroll the mousse. Slice the mousse into six 1-inch-thick slices, cover and refrigerate until ready to use. Allow to come to room temperature before heating.

FOR THE ROASTED HEN BONE SAUCE

Preheat the oven to 350°F (180°C). Spread the chicken wings on a baking sheet and roast, stirring occasionally, until golden brown, about 20 minutes.

In a medium saucepan, melt the butter over medium-low heat. Add the shallots, mushrooms and garlic and gently cook until wilted and tender. Add the roasted chicken wings, bay leaves, black peppercorns, thyme and parsley. Stir to mix. Pour ½ cup of the Madeira into the baking sheet and use a wooden spoon or rubber spatula to scrape all the roasted bits off the pan; add to the saucepan. Increase the heat to medium-high, pour in the remaining 2½ cups Madeira and reduce until almost dry. Add the chicken stock and reduce to almost dry again. Add the veal jus

and reduce to two-thirds. Add the cream and bring to a simmer. Reduce the heat to medium-low and simmer gently until the sauce is thick and creamy, about 10 minutes. Strain through a fine-mesh sieve into a clean medium saucepan, cover and keep warm. Discard the solids.

FOR THE SAUTÉED MUSHROOMS

Break the lion's mane and hen-of-the-woods mushrooms into 1-inch clusters. Slice the king oyster mushrooms in half and gently score the cut side in a crisscross design. In a medium frying pan, heat the vegetable oil over medium heat. Add the mushrooms and crushed garlic. Season with salt and fry, stirring occasionally, for 1 minute to caramelize the mushrooms. Reduce the heat to low and add the butter, shallot and thyme. Cook, stirring frequently, for 1 to 3 minutes longer, until the butter is foaming and starting to brown and the mushroom are cooked through. Using a slotted spoon, transfer the mushrooms to paper towel to absorb excess oil.

TO SERVE

Bring the roasted hen bone sauce to a simmer over medium heat. Lower the sliced hen mousse portions into the sauce, reduce the heat to low and warm the mousse gently just under a simmer until warmed through, about 2 minutes. Using a slotted spoon, transfer the warm mousse to heated plates. Arrange the cooked mushrooms to the side of the mousse. Spoon a mound of chicken skin crumb between the mousse and mushroom to garnish. Using an immersion blender, froth the hen bone sauce to create a bubbly cream, and finish the dish with some of the tasty bubbles for a contrast in colour and textures.

JB'S TIPS

We use a mix of heritage-breed hens from a farm down the way, but any good-quality farmed chicken works just as well. Also, feel free to use any of your favourite mushrooms. Button, oyster and shiitake will all work.

BLUEBERRY AND LEMON FUDGE

HERE IS A SIMPLE, FUN sweet recipe that would be great to do with the kids. I like it because it's something sweet that's not store-bought and you can control the quality of the ingredients that go into it. The recipe comes together quickly, as you basically melt chocolate, add some condensed milk, lemon zest and kosher salt, and then simply decorate the top with whatever flavour you want to go with for the day. In this recipe we use dried blueberries and candied lemon, but you could use dried cranberries, banana chips, nuts or seeds, or fresh fruit for that matter. Once chilled, just cut it into squares or break it into chunks and you're ready to go.

MAKES 1 (9 X 6-INCH) SHEET OF FUDGE

Blueberry and Lemon Fudge

8.3 ounces (235 g) white chocolate, chopped (1⅓ cups)

¾ cup condensed milk

½ cup roughly chopped dried blueberries

2 tablespoons lemon zest

⅛ teaspoon kosher salt

½ cup finely diced Candied Lemon Peel (page 33)

FOR THE BLUEBERRY AND LEMON FUDGE

Line the bottom of a 9 × 6-inch baking sheet with parchment paper.

In a medium saucepan, bring a few inches of water to a simmer over medium heat to create steam. In a medium heatproof bowl (big enough to sit on the saucepan but not in the water), combine the chopped white chocolate and condensed milk. Place the bowl over the simmering water and melt the chocolate into the condensed milk, stirring with a heatproof rubber spatula until thoroughly combined.

Remove from the heat and stir in the dried blueberries, lemon zest and salt. Immediately pour the fudge onto the prepared baking sheet, spreading it out evenly with the rubber spatula. Sprinkle with the candied lemon peel and allow to cool. When cool, cover and chill overnight in the refrigerator.

With a paring knife, cut the sides of the fudge away from the pan and slide out onto a cutting board. Portion into desired shapes and store in an airtight container between layers of parchment paper. The fudge will keep in the refrigerator for up to 1 week.

CHERRY CHEESECAKE

with cherry compote, graham cracker crust and mascarpone

WE'RE REALLY FORTUNATE TO BE so close to Niagara, a region that produces so much amazing stone and vine fruit. The cherries from there are one of my favourites and they were the inspiration for this modern take on cheesecake. This recipe is not baked and set like a mousse, resulting in a light and fresh finish on the palette. If you can't find fresh or frozen sour cherries, you can get away with a sour cherry concentrate or even preserves. If you already have some sour cherry compote on hand, this dessert comes together in a flash.

SERVES 8

Cherry Compote

1½ cups fresh or frozen pitted sour cherries

2 tablespoons sugar

2 tablespoons sour cherry concentrate (I use Cherry Lane)

Graham Cracker Base

1 cup graham cracker crumbs

⅛ teaspoon kosher salt

3 tablespoons unsalted butter, melted, at room temperature

Cheesecake Filling

1½ cups mascarpone cheese, at room temperature

½ cup cream cheese, at room temperature

⅔ cup + ½ cup icing sugar, divided

½ cup whipping (35%) cream

2 teaspoons apple pectin powder

Garnish

Elderflower blossoms

FOR THE CHERRY COMPOTE

In a small saucepan, stir together the cherries, sugar and cherry concentrate and cook, stirring frequently, over medium heat. The cherries will start to release their juices and the sugar will dissolve. Continue to cook until the juices are thick enough to coat the back of a spoon, about 5 minutes. Remove from the heat and allow to cool before serving.

FOR THE GRAHAM CRACKER BASE

Preheat the oven to 325°F (160°C).

In a small bowl, stir together the graham cracker crumbs, salt and butter. The mixture should be wet and hold together like a paste when pressed. Place eight 3¼-inch tart rings on a baking sheet lined with parchment paper or a silicone mat. Evenly press 2 tablespoons of the graham cracker mixture into each tart ring. Bake until the base is golden brown and firm, about 10 minutes. Remove from the oven and allow to cool before removing the rings. Clean the rings to use for the cheesecake filling.

FOR THE CHEESECAKE FILLING

In the bowl of a stand mixer fitted with the paddle attachment, combine the mascarpone, cream cheese and ⅔ cup of the icing sugar. Beat on low speed until no lumps remain, about 2 minutes. Scrape down the bowl and the paddle with a rubber spatula. Mix again to make sure no lumps remain.

In a small saucepan over medium-low heat, bring the cream, the remaining ½ cup icing sugar and the apple pectin to 194°F (90°C), whisking occasionally. Strain through a fine-mesh sieve into the cream cheese mixture. Mix on low speed until combined.

Place the tart rings on a baking sheet lined with parchment paper or a silicone mat. Pour the filling mixture into the tart rings, cover with plastic wrap and chill until firmly set, at least 2 hours.

TO SERVE

Place a graham cracker base on each plate. Using a paring knife, cut around the rim of the tart ring and remove the cheesecake. Place the cheesecake on top of the graham base. Top the cheesecake with cherry compote. Garnish with elderflower blossoms.

SWEET CORN AND MUSTARD CARAMEL

with brown butter pound cake and popped sorghum

THE BEGINNING OF A MEAL is an opportunity to have fun and serve something that's going to give people a lasting impression of their experience. I love the sweetness in corn, and although it works amazingly with roast chicken or in a soup or with seafood, it's also fantastic in a dessert. In this case we've gone with a corn sorbet along with a brown butter pound cake with popped sorghum and marjoram. The combination of corn and marjoram is really interesting. The floral flavour of the marjoram pairs perfectly with the sweetness of the corn. The sorghum—mini popcorn—is there as a way of featuring the ingredient in all its forms and going back to having something playful and nostalgic.

SERVES 6

Corn Sorbet

10 cups fresh or thawed frozen corn kernels (14 to 16 cobs)

1 cup sugar

½ cup corn syrup

6 tablespoons dextrose

1 teaspoon kosher salt

Brown Butter Pound Cake

1⅓ cups all-purpose flour

½ teaspoon baking powder

½ teaspoon kosher salt

1 cup + 2 tablespoons Brown Butter (page 280), at room temperature

1 cup sugar

4 large eggs

½ tablespoon pure vanilla extract

Caramel Mustard Sauce

1¾ cups sugar

6 tablespoons glucose syrup

1 cup whipping (35%) cream

1 teaspoon grainy mustard

Popped Sorghum

1 tablespoon vegetable oil

½ cup whole-grain sorghum

Pinch of kosher salt

Garnish

1 tablespoon fresh marjoram leaves

FOR THE CORN SORBET

In a medium saucepan over medium-low heat, gently cook the fresh corn kernels, covered, until they are very tender. (If using frozen kernels, skip this step and go straight to puréeing the corn.) Transfer to a high-speed blender and process to a smooth purée. Pass the purée through a fine-mesh sieve into a clean medium saucepan. Add the sugar, corn syrup, dextrose and salt and heat gently, stirring with a rubber spatula, until the sugar is completely dissolved. Remove from the heat and allow the mixture to cool to room temperature. Cover and refrigerate until chilled, about 2 hours.

To finish the sorbet, transfer the corn mixture to an ice-cream maker and process according to the manufacturer's instructions until the sorbet has a soft-serve consistency. Scrape into a chilled airtight container and freeze until hard, about 4 hours. Keep frozen until ready to use.

FOR THE BROWN BUTTER POUND CAKE

Preheat the oven to 325°F (160°C). Grease an 8½ × 4½-inch loaf pan.

In a small bowl, stir together the flour, baking powder and salt. In the bowl of a stand mixer fitted with the paddle attachment, beat the brown butter on medium speed until smooth and creamy. Add the sugar and beat on high speed until smooth and the sugar is incorporated, about 3 minutes. Reduce the speed to medium and add the eggs, one at a time, mixing well after each addition. Add the vanilla and mix until well incorporated. Add the dry ingredients and mix on low speed to just blend together. Do not overmix. Pour the batter into the greased loaf pan.

RECIPE CONTINUES . . .

Bake until you have a golden brown crust and a cake tester or wooden skewer inserted in the middle comes out clean, 45 to 60 minutes.

FOR THE CARAMEL MUSTARD SAUCE

In a medium nonstick saucepan, combine the sugar and glucose syrup. Give the pan a shake to spread the sugar in an even layer across the bottom, then heat over medium-low heat. The sugar will begin to melt and caramelize at the edges of the saucepan. When the edges of the sugar are caramelizing, using a heatproof rubber spatula, bring the caramelized parts into the middle of the pan to where the sugar hasn't melted completely yet. Press the sugar lumps against the sides of the pan with the spatula, if necessary, to ensure a smooth consistency. When you have pulled the edges into the centre, keep stirring with the rubber spatula until all the sugar has melted and is a golden caramel colour. Increase the heat to medium and continue cooking the caramel until it turns a dark amber colour or reaches a temperature of 340°F (170°C) when tested with a sugar thermometer. Immediately remove from the heat and stir in the cream a little at a time, being careful to avoid any hot sugar splashes when the cream connects with the hot sugar. Once the cream is smoothly mixed into the caramel, add the grainy mustard and stir until fully incorporated.

FOR THE POPPED SORGHUM

In a heavy medium saucepan, heat the vegetable oil with a few sorghum grains over medium heat. Cover the pot with a lid and wait for the grains to pop, about 2 minutes. Meanwhile, line a medium bowl with paper towel.

Once the kernels pop, remove the saucepan from the heat and, using a slotted spoon, transfer the popped sorghum to the prepared bowl. Pour the remaining sorghum into the hot oil. Cover with a lid and give the saucepan a little shake to distribute the sorghum evenly. Place the saucepan back over medium heat and continue cooking the sorghum, carefully shaking the pot occasionally to cook the grains evenly. Once the sorghum starts popping, tip the lid just a touch to allow steam to escape. Continue cooking until the popping slows to about one pop every few seconds. Dump the popped sorghum into the prepared bowl. Season with the salt.

TO SERVE

Slice the brown butter pound cake into three 1-inch slices. Remove the crust and tear the cake into large pieces. Arrange one piece of the cake on each of the plates. Garnish with the fresh marjoram leaves. With the remaining cake, rub the cake between your fingers to break it down into a large crumb texture. Place a teaspoon of the crumb onto the plate to set the corn sorbet onto. Spoon the corn sorbet onto the brown butter pound cake crumbs. Finish the dish with a spoonful of caramel mustard sauce and serve with some popped sorghum.

COFFEE ICE CREAM

with white chocolate granola, brown butter honey tuile and chocolate rocks

CHOCOLATE AND COFFEE IS A classic combination. A perfect espresso or cup of coffee with a nice piece of chocolate is always comforting and provides so much pleasure. I find it really exciting when we add some texture or punch to our ice creams. In this case we've added white chocolate and crushed cocoa nibs to a chewy, crunchy, nutty baked granola that serves as the base for the ice cream. For an additional textural element, we add a honey and brown butter tuile. Finally, we had a bit of fun with a molecular-type preparation where we make milk chocolate rocks by melting the chocolate and adding maltodextrin, which makes the chocolate into something like an Aero bar but more like a powdery solid candy.

SERVES 6

White Chocolate Granola

1¼ cups large-flake rolled oats

2 tablespoons cocoa nibs

⅓ cup packed brown sugar

3 tablespoons honey

1 tablespoon canola oil

½ teaspoon pure vanilla extract

4.1 ounces (115 g) white chocolate, finely chopped (⅔ cup)

½ tablespoon fleur de sel

Coffee Ice Cream

3½ cups whipping (35%) cream

½ cup whole milk

¼ cup ground espresso

5 large egg yolks

¾ cup sugar

Brown Butter Honey Tuile

¼ cup Brown Butter (page 280), at room temperature

¼ cup honey

2 tablespoons egg whites (about 1 large egg white)

½ cup sugar

⅓ cup all-purpose flour

⅛ teaspoon kosher salt

Chocolate Rocks

3.1 ounces (90 g) milk chocolate, chopped (½ cup)

¾ cup maltodextrin

1 teaspoon kosher salt

FOR THE WHITE CHOCOLATE GRANOLA

Preheat the oven to 250°F (120°C). Line a baking sheet with parchment paper or a silicone mat.

In a medium bowl, stir together the oats and cocoa nibs. In a separate medium bowl, stir together the brown sugar, honey, canola oil and vanilla. Pour the wet ingredients over the dry ingredients and mix well with a spoon or spatula. Spread the mixture evenly on the prepared baking sheet and bake for 1 hour, stirring every 15 minutes. The granola is ready when it is golden brown.

In a medium bowl, stir together the hot granola, chopped white chocolate and fleur de sel. Spread this mixture onto a baking sheet lined with parchment paper or a silicone mat to cool. Once cooled, break up any large pieces and store in an airtight container for up to 1 week.

FOR THE COFFEE ICE CREAM

In a heavy medium saucepan, stir together the cream, milk and ground espresso. Bring to a simmer over medium heat, then remove from the heat and let steep for 10 minutes. Strain the mixture through 4 layers of cheesecloth into a clean medium saucepan. Discard the coffee grounds.

In a medium bowl, whisk together the egg yolks, sugar and 1 cup of the warm cream mixture. Over low heat, bring the remaining cream mixture back up to a simmer. Slowly pour it into the egg mixture while whisking continuously. Return the mixture to the saucepan and stir with a rubber spatula until the mixture reaches 180°F (82°C). Do not boil. Strain through a fine-mesh strainer into a clean medium bowl. Place plastic wrap directly on the surface so no skin develops on the top. Set the bowl in a larger bowl of ice to chill until the custard is cold.

RECIPE CONTINUES . . .

Pour the custard into an ice-cream maker and process according to the manufacturer's instructions until the ice cream has a soft-serve consistency. Scrape into a chilled airtight container and freeze until hard, about 4 hours. Keep frozen until ready to use.

FOR THE BROWN BUTTER HONEY TUILE

In a medium bowl, whisk together the brown butter, honey, egg whites, sugar, flour and salt. Cover the batter and chill for at least 1 hour in the refrigerator.

Preheat the oven to 325°F (160°C). Line a baking sheet with parchment paper or a silicone mat.

Using an offset palette knife or spatula, spread the chilled mixture very thinly, until almost translucent, on the prepared baking sheet. Bake until golden brown and crispy, 10 to 15 minutes. Allow to cool on the baking sheet to room temperature.

FOR THE CHOCOLATE ROCKS

Melt the chocolate in a small bowl over a double boiler or in the microwave. In a medium bowl, stir together the maltodextrin and salt. Once the chocolate has melted, using a rubber spatula, scrape it into the maltodextrin and stir until no white powder remains. You can use it as is or you can press small amounts together with your hands to form small rocks or pebble shapes. Place on a baking sheet lined with parchment paper or a silicone mat, cover and let sit overnight at room temperature to set before serving.

TO SERVE

Spoon a couple tablespoons of the white chocolate granola into an ice cream bowl or serving dish. Scoop the coffee ice cream and place it gently in the centre of the granola. Add pieces of the chocolate rocks around the ice cream and break shards of the brown butter honey tuile to serve one as a garnish on each dish.

JB'S TIP

When developing this recipe, instead of doing the usual vanilla ice cream served with a cup of coffee, we thought it would be fun to switch it around and feature the coffee in the ice cream component. It turned out so well we've since found all sorts of ways to use it. Pour a shot of espresso over a nice scoop of this coffee ice cream, for example, and you have the ultimate affogato.

PÂTES DE FRUITS

"PÂTES DE FRUITS" IS BASICALLY a fancy name for a grown-up jujube or gummy bear. You might not think of making your own pâtes de fruits at home, but this is an easy recipe to do, especially if you're already making your own preserves and jams. They make a fresh little treat for a fancy dinner party, but can also just be some candy for the kids that aren't full of preservatives. They're wholesome and delicious and you can't beat the flavour.

The method is the same regardless of what kind of fruit you're using, but the different sweetness levels and viscosity of the fruit means the amounts of juice, sugar, pectin, citric acid and water will be different.

When cooking, be careful not to get any hot mixture on your skin. Long sleeves are recommended.

EACH VARIATION MAKES 18 TO 20 PIECES

Blood Orange Pâtes de Fruits

2 cups fresh blood orange juice

½ cup apple juice

2¾ cups + 1 cup (for coating) sugar, divided

2 tablespoons apple pectin powder

⅓ cup glucose syrup

1¾ teaspoons citric acid

1¾ teaspoons water

Blackberry Pâtes de Fruits

2 cups blackberry purée

¾ cup apple juice

2½ cups + 1 cup (for coating) sugar, divided

2 tablespoons apple pectin powder

⅓ cup glucose syrup

1¼ teaspoons citric acid

1¼ teaspoons water

Apricot Pâtes de Fruits

2 cups apricot purée

⅓ cup apple juice

2¾ cups + 1 cup (for coating) sugar, divided

3 teaspoons apple pectin powder

⅓ cup glucose syrup

½ tablespoon citric acid

½ tablespoon water

FOR THE PÂTES DE FRUITS

Line the bottom of a 9 × 6-inch baking sheet with parchment paper.

In a medium saucepan with high sides, bring your chosen juice or purée and the apple juice to a boil over medium heat, stirring occasionally.

In a small bowl, stir together ¼ cup of the sugar and the apple pectin, then whisk into the boiling liquid. This helps keep your pâte de fruit from having lumps of pectin. Bring the mixture back up to a boil. Add the remaining sugar (excluding the sugar for coating) and the glucose syrup and stir until the sugar has dissolved. Continue to cook, stirring occasionally, over medium heat until the temperature reaches 225°F (107°C). The fruit mixture will bubble vigorously and grow in volume. Once this temperature is reached, remove from the heat.

In a small bowl, stir together the citric acid and water, then whisk into the hot fruit mixture. Using a heatproof rubber spatula, immediately scrape the mixture onto the prepared baking sheet. The mixture should be ¼ to ½ inch thick. Let the mixture sit at room temperature until cool and set.

Lightly coat a cutting board or cool marble work surface with nonstick spray to prevent sticking. With a paring knife, cut the sides of the pâte de fruit from the pan and turn out onto the cutting board. Portion into desired shapes with a knife or small cookie cutter. If serving immediately, toss as many pieces as you are serving in a medium bowl with the remaining 1 cup sugar to coat, shaking off excess sugar. Alternatively, store cut pieces in an airtight container at room temperature for up to 1 week. Coat in the sugar just before serving.

JB'S TIPS

When making a confection like this, it is important to have all your equipment organized and ingredients measured out before beginning to cook.

Before measuring glucose, spray the inside of the measuring cup with nonstick spray to allow the glucose to easily pour.

CHOCOLATE TERROIR

IN 2016, JASON AND I were invited by chocolate producer Cacao Barry to the prestigious Or Noir Laboratory in Paris and given the opportunity to create a signature chocolate. It was an incredible honour, and we were one of the only chef/pastry chef duos ever to make the trip together. We both knew that getting the blend right was crucial to capturing flavours that spoke to the terroir of Langdon Hall, and we spent a lot of time studying and dreaming of ways we could make that work.

I'm really lucky because I have a window in my pastry kitchen with a beautiful view out over the grounds. At the time we were starting to think about developing the chocolate it was coming on winter, so I could see the leaves on the ground and smell the smoke coming from the fireplaces. That view got me thinking about earth and smoke and wood as flavours I wanted to sense in the finished product. I knew it had to be dark and have some sort of depth to it and speak to the property and how we strive to achieve a certain level of sophistication.

Once we got there, we were given an opportunity to taste all the raw chocolates that they had on offer. The entire process is so magical. You're in a room full of just chocolate and you can create whatever you want. I think there were close to twenty different kinds in total, from all around the world. It was a bit overwhelming, in a way, because you have the opportunity to make something that no one else has ever created before. You can do whatever you want. There's no limitation whatsoever given to you.

We also knew that we needed to get a lot out of this chocolate. It wasn't just going to be an eating chocolate. It had to be something we could cook with. We needed to be able to temper it, bake with it, it needed to go into brownies, it had to go into a ganache, it had to be able to work as a mousse. It had to be a very specific ingredient that we could then use to produce everything that we do here. We needed something that was multi-purpose yet distinguishable. We were lucky because we pinpointed quite early what we did and didn't like, so we had a pretty good idea of what we were looking for. We did our actual tastings separately, but it turned out that we both ended up picking the exact same chocolates. The result is two distinct, unique chocolates. Our Terroir Noir is 70 percent dark chocolate and our Terroir au Lait is 40 percent milk chocolate.

By doing both the dark and the milk, I think we nailed it. We went over with just the dark in mind, but once we tasted the milk chocolate and saw what we could do with both of them we just hit magic, because we can take our milk chocolate, which is a bit milkier and caramel-like, and mix it with our dark chocolate, which has more tobacco, molasses and wine notes, to create something else altogether. It's like we have three chocolates: dark, light and blended. We even use our milk chocolate as a sweetener instead of sugar in combination with the dark chocolate to create something with a really intense, pure chocolate flavour.

—RACHEL NICHOLSON, PASTRY CHEF

TERROIR NOIR TRUFFLES

IT DOESN'T TAKE A WHOLE lot of skill to make truffles, and for anyone who wants to get into chocolate work, truffles are a great way to start. The focus here, as in any recipe, is on finding the best ingredients: the best chocolate, the best cream and the best cocoa powder. We usually serve these truffles at the end of a meal with coffee to thank our guests for coming and to send them off with one last little sweet treat.

MAKES ABOUT 24 TRUFFLES

Chocolate Truffles

3.1 ounces (90 g) 70% dark
  chocolate, chopped (½ cup)

⅓ cup whipping (35%) cream

1½ tablespoons glucose syrup

1 tablespoon unsalted butter, at
  room temperature

1 cup good-quality cocoa powder

FOR THE TRUFFLES
Place the chocolate in a medium bowl. In a small saucepan, bring the cream and glucose to a simmer over medium heat. Pour the simmering cream over the chocolate and stir gently with a rubber spatula until the chocolate has melted completely and the mixture is smooth. Add the butter and stir until it melts and the mixture is smooth. Pour into a container with a lid and chill overnight in the refrigerator.

The next day, scoop portions with a small ice-cream scoop or melon baller and roll between your palms into bite-size balls. Roll the balls in dark cocoa powder, shaking off the excess. Keep chilled for up to 2 days.

TO SERVE
Approximately 1 hour before serving, place the truffles on a plate and allow them to come up to room temperature.

SNOW COVER

A S'MORES PARTY IS IN FULL SWING beside the firepit. Guests bundled in Moncler puffers and Canada Goose parkas huddle together and roast vanilla bean marshmallows on bespoke toasting skewers, squishing the caramelized morsels between fresh graham biscuits and Langdon Hall's own terroir au lait chocolate. "These s'mores . . ." one guest says, trailing off in rapture between bites. "Mmmnnnn," groans her friend in agreement. A dog looks pleadingly at the treats for a minute before giving up and loping away for a romp.

Earlier in the day the first significant snowfall of the season left behind a thick blanket of white, but now the skies have cleared and bright moonlight illuminates a transformed landscape. At this time of year, on a night such as this, it might seem like there's nothing much happening in the garden. The snow weighs heavy on the vegetable and herb beds, the trees are stark and leafless, and the reflecting pool is a sheet of ice.

Even on the shortest, coldest days, though, a closer look reveals life throughout the grounds. The gardening team purposely doesn't cut a lot of things back in the winter. This allows guests to see the wind still moving the branches, their movement giving them a sense of life. The goal is to create harmony, so that as a person walks through the garden, there's always a feeling of something flowing.

Bright red coralberries glow like Christmas ornaments even through the dusting of snow that clings to their branches. Rows of lavender, stately beneath their frosty domes, offer a sense of formality and tranquility. The ancient Camperdown elm may have lost its heavy foliage, but now it sports a garland of pendant lights.

The gardeners might not be planting anything in the frozen earth right now, yet that spot over by the edge of the forest where they were burning brush earlier in the day will welcome a bonanza of morels in the spring.

Inside the greenhouse, spring has already arrived. Trays upon trays of seedlings bristle with their first tender young shoots. Crowds of lush ferns, plump succulents in tiny pots and even a banana plant, in combination with the warmth and humidity, make the space feel downright tropical. All the citrus plants—lemongrass, geranium, citronella—are still producing. Marigolds, basil and mint are starting to come to life. A great aromatic rosemary bush—a gift from a friend of Bill and Mary's who nearly forty years ago smuggled a cutting back from France in a shirt pocket, disguising it as a boutonniere—presides over the scene like a head of state.

The cold also brings out the full coziness of the house. Push open the heavy front door and immediately the warm scent of hearth mingled with the aroma of fresh-baked bread replaces the blank smell of cold and snow. Billiard balls ricochet into one another and thud against the felt, providing a percussive accompaniment to the pianist's rendition of "Polka Dots and Moonbeams." In Wilks' Bar, couples sit a little closer together, speak a little more intimately and admire each other in the glow of the fireplace while the portraits of Langdon Hall's founding family discreetly look away.

For a kitchen that relies so heavily on the bounty of the garden and the surrounding forest, winter might be considered a challenging time, but Jason and his team are more inspired than daunted by the season.

"To be able to create something when there's nothing, when the ground is covered in snow, that has so much value," Jason says. "I think everyone thinks of Langdon Hall cuisine as being very floral and light and fresh, and in the cold months people often ask us, 'What can you possibly do in winter?' What we do is move away from those crisp, fresh and floral flavours and turn more toward elements of smoke, earth and pine." As the essence of the property itself changes, when the hearths are up and running in all of the rooms and around the grounds outside, that transformation is reflected in the dishes as well. The smoker gets fired up more often and the smells of applewood and roasted meat and vegetables fill the kitchen.

Jason also points out that, mixed in with the game roasts and rich braises, there are still plenty of beautiful root vegetables around in the cellar and there's a lot of life left in the preserves the brigade put up earlier. "We're preserving throughout the year," he notes, "from the earliest arrivals like wild leek bulbs and wild ginger in spring, and we can use those things well into the winter. Whenever we find that something is coming to the end of its season, there's always this moment when we say, 'Okay, let's make sure we preserve some of this.' So at the end of the year we've got a kind of library of all the cool things that were growing, from the first spring shoots right until we close the garden."

For the kitchen brigade and the gardeners, the last harvests before winter are some of the most interesting, not only for their bounty but also because they are often a race against that first big snowfall. "Everyone wants to make sure nothing goes to waste," Jason says, "so they want to find ways to utilize everything that's coming in, and if the season was a good one, that's quite a lot." There are tomatoes to sauce, radishes to pickle, cabbages to ferment. Just about everything that produces seeds—from coriander to fennel to Queen Anne's lace—gets saved.

Even beyond individual ingredients, the garden and the Carolinian forest are celebrated in other ways. A large sheet of bark that's fallen away from a black walnut tree becomes a serving vessel for a selection of canapés. Moss that was growing around the edges of the garden garnishes an elaborate appetizer along with a bouquet of pine cones and cedar boughs. Aromatic citrus from the greenhouse become tea, and dried wild mushrooms flavour an earthy broth.

"The start of a new year to me is always exciting," Jason says. "We've gotten through the really, really busy time around the holidays and automatically I'm realizing spring is just around the corner and that means the birth of a new menu. I love that."

TRUFFLE SOUP
with savoury parmesan shortbread

A GREAT CHEF ONCE TOLD me you can always tell the quality of a chef by their soups. It seems like one of the easiest things to make, but great soup takes time and an understanding of the ingredients, techniques and the art of layering flavours.

I credit two chefs and the British royal family for helping to inspire this soup. In the early 1990s I was working in the pastry kitchen at the King Edward Hotel in Toronto as an apprentice to John Higgins, a former chef to the royal family. He used to serve shortbread cookies to the Queen and her corgis for tea. One of the first recipes I learned in the pastry kitchen was the Buckingham Palace shortbread biscuits. The biscuits in this recipe are a savoury version of those.

The idea for the soup came later, when I was working in London for Anton Mosimann, one of the official caterers for the royal family. His mushroom risotto was one of Princess Di's favourite dishes. While working for Mosimann, I made the dish over and over, at all sorts of events across Europe. It became very special to me. Here are all the luxurious ingredients from Mosimann's risotto—transformed into soup.

SERVES 6 TO 8

Truffle Soup

2 tablespoons olive oil

1 cup sliced white onions

1 cup thinly sliced leeks (white part only)

½ cup thinly sliced celery

6 garlic cloves, sliced

1 tablespoon fresh thyme leaves

½ tablespoon fresh rosemary leaves

2 fresh bay leaves

1 teaspoon kosher salt

1 tablespoon minced fresh truffle (optional)

1 pound (450 g) portobello mushrooms, sliced (5 cups)

1 cup Madeira

4 cups mushroom stock

4 tablespoons cold unsalted butter, cut into 1-inch cubes

3 tablespoons truffle oil

Mushroom Cream

1 tablespoon vegetable oil

1 pound (450 g) chicken wings, roughly chopped (2 cups)

1 cup sliced shallots

2 garlic cloves, sliced

1 tablespoon minced fresh truffle (optional)

1 tablespoon fresh thyme leaves

2 sprigs fresh flat-leaf parsley

1 sprig fresh rosemary

1 fresh bay leaf

½ pound (225 g) button mushrooms, sliced (3 cups)

1 teaspoon kosher salt

½ teaspoon white peppercorns

½ cup dry white wine

2 cups mushroom stock or Chicken Stock (page 286)

4 cups whipping (35%) cream

1 tablespoon good-quality truffle oil

Parmesan Shortbread

¾ cup all-purpose flour

½ cup cold unsalted butter, cubed

½ cup finely grated Parmigiano-Reggiano

¼ teaspoon kosher salt

Garnishes

Wild mushroom powder

Bite-size chunks of Parmigiano-Reggiano

FOR THE TRUFFLE SOUP

In a large saucepan or Dutch oven, heat the olive oil over medium heat. Add the onion, leeks, celery, garlic, thyme, rosemary and bay leaves and cook gently without browning, stirring frequently, until wilted and softened, about 5 minutes. Add the salt, truffle (if using) and mushrooms and continue cooking gently, stirring occasionally, until the juices released by the

RECIPE CONTINUES . . .

mushrooms have reduced almost completely. Increase the heat to medium-high, stir in the Madeira and cook until the liquid is evaporated. Add the mushroom stock and bring to a simmer. Reduce the heat to low and simmer until the stock has reduced by one-third, about 15 minutes.

Remove the pot from the heat and let cool slightly. Remove the bay leaves from the pot and discard. Transfer the soup to a high-speed blender and purée, adding the cold butter, one piece at a time, alternating with light drizzles of truffle oil, letting each addition emulsify completely before proceeding to the next. Pass the soup through a fine-mesh sieve into a clean large saucepan. Taste and adjust the salt or other seasonings, if needed. If the purée is too thick, whisk in a little more stock. Cover the soup and keep warm until ready to serve.

FOR THE MUSHROOM CREAM
In a medium saucepan, heat the vegetable oil over medium-high heat. Add the chicken wings and fry until caramelized and golden brown, stirring frequently to avoid burning, about 4 minutes. Reduce the heat to medium-low and add the shallots, garlic, truffle (if using), thyme, parley, rosemary, bay leaf, mushrooms, salt and white peppercorns. Cook gently until the vegetables are tender and the mushrooms release their juices, about 5 minutes. Reduce the mushroom juice until it has reduced almost completely. Add the white wine and reduce by two-thirds. Add the mushroom stock and again reduce by two-thirds. Add the cream to just cover the vegetables. Bring to a gentle simmer and cook for another 10 minutes.

Strain the sauce through a fine-mesh sieve back into a clean medium saucepan. Taste and adjust the salt, if needed. Whisk in the truffle oil.

FOR THE PARMESAN SHORTBREAD
Preheat the oven to 360°F (185°C). Line a baking sheet with parchment paper.

In a medium bowl, combine the flour, cold butter, cheese and salt. Mix together using your hands (or in a stand mixer fitted with the paddle attachment) until a dough begins to form. Turn the dough out onto a lightly floured work surface and knead for about 30 seconds, just until smooth. Roll the dough into a ball, cover with plastic wrap and set aside to rest in a cool spot for at least 30 minutes.

On a lightly floured work surface, and using a rolling pin, roll out the dough to a thickness of about ¼ inch. Using a 2-inch round cutter, cut out discs and transfer to the prepared baking sheet. Bake until golden, about 15 minutes.

TO SERVE
Pour the hot soup into warmed bowls. Using an immersion blender or whisk, froth the mushroom cream. Skim the froth with a spoon and transfer those collected bubbles to the surface of the soup. Dust with mushroom powder. Serve with a Parmesan shortbread and a nice piece of Parmigiano-Reggiano on the side.

JB'S TIPS
You can use other varieties of mushroom in place of the portobello in the soup, but I find it offers the best result in this recipe.

This is a great dish to shave fresh truffle onto at the table if you have some to use.

CAULIFLOWER SOUP
with raw and pickled brassicas, toasted hazelnuts and sumac

IN THIS VERY SIMPLE VEGETARIAN soup we stay really true to the vegetable. The soup is light and fresh, and because the flavour of the cauliflower is so delicate we've used minimal aromatics. Where we play a little bit with the acidity and texture is in the garnish, where we use different-coloured cauliflowers and Romanesco, raw and pickled, along with toasted hazelnuts and sumac. The contrast of the raw, cooked and pickled brassicas with the toasted nuts and sour sumac makes for a really interesting dish. I think cauliflower is extremely versatile and I'm glad to see that it's making a comeback now, as it was overlooked for a long time. With vegetarian cuisines becoming much more relevant, it's a real leader in the pack.

SERVES 4

Pickled Cauliflower

1 cup cauliflower or Romanesco florets (preferably mixed colours)

⅔ cup white wine vinegar

¼ cup water

2 tablespoons sugar

1 teaspoon coriander seeds

¾ teaspoon kosher salt

1 fresh bay leaf

Cauliflower Soup

2½ tablespoons unsalted butter, divided

4 cups roughly sliced cauliflower

1 teaspoon fresh thyme leaves

1 teaspoon salt

4 cups whipping (35%) cream

1 tablespoon fresh lemon juice

Garnishes

Shaved raw cauliflower (preferably mixed colours)

Toasted hazelnuts

Small, tender cauliflower leaves

Sumac powder

FOR THE PICKLED CAULIFLOWER
Place the cauliflower florets in a 2-cup mason jar. In a small saucepan, combine the white wine vinegar, water, sugar, coriander seeds, salt and bay leaf. Bring to a simmer over medium heat and cook for 2 minutes. Pour the hot pickling liquid into the jar to cover the cauliflower. Allow to cool, cover with a lid and refrigerate for at least 48 hours before using.

FOR THE CAULIFLOWER SOUP
Melt 1 tablespoon of the butter in a medium saucepan over medium heat. Add the cauliflower, thyme and salt. Cook gently for 4 minutes. Add the cream, bring to a simmer, then reduce the heat to low, partially cover with a lid and simmer until the cauliflower is tender, 20 to 30 minutes.

Strain the cream into another container, reserving it for adjusting the consistency of the soup. In a high-speed blender, purée the cauliflower, adding enough of the cream in a slow, steady stream while blending to achieve a smooth, velvety consistency. Once processed, add the remaining 1½ tablespoons butter and the lemon juice. Adjust the seasoning with salt, if needed. Strain through a fine-mesh sieve back into the saucepan. Warm gently before serving.

TO SERVE
Remove the pickled cauliflower from the jar and drain on paper towel. In warmed soup bowls, arrange the shaved raw cauliflower and pickled cauliflower. Scatter the toasted hazelnuts and the tiny cauliflower leaves on top. Pour in the hot soup at the table and dust with sumac powder.

JB'S TIP
This soup is a great canvas for all kinds of garnishes. I've garnished it with truffles, lobster, lemon brioche croutons, cheddar cheese biscuits and even braised oxtail.

LEMONGRASS PANNA COTTA

with caviar and Orange Gem marigold

AS LOCAL FOCUSED AS WE are here at Langdon Hall and as much as we talk about what is Ontario or Canadian cuisine, having a greenhouse gives us a great opportunity to use some ingredients that aren't entirely indigenous. This panna cotta is a perfect example of that. Here we take all of the citrus-type plants we grow in the greenhouse—lemongrass, geranium, key lime—and incorporate them into a panna cotta that's set just to the point where it melts in the mouth. We use the buttermilk from our butter production. A garnish of Canadian sturgeon caviar and lake trout roe transforms a dish most often associated with dessert into something that plays on the savoury side.

SERVES 4

Lemongrass Panna Cotta

2½ gelatin leaves

⅔ cup whipping (35%) cream

1 lemongrass stalk, tough outer leaves and stems discarded, roughly chopped

1 teaspoon lime zest

2 cups buttermilk, at room temperature

1 teaspoon shoyu

Garnishes

2 tablespoons sturgeon caviar

½ tablespoon salt-cured trout roe

Orange Gem marigold leaves and flowers

Tiny lemon verbena leaves

Baby geranium leaves

FOR THE LEMONGRASS PANNA COTTA
In a medium bowl, bloom the gelatin leaves by submerging them in cold water until soft, about 5 minutes. Lift the softened gelatin leaves from the bowl and squeeze out the water. Discard the water.

Combine the cream, lemongrass and lime zest into a small saucepan and warm gently over low heat. Strain the lemongrass cream through a fine-mesh sieve into a clean small saucepan and warm gently over low heat. Add the softened gelatin to the cream and whisk until it is completely dissolved. Whisk in the buttermilk. Season with the shoyu. Strain through a fine-mesh sieve to be sure no debris has

made it through the previous straining and any gelatin that did not dissolve is removed, then transfer into a pouring jug and divide evenly among serving dishes. Chill in the refrigerator until the panna cotta is set, about 6 hours. Cover and store in the refrigerator for up to 3 days.

TO SERVE
Spoon ½ tablespoon of caviar along the rim of each dish. Continue to garnish with trout roe, Orange Gem marigold leaves and flowers and tiny lemon verbena and baby geranium leaves.

SPICED SHRIMP FRITTER

with spring onion, pickled chili and coriander

THIS FUN, TASTY LITTLE SNACK showcases the local Ontario farmed shrimp that we started cooking with a few years ago. I know that Ontario isn't the first place most people think of when they think of shrimp, but the fishery is doing something really special that ties nicely into our ideas of sustainability and ethical food sourcing without harming the environment or wild populations. Besides the green goddess sauce, there are a number of different dips you can serve with these fritters. Try a Pineapple Yogurt (page 185) or a Lemon Gel (page 284). Or you can enjoy them just on their own.

SERVES 8

Pickled Chili

¼ cup thinly sliced Anaheim chili

¼ cup lightly packed fresh cilantro leaves

1 cup rice wine vinegar

¼ cup honey

1 lemongrass stalk, tough outer leaves and stems discarded, roughly chopped

1 teaspoon minced peeled fresh ginger

1 teaspoon kosher salt

½ teaspoon minced garlic

Green Goddess Sauce

1 cup Mayonnaise (page 280)

1 cup sour cream

2 anchovy fillets packed in olive oil, patted dry

2 cups lightly packed chopped fresh flat-leaf parsley

1 cup lightly packed chopped fresh tarragon leaves

1 tablespoon chopped fresh chives

1 garlic clove, thinly sliced

1 teaspoon kosher salt

¼ cup fresh lemon juice

Fritters

1 cup chickpea flour

¼ cup rice flour

2½ teaspoons ground cumin

2½ teaspoons ground ginger

½ tablespoon kosher salt

1 teaspoon garlic powder

1 teaspoon onion powder

1 teaspoon cayenne pepper

1 teaspoon baking soda

½ teaspoon baking powder

1 cup water (just enough to make a thick batter)

6 cups vegetable oil, for deep-frying

1 cup peeled and roughly diced fresh shrimp

¼ cup thinly sliced spring onion

¼ cup grated green zucchini

¼ cup grated yellow zucchini

¼ cup grated peeled carrot

¼ cup chopped fresh cilantro leaves and stems

¼ cup chopped fresh chives

¼ cup chopped fresh flat-leaf parsley

1½ tablespoons lime zest

Garnishes

Scallions

Coriander leaves and flowers

FOR THE PICKLED CHILI

Place the sliced chili and cilantro leaves in a 2-cup mason jar. In a small saucepan, combine the rice wine vinegar, honey, lemongrass, ginger, salt and garlic. Bring to a simmer over medium heat. Pour the pickling liquid into the mason jar to cover the chilies. Allow to cool, seal with the lid and refrigerate for at least 24 hours before using.

FOR THE GREEN GODDESS SAUCE

Place all the ingredients in a high-speed blender. Starting on a low speed, blend by pulsing the blender. Increase the speed to mix and process to make a smooth purée, about 2 minutes. Using a rubber spatula, scrape the sauce into a 4-cup mason jar, cover with a lid and store in the refrigerator for up to 1 week.

RECIPE CONTINUES . . .

FOR THE FRITTERS

In a large bowl, whisk together the chickpea flour, rice flour, cumin, ginger, salt, garlic powder, onion powder, cayenne, baking soda and baking powder. Whisk in just enough water to make a thick pancake-like batter.

Fill a medium saucepan with the vegetable oil and heat to 350°F (180°C).

Fold the shrimp, spring onion, green and yellow zucchini, carrot, cilantro, chives, parsley and lime zest into the batter. Working in batches, carefully drop tablespoonfuls of the batter into the hot oil. Fry until golden brown, turning occasionally, about 3 minutes. Using a slotted spoon or spider, transfer the fritters to paper towel to drain excess oil. Keep warm.

TO SERVE

Remove the pickled chilies from the jar and drain on paper towel. Place a generous pool of the green goddess sauce on the base of each plate, then arrange fritters on the sauce. Place a few pickled chilies on and around the fritters and garnish with scallions and coriander leaves and flowers.

SEA SCALLOP IN THE FOREST

with bay leaf cream, citronella and ocean mist

ON MY MENUS I ALWAYS have some representation of my childhood, a dish I think of as an homage to my heritage and my journey into the world of food. The creation and presentation of this dish, almost more than any other, is all about my experiences growing up in Ontario and Nova Scotia where I first fell in love with food. By drawing on those experiences and filtering them through the beautiful ingredients available to me now, this recipe also serves as a simple introduction to the philosophy of the cuisine at Langdon Hall. The presentation brings together the taste of the forest and the ocean.

I've included the full presentation as we serve it in the dining room, dry ice and all, but I understand that carbon dioxide in its solid form might not be in everybody's pantry. Don't worry: the dry ice is only there for dramatic effect. The idea is to simulate a fragrant mist that conjures the essence of the ocean and forest. Of course you can do the presentation without the dry ice and it will still smell great and be very impressive to the eye. If you do want to use dry ice, read up on how to properly store and handle it.

SERVES 6 AS AN AMUSE-BOUCHE

6 large (U-10) fresh dry sea scallops, side muscle removed for the bay leaf cream, at room temperature

Bay Leaf Cream

1 tablespoon unsalted butter

2 cups sliced shallots

½ cup thinly sliced garlic

6 fresh bay leaves

2 star anise

1 teaspoon coriander seeds

1 teaspoon kosher salt

Reserved scallop side muscles (see above)

1 cup dry white wine

1 cup Fish Stock (page 287)

4 cups whipping (35%) cream

1 tablespoon fresh lemon juice

Citronella Tea

4 cups water

4 lemongrass stalks, tough outer leaves and stems discarded, roughly chopped

1 cup lightly packed citronella geranium leaves (optional)

16 fresh lemon verbena leaves

12 juniper berries, crushed

For presentation

1 pound (450 g) fresh cold-water seaweed

6 large soup bowl–sized stone mortars or heavy soup bowls

Eighteen 6-inch branches of fresh juniper, balsam fir or pine

Six 4-inch citronella geranium branches

3 cups dry ice

6 scallop shells

FOR THE BAY LEAF CREAM

Heat the butter in a heavy medium saucepan over low heat. Add the shallots, garlic, bay leaves, star anise, coriander seeds, salt and scallop side muscles and cook, stirring frequently, until the shallots are tender and translucent, about 5 minutes. Increase the heat to medium-high, add the white wine and reduce the wine until almost completely evaporated. Add the fish stock and reduce by two-thirds. Add the cream and bring to a simmer. Reduce the heat to medium-low and simmer gently for 10 minutes to infuse all the flavours into the cream. Strain the sauce through a fine-mesh sieve into a clean medium saucepan. Discard the solids. Whisk in the lemon juice, taste, and add more salt, if needed. Cover and keep warm.

FOR THE CITRONELLA TEA

In a small saucepan, bring the water to a boil over medium heat. When the water is boiling, add the lemongrass, citronella geranium, lemon verbena and juniper berries. Reduce the heat to low and simmer for 5 minutes. Remove the saucepan from the heat

RECIPE CONTINUES . . .

and allow the tea to steep for another 10 minutes. Strain the tea through a fine-mesh sieve, return it to the saucepan and keep warm. Discard the solids.

FOR THE OCEAN MIST PRESENTATION
Carefully lay the seaweed in the base of each serving bowl until it just reaches the rim. Insert fresh juniper and citronella geranium branches around the rim of the bowl in a jaunty way.

Just before poaching the scallops, carefully lift the seaweed to one side and, using a stainless steel spoon or tongs, place ½ cup of dry ice under the seaweed. Put the seaweed back into place, ensuring at least 1 inch of seaweed covers the dry ice. Place a scallop shell on top of the seaweed in the centre of the bowl.

TO SERVE
Bring the bay leaf cream to a simmer, then remove from the heat. Lower the scallops into the cream and allow them to gently poach off the heat for 2 minutes. The scallops should still be undercooked slightly in the centre.

Using a slotted spoon, place a scallop onto each scallop shell. Using an immersion blender or whisk, froth the bay leaf cream, then spoon the aerated bubbles and sauce over the scallops. Pour an ounce or two of the citronella tea slowly into the seaweed from the side until a mist begins to rise, being careful not to get any tea in the scallop shell.

JB'S TIPS
For the seaweed, rockweed or knotted kelp are usually available wherever you can buy oysters.

The bay leaf cream is a versatile sauce that can be used with many fish and shellfish preparations.

The citronella tea is a great herbal tea to enjoy just on its own. If you have these plants growing in your garden, give it a try.

ROSEMARY POTATOES
with garlic confit purée and rosemary flowers

MY IDEA HERE WAS TO showcase all the different types of potatoes we grow in southern Ontario and how beautiful they are. We've grown some potatoes over the years that really did well in the garden, and we have a thirty-year-old rosemary tree that supplies us with beautiful sweet flowers a couple times a year. You don't always have to stick to the same kind of potato you get at the grocery store. Go to a farmers' market and seek out some of the more uncommon and heritage varieties and I think you'll find that they taste better. In the past, we've served this dish with a smoked parsnip purée, some slow-cooked onions or our Coal-Roasted Savoy Cabbage (page 242), but ultimately we just want to let the flavour of the potatoes and the hard work of the farmer really shine through.

SERVES 4

Rosemary Potatoes

1 pound (450 g) heirloom, new or
  marble potatoes, scrubbed

1 tablespoon kosher salt

4 sprigs fresh rosemary

Garlic Confit Purée

1½ cups garlic cloves

2 sprigs fresh rosemary

2 cups vegetable oil

2 tablespoons water or Vegetable
  Stock (page 285), as needed

1 teaspoon kosher salt

Garnishes

1 tablespoon flaky sea salt

Fresh rosemary flowers

FOR THE ROSEMARY POTATOES

Remove the steamer basket from a medium steamer pot. Place a kitchen towel in the basket and rest the cleaned potatoes on top. Half-fill the steamer pot with water, add the salt and rosemary and bring to a boil over medium-high heat. Reduce the temperature to medium-low to maintain a simmer, then place the steamer basket in the pot, cover tightly with a lid and steam the potatoes until they are fork-tender, about 10 minutes, checking them at the 5-minute mark to gauge how they are doing. Cooking time will depend on the size of the potatoes and the variety. When the potatoes are cooked, place the steamer basket on a large plate, remove the lid and allow the potatoes to cool slightly. Put the lid back on to keep the potatoes warm.

FOR THE GARLIC CONFIT PURÉE

Combine the garlic, rosemary and vegetable oil in a small saucepan. The garlic should be fully submerged. Bring the oil to a low simmer over medium-low heat and cook gently until the garlic is fork-tender, 15 to 20 minutes. Remove the rosemary and discard. Using a slotted spoon, transfer 8 whole garlic cloves to a small bowl with 2 tablespoons of the rosemary-flavoured oil; cover and set aside. Using a slotted spoon, transfer the remaining garlic to a high-speed blender. (Allow the remaining oil to cool to room temperature. Transfer to a mason jar, seal with a lid and keep for another use in the refrigerator for up to 1 month.)

Purée the garlic, adding enough of the water or vegetable stock in a slow, steady stream while blending to achieve a smooth, thick, creamy consistency. When processed, season with the salt. Pass through a fine-mesh sieve into a clean small saucepan. Heat gently when ready to serve.

TO SERVE

Remove the warm potatoes from the steamer basket. Place them in a medium bowl and drizzle the reserved rosemary-flavoured oil over them. Season with the flaky sea salt.

Place 1 tablespoon of the garlic confit purée on each plate and spread it across the plate with an offset palette knife or large spoon. Arrange the potatoes and whole confit garlic cloves on the purée. Garnish with the rosemary flowers.

BLACK TRUFFLE LI'L DEVILS

TRUFFLES ARE DEFINITELY A LUXURY ingredient, but this recipe is just as much about celebrating the beautiful hen eggs our kitchen gets from Murray's Farm as it is about the über-tuber. Eggs are a great neutral canvas for ingredients that have more flavour and character, like mustard, cheese, acidic chutneys and ketchups. When you combine neutral eggs with pungent, petrol-y, earthy truffle and season it to give it some zing, you put the emphasis on the texture of the egg and on the umami flavour of the truffle.

SERVES 6 TO 12

Truffle Aïoli (makes extra)

2 large egg yolks

½ garlic clove, finely minced or grated with a microplane

1 tablespoon fresh lemon juice

2 teaspoons white wine vinegar

1 teaspoon Dijon mustard

⅔ cup vegetable oil

⅓ cup truffle oil

1 teaspoon kosher salt

Devilled Eggs

6 large eggs, simmered for 10 minutes, cooled and peeled

2 tablespoons Truffle Aïoli (recipe at left)

1 teaspoon Dijon mustard

¼ teaspoon kosher salt

Garnish

Shaved fresh black or white truffle

FOR THE TRUFFLE AÏOLI

In a medium bowl, whisk the egg yolks with the garlic, lemon juice, white wine vinegar and mustard to mix well. While whisking, add the vegetable oil in a thin stream, followed by the truffle oil, whisking continuously to emulsify. The aïoli will thicken to the texture of a silky mayonnaise. If it becomes too thick, thin it with a few drops of room-temperature water. Stir in the salt. Transfer the aïoli to a covered container and refrigerate for up to 5 days.

FOR THE DEVILLED EGGS

With a sharp knife, cut a thin slice from the top and bottom of each egg so they will sit upright once halved. Evenly slice the eggs in half crosswise. Remove the yolks and reserve for the filling. The egg white should have a cup shape. Rinse the egg whites in water to clean out any remaining yolk and dry them on paper towel.

In a food processor, purée the reserved egg yolks with the truffle aïoli and mustard until you have a smooth, creamy texture without lumps. If there are lumps, pass the mixture through a fine-mesh sieve. Season with the salt.

TO SERVE

Transfer the yolk mixture to a piping bag fitted with a plain tip and pipe the yolk mixture into the egg white cups. Garnish the top with shaved fresh black or white truffle.

JB'S TIPS

With all the fresh truffle that we go through in the kitchen, we end up with a lot of bits and pieces that all get minced and used in a variety of preparations. Here, we would fold them into the finished yolk mixture. Not everybody has access to fresh truffles, of course, and so this recipe is a great way to use that truffle oil or paste in your cupboard that you're not sure what to do with.

This aïoli is the truffle bomb. Put it on burgers, it's fab as a dip for fries or chips and it goes great on a roast beef or chicken sammy.

COAL-ROASTED SAVOY CABBAGE

THIS METHOD OF COOKING CABBAGE, whole with the stem and outer leaves still on, turns a humble brassica into a full-on umami bomb, smoky and caramelized. The juices intensify and reduce inside the leaves, and when you cut open the cabbage, it just oozes deliciousness. We save all that juice and combine it with butter to make a glaze and it's crazy how good the finished dish is: chewy, almost gummy, with little crispy bits on the outside and then soft and delicate inside. You could easily serve this on its own as a vegetarian dish, but it's also great alongside a piece of perfectly roasted chicken, pork or fish. Cabbage is not necessarily fashionable—it's one of those "animal feed" vegetables—but prepared properly, I would choose it over meat any day.

SERVES 8 TO 10

Roasted Cabbage
1 large head of savoy cabbage
2 tablespoons vegetable oil
1 teaspoon kosher salt
1 tablespoon unsalted butter
Freshly ground black pepper

FOR THE ROASTED CABBAGE

Start a fire using whatever hardwood you prefer. I love the taste of maple wood in this preparation, as it adds a slightly sweet flavour to the smoke. You can use a variety of means to roast the cabbage, from a charcoal barbecue, to a home smoker, to a backyard firepit.

Rub the cabbage liberally with the vegetable oil and salt, then wrap it entirely in 2 layers of foil. Once the fire's flames have died down and you are left with hot white coals, place the foil-wrapped cabbage in the fire and cover with the hot coals. Allow the cabbage to slowly cook in the coals for 1½ to 2 hours, depending on the size of the cabbage, until it is tender all the way through when poked with a long knife or skewer.

Remove the cooked cabbage from the coals and allow to cool until you can comfortably touch it with your hands, 10 to 15 minutes. Working over a large bowl to catch the juices, remove the foil and peel off and discard the burnt outer layers until you are left with the tender, smoky inner cabbage. Reserve the cooking juices.

TO SERVE

Cut the cabbage into wedges or small rustic chunks. Melt the butter in a large, wide saucepan or frying pan over medium heat. Add 1 cup of the reserved cooking juices, then carefully add the cabbage. Gently baste the cabbage to warm it with the juice and butter. Adjust the seasoning with salt and freshly ground pepper.

JB'S TIPS
There are a million variations on this basic recipe. We've added miso, juniper truffle or smoked bacon to the butter. For the garnish we might play with the brassica theme and add vinaigrette-tossed raw Brussels sprout leaves or maybe some mustard flowers. A dollop of sour cream spiked with chopped juniper berries would work magic here as well. This is a base—have fun and make it your own.

CHAMPAGNE EGGS
with sourdough crisps and chickweed

I LEARNED THIS ELEGANT WAY to cook eggs when I worked in London, England, where it was the kind of thing we would make when we did breakfasts for the royal family. The eggs are cooked very slowly in a bowl over a bain-marie (water bath) and you're constantly moving them as they slowly curdle. Just when they're cooked perfectly, you add a splash of Champagne to slow down the cooking and add a little acidity and flavour to the eggs. At the end you have a beautiful, almost custard texture with small pieces of cooked egg throughout. Since nothing is getting direct heat, you end up with incredibly supple and soft eggs. In this recipe we garnish the finished dish with thin shards of seasoned sourdough toast and herbs from the garden, but if you have some fresh truffles kicking around or some quality caviar you'd like to enjoy, that is a great way to go.

This style of scrambled eggs is quite luxurious. The ingredients are key here, as in all our recipes. The flavour from a top-quality yolk is divine. At the restaurant, we will use Champagne on occasion or a great sparkling wine from the Niagara region. Technique and timing are very important here as well. Don't rush. Take your time, connect with the process, and maybe enjoy some bubbly while you are at it. Perfect for a Sunday brunch.

SERVES 4

Sourdough Crisps

4 wafer-thin slices of day-old sourdough bread (page 263)

Olive oil

Champagne Eggs

8 heritage hen eggs

1 teaspoon kosher salt, more for seasoning

2 tablespoons Champagne or sparkling wine

1 tablespoon finely chopped fresh chives

Garnish

12 sprigs fresh chickweed or chervil

FOR THE SOURDOUGH CRISPS

Preheat the oven to 325°F (160°C). Line a baking sheet with parchment paper.

Brush the bread with olive oil and place on the prepared baking sheet. Top with another sheet of parchment paper and another baking sheet to weigh down the bread slices. Bake the bread slices until toasted golden brown and crispy, 5 to 8 minutes.

FOR THE CHAMPAGNE EGGS

In a medium saucepan, bring a few inches of water to a simmer over medium heat to create steam. Crack the eggs into a medium heatproof bowl (big enough to sit on the saucepan but not in the water) and whisk to break the yolks. Add the salt and continue to whisk until the egg yolks and whites are well combined. Place the bowl over the simmering water and, using a rubber spatula or wooden spoon, stir the eggs continuously, making sure to scrape the bottom and sides of the bowl to prevent sticking. The steam will cook the eggs from the bottom, so you want to scrape the cooked egg off the bottom of the bowl and mix it into the uncooked egg. Continue stirring this way until the eggs are creamy like a porridge, 5 to 8 minutes. Low and slow and constant movement is the key. When the eggs are cooked, stir in the Champagne to stop the cooking. Season with more salt, if necessary, and the finely chopped chives. Serve immediately.

TO SERVE

Spoon the eggs into warm bowls or shallow coupe plates. Garnish with the chickweed and sourdough crisps.

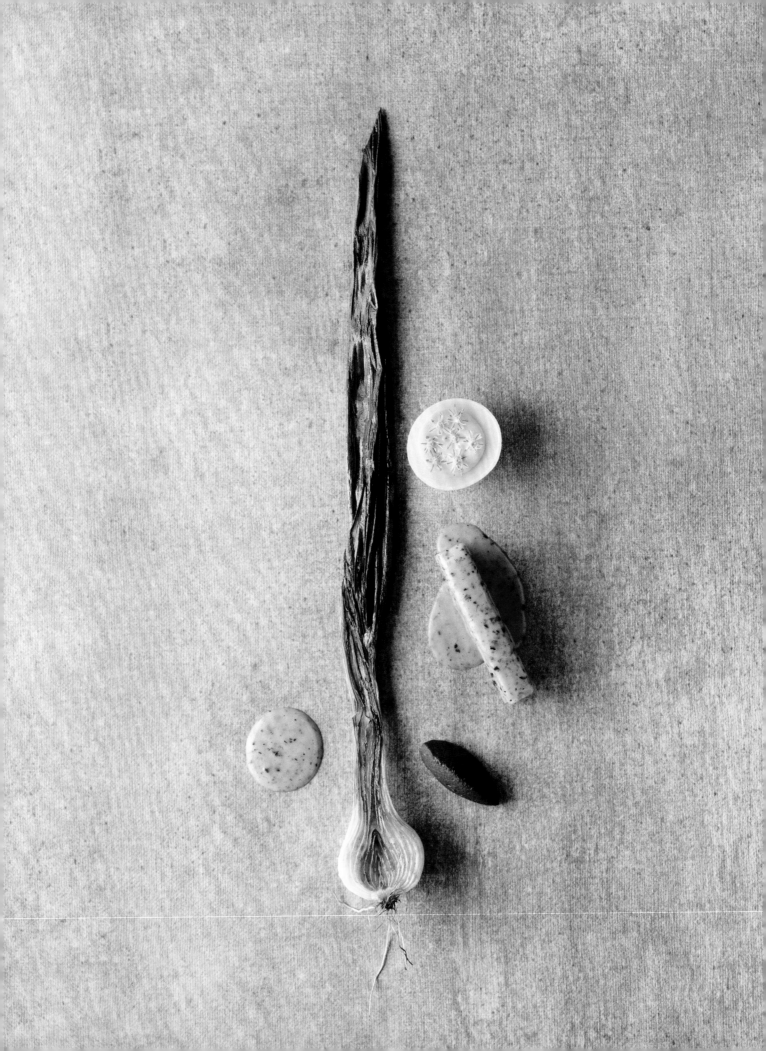

TASTY TUBERS, LEAVES AND ROOTS
roasted onion, truffle potato and watercress purée

HERE WE ARE CELEBRATING THE ONION and giving it the starring role. There's a roasted Barletta onion, and a sweet Vidalia-type onion poached until it's really tender and cut into cups, then filled with milky, silky, buttery mashed potato purée. There's also a warm pressed potato terrine glazed in Madeira truffle butter and a quenelle of rich, creamy watercress purée. Onion, potato and watercress—it's the perfect Sunday supper for a vegetarian, but also a great match to a Sunday supper with braised or roasted meats or your favourite fish.

SERVES 4

Potato Pavé

12 russet potatoes

2 cups whipping (35%) cream

1½ cups thinly sliced shallots

10 garlic cloves, thinly sliced

2 tablespoons chopped fresh thyme, divided

6 fresh bay leaves

1 tablespoon unsalted butter

2 tablespoons kosher salt

1 tablespoon freshly ground black pepper

Watercress Purée

1 tablespoon kosher salt, more for seasoning

12 cups loosely packed watercress leaves

3 cups whipping (35%) cream

Potato Purée

1½ tablespoons kosher salt, divided

2 cups thickly sliced peeled potato

½ cup whole milk, at room temperature

⅛ teaspoon nutmeg

1 cup unsalted butter, at room temperature

Poached Onion

1 large sweet white onion, peeled

4 cups whole milk

1 garlic clove, crushed

¼ cup loosely packed fresh flat-leaf parsley

1 tablespoon fresh thyme leaves

2 fresh bay leaves

5 whole cloves

1 teaspoon kosher salt

1 teaspoon black pepper

Roasted Onion

2 small spring onions, tops and roots attached (or trimmed whole leeks)

½ tablespoon vegetable oil

1 tablespoon unsalted butter, softened

½ teaspoon kosher salt

⅛ teaspoon freshly ground black pepper

1 tablespoon fresh thyme leaves

Truffle Butter Sauce

1 tablespoon minced shallots

½ teaspoon minced garlic

1 fresh bay leaf

½ cup Madeira

2 tablespoons sherry vinegar

1½ cups unsalted butter, cubed

1 tablespoon minced black truffle or truffle paste

1 teaspoon chopped fresh thyme

Pinch each of kosher salt and freshly cracked black pepper

Garnish

Spring onion, chive, leek or garlic flowers

FOR THE POTATO PAVÉ

Peel the potatoes and place them in a large container of cold water. Reserve the potato peels. Cover the potatoes and store in the refrigerator overnight.

In a medium saucepan, combine the cream with the shallots, garlic, 1 tablespoon of the thyme, reserved potato peels and bay leaves. Bring to a simmer over medium heat and cook gently, stirring occasionally, for 5 minutes. Remove from the heat, cover and let steep in the refrigerator overnight.

The next day, preheat the oven to 325°F (160°C). Rub the butter over the bottom and sides of a 10 × 6-inch loaf pan or a deep-dish casserole and line with parchment paper.

RECIPE CONTINUES . . .

Strain the cream mixture through a fine-mesh sieve into a large bowl. Discard the vegetables and other aromatics. Add the remaining 1 tablespoon thyme, salt and pepper to the seasoned cream.

Using a mandoline or a very sharp knife, thinly slice the potatoes lengthwise into even 1/16-inch slices. Add the potato slices to the bowl of seasoned cream as you work. Toss the potatoes in the cream to coat. Arrange an even layer of potato slices on the bottom of the prepared pan, being sure not to overlap. Lay the next layer perpendicular to the first layer. Repeat, alternating the direction of layers, until all the potatoes are used. Pour any remaining cream over the top layer. Wrap with plastic wrap and again with foil.

Bake for 1¼ hours or until you are able to run a small knife or fork with no resistance through the potatoes. Remove from the oven and allow to cool for 10 minutes. Place another loaf pan or dish on top and add about 3 pounds (1.4 kg) of weight (canned goods work well here) to compress the cooked potatoes. Refrigerate overnight.

The next day, remove the weights, unwrap the potato pavé and turn out onto a cutting board. Cut into four 3 × 1-inch rectangles. Arrange on a baking sheet lined with parchment paper, cover with plastic wrap and store in the refrigerator. Allow to come to room temperature before heating.

FOR THE WATERCRESS PURÉE

Fill a medium bowl with ice water. Half-fill a large saucepan with water and add the salt. Bring to a boil over high heat. When the water is boiling, blanch the watercress leaves for 60 seconds. Drain the blanched leaves and plunge them into the ice water, stirring to cool rapidly. Once cooled, remove the leaves from the ice water and squeeze as much liquid as possible from them. Place on a kitchen towel and squeeze again to absorb any additional moisture.

In a small saucepan, bring the cream to a simmer over medium heat, then reduce the heat to low and gently reduce to ½ cup. Transfer the reduced cream and the blanched watercress to a high-speed blender. Blend until a thick purée is formed, scraping the sides of the blender periodically with a rubber spatula, about 3 minutes. Pass the purée through a fine-mesh sieve into a clean small saucepan. Season with salt, if needed, and cover. Warm gently before serving.

FOR THE POTATO PURÉE

Half-fill a medium saucepan with water and add 1 tablespoon of the salt. Add the potatoes and bring to a boil over high heat. Boil for 30 minutes or until the potatoes are tender. Drain the potatoes in a colander and allow to dry in the colander for about 5 minutes. Meanwhile, in a small saucepan, bring the milk, the remaining ½ tablespoon salt and nutmeg to a simmer over medium heat, then remove from the heat.

Place the butter in a medium bowl. Pass the potatoes through a food mill or potato ricer into the bowl with the butter. Add the warm seasoned milk and gently fold together with a rubber spatula until combined. The purée should be smooth and buttery, not like a typical stiff mashed potato. Adjust the seasoning if necessary with salt and nutmeg. Transfer to a saucepan, cover and keep warm until ready to serve.

FOR THE POACHED ONION

Cut the onion in half crosswise. Slide a toothpick or small skewer through each half of the onion from one side to the other to keep the layers in place during cooking.

Place the onion halves in a medium saucepan and add the milk, garlic, parsley, thyme, bay leaves, cloves, salt and pepper. Bring to a simmer over medium heat and cook, covered, for 20 minutes or until the onion is completely tender. Allow the onion to cool in the milk.

Transfer the onion to paper towel to dry. Reserve the milk. Remove the toothpicks and gently separate the layers of the onion. Set aside 4 "cups" of similar size from the middle section of the onion and return to the milk.

FOR THE ROASTED ONION

Preheat the oven to 350°F (180°C). Line a small baking sheet with parchment paper.

Cut the onions in half lengthwise, keeping the greens intact. Drizzle the onions and prepared baking sheet with the vegetable oil. Brush the softened butter on the cut side of the onions, season with the salt and pepper and then dust with the thyme leaves. Place the seasoned onions cut side down on the prepared baking sheet. Cover with foil and roast for 25 minutes or until lightly caramelized and tender. Keep the oven on.

FOR THE TRUFFLE BUTTER SAUCE

In a small saucepan, combine the shallots, garlic and bay leaf. Add the Madeira and sherry vinegar and bring to a boil over medium-high heat. When boiling, reduce the heat to low and gently simmer until the liquid is reduced to about ¼ cup. Whisk in the butter, a few cubes at a time, until all the butter has melted and an emulsified sauce has formed. Be careful not to let the sauce simmer. Stir in the truffle and thyme. Season with salt and pepper. Cover and keep in a warm place until ready to use.

TO SERVE

Warm the potato pavé slices in the oven for 6 minutes at 350°F (180°C). Warm the poached onion cups, then drain on paper towel. Place a roasted onion half, cut side up, on each plate slightly to the left of centre. Quenelle some warm watercress purée to the right of the onion. When the potato pavé is warm, lay a slice next to the watercress purée and spoon some warm truffle butter sauce over it. Place the poached onion cups on the plates and fill with potato purée. Garnish the potato purée with the onion flowers.

BEEF SHORT RIB AND RUTABAGA
with black truffle and Madeira jus

WE DEVELOPED THIS RECIPE TO showcase the beautiful beef we get from farmer Bryan Gilvesy at YU Ranch. Most of the beef we use comes from a co-op of farms in our area, but Farmer Bryan and his family raise Texas Longhorn cattle in a very special way. Their cattle are allowed free range across their Tillsonburg property, a beautiful slice of Carolinian forest, wetlands and tall grassland that has been enriched and restored by allowing it to revert to its natural state with an abundance of native plants, grasses and flowers that make up the feed for the herd. It's not uncommon to visit the farm and find the cattle sitting in the forest or wading in the ravine. They are gorgeous animals, and the meat is lean, high in protein and delicious. The farm only harvests a few head a month, so we use different cuts throughout the year.

The dish also celebrates a much more humble ingredient: rutabaga. Rutabaga is so amazing. It has such an umami flavour, whether it's roasted or raw in a salad. I love it in broths and stocks. It has a natural sweetness and earthiness that is unmistakable if you are familiar with the vegetable. Here we serve it three ways: puréed, roasted whole and, because our rutabaga was cellared over the winter and grew all these lovely greens, as a salad with truffle and a splash of vinaigrette to balance the richness of the dish.

If you don't have a sous vide cooker, see page 291 for the Traditional Method of Braised Beef Short Rib.

SERVES 4

Beef Short Rib
1 pound (450 g) boneless beef short ribs

1 tablespoon kosher salt

1 teaspoon freshly cracked black peppercorns

3 tablespoons vegetable oil, divided

1 clove unpeeled garlic, crushed

2 sprigs fresh thyme

2 tablespoons unsalted butter

Madeira Jus
1 pound (450 g) chicken wings, roughly chopped (2 cups)

1 tablespoon unsalted butter

½ cup sliced shallots

½ cup sliced button mushrooms

1 tablespoon minced black truffle

½ tablespoon minced garlic

¼ cup chopped fresh thyme

¼ cup chopped fresh flat-leaf parsley

¼ teaspoon black peppercorns

1 fresh bay leaf

1 cup Madeira, divided

2 cups Veal Jus (page 289)

1 teaspoon kosher salt

Rutabaga Purée
2 cups peeled and diced rutabaga

2 cups whipping (35%) cream

1 tablespoon kosher salt

Roasted Rutabaga
1 small rutabaga

1 tablespoon vegetable oil, divided

1 teaspoon kosher salt

½ tablespoon fresh thyme leaves

1 tablespoon unsalted butter

Garnishes
Flaky sea salt

2 cups rutabaga and turnip greens

16 slices shaved black truffle (4 slices per portion)

½ tablespoon Shallot Vinaigrette (page 282)

FOR THE BEEF SHORT RIB

Set a sous vide water bath to 149°F (65°C).

Trim the short ribs of any excess exterior fat and connective tissue. Reserve the trimmings. Season the short ribs with the salt and pepper. In a 10-inch cast-iron skillet or frying pan, heat 2 tablespoons of the vegetable oil over high heat. Sear the beef on all sides until golden brown, 1 to 2 minutes per side. Remove the beef from the pan and rest on a small baking sheet. Add the reserved beef trimmings to the pan and fry until golden brown, about 3 minutes.

RECIPE CONTINUES . . .

Transfer the short ribs and caramelized trimmings to a sous vide bag. Vacuum-seal on full pressure. Add the beef to the water bath, reduce the temperature to 133°F (56°C) and cook for 48 hours. (If not using immediately, chill in an ice bath and store in the refrigerator until ready to serve or for up to 1 week.)

FOR THE MADEIRA JUS

Preheat the oven to 350°F (180°C). Spread the chicken wings on a baking sheet and roast, stirring occasionally, until golden brown, about 20 minutes.

In a medium saucepan, melt the butter over medium-low heat. Add the shallots, mushrooms, truffle and garlic and gently cook until wilted and tender. Add the roasted chicken wings, thyme, parsley, black peppercorns and bay leaf. Stir to mix. Pour ½ cup of the Madeira into the baking sheet and use a wooden spoon or rubber spatula to scrape all the roasted bits off the pan; add to the saucepan. Increase the heat to medium-high, pour in the remaining ½ cup Madeira and reduce until almost dry. Add the veal jus and bring to a simmer, then reduce the heat to medium-low and reduce the jus at a gentle simmer until thick enough to coat the back of a spoon, another 8 to 10 minutes. Strain through a fine-mesh sieve into a small saucepan. Discard the solids. Season the jus with the salt, cover and keep warm (or allow to cool and store in an airtight container in the refrigerator for up to 5 days).

FOR THE RUTABAGA PURÉE

In a medium saucepan, combine the rutabaga and cream. Cover, bring to a simmer over medium-low heat and cook, stirring often, until tender, about 30 minutes. Strain the cream into another container, reserving it for adjusting the consistency of the purée, if needed. In a high-speed blender, purée the rutabaga, adding enough of the cream in a slow, steady stream while blending to achieve a smooth, velvety consistency. Once processed, adjust the seasoning with salt, if needed. Strain through a fine-mesh sieve into a small saucepan. Warm gently before serving.

FOR THE ROASTED RUTABAGA

Preheat the oven to 325°F (160°C).

Rub the root liberally with ½ tablespoon of the vegetable oil and the salt, then wrap it entirely in 2 layers of foil. Place on a baking sheet and roast until it is tender all the way through when poked with a long knife or skewer, about 1½ hours. Cooking time will depend on the rutabaga's size and density.

Remove from the oven and allow to cool for 30 minutes or until you can comfortably touch it with your hands. Remove the foil and transfer the root to a cutting board. Slice the rutabaga down the middle and cut into wedges. Season with salt and keep warm.

Just before serving, heat the remaining ½ tablespoon vegetable oil in a large frying pan over medium-high heat. Add the rutabaga wedges and caramelize on both sides, about 30 seconds per side. Once nicely caramelized, reduce the heat to low and add the thyme and butter. The butter will melt quickly and begin to brown and bubble. Baste the wedges with the butter. Season with salt. Remove from the heat and keep warm.

FINISH THE BEEF SHORT RIB

Remove the beef from the sous vide bag and dry with paper towel. Season again with salt and pepper. In a 10-inch cast-iron skillet or frying pan, heat the remaining 1 tablespoon vegetable oil over medium-high heat. Add the beef, garlic and thyme and brown the beef until golden brown on all sides, about 30 seconds per side. Add the butter, and when it is bubbling, baste the beef with the butter for 2 minutes. Transfer the beef to a cutting board.

TO SERVE

Carve the beef and season with flaky sea salt. In a small bowl, toss the rutabaga and turnip greens with the shaved truffle and shallot vinaigrette, then season with freshly ground pepper and salt. Divide the salad garnish among warm dinner plates. Arrange the roasted rutabaga and the carved beef on the plates. Add 1 tablespoon of the rutabaga purée to each plate and finish with the Madeira jus.

VEAL TARTARE

with Jerusalem artichoke, raisin and nasturtiums

THIS IS MY REIMAGINING OF a purely classic tartare. The concept remains the same, but the recipe draws heavily on the bounty of the surrounding farms and the terroir of Langdon Hall itself. In this recipe the artichokes are fried into thin, crispy strips to add a nutty element of texture that really complements the delicacy of the veal. We pick the nasturtiums fresh every day before dinner service, so they are vibrant and add a colourful punch of peppery green spice and a bright floral flavour to the dish.

SERVES 4

Raisin Purée

1 cup Simple Syrup (page 284)

1 good-quality Earl Grey tea bag

1 cup golden raisins

½ teaspoon kosher salt

Jerusalem Artichoke Chips

2 large Jerusalem artichokes

4 cups vegetable oil, for deep-frying

½ teaspoon kosher salt

Veal Tartare

1 pound (450 g) milk-fed veal tenderloin, cleaned

¼ cup Pickled Mustard Seeds (page 283), drained

3 tablespoons minced drained capers

3 tablespoons thinly sliced fresh chives

3 tablespoons thinly sliced fresh flat-leaf parsley

2 teaspoons freshly ground grains of paradise

2 tablespoons minced shallot

2 tablespoons smooth Dijon mustard

2 tablespoons extra-virgin olive oil

2 teaspoons kosher salt

24 nasturtium leaves

FOR THE RAISIN PURÉE

In a small saucepan, bring the simple syrup and tea bag to a simmer over medium heat. Add the raisins and bring to a boil. Remove from the heat and allow to steep for 20 minutes or until the raisins are plump and hydrated. Remove the tea bag and strain the raisins, reserving the syrup in another container. Discard the tea bag.

In a high-speed blender, purée the raisins with half of the syrup until a smooth, thick sauce consistency is achieved, about 2 minutes. Press through a fine-mesh sieve into a small bowl to remove any skin and seeds. Season with the salt. Transfer to an airtight container and store in the refrigerator until ready to use.

FOR THE JERUSALEM ARTICHOKE CHIPS

Slice the artichokes as thinly as possibly on a mandoline or with a sharp knife. You'll need 8 to 12 chips per plate.

In a medium saucepan, heat the vegetable oil over medium heat to 250°F (120°C). In small batches,

so the chips don't stick together or clump, deep-fry the artichoke slices until they are a rich golden colour and crispy all the way through, 6 to 8 minutes. Using a slotted spoon, transfer the chips to paper towel to drain. Season with the salt.

FOR THE VEAL TARTARE

Finely dice the veal and place it in a medium bowl. Add the pickled mustard seeds, capers, chives, parsley, grains of paradise, shallot, mustard, olive oil and salt. Mix with a rubber spatula or a large spoon until the ingredients are well incorporated.

TO SERVE

Spoon 2 mounds, each 1 tablespoon, of the veal tartare onto each plate. Garnish one mound with 8 to 12 artichoke chips to completely cover the meat. Cover the other mound with 6 green peppery nasturtium leaves. Spoon a pool of the raisin purée onto each plate to finish.

JB'S TIPS

Always be sure to use fresh meat for a tartare preparation. It is a good idea to let the butcher know what you are planning so they can help you select the best product they have to offer.

You can use beef in this recipe, although I find the ingredients dance much more elegantly with veal.

Jerusalem artichoke, also called sunroot, sunchoke or earth apple, is actually a species of daisy tuber that's native to eastern Canada. Here at the property it grows wild in the garden beside the pool and supplies the kitchen with earthy, sweet garden jewels and the guests with beautiful yellow sunflowers.

Grains of paradise are a dried floral seed from the ginger family that I often use in place of peppercorns. Freshly ground black pepper can be used instead.

SQUAB POACHED IN DUCK FAT

with spiced chocolate and Jerusalem artichoke

THE TRICKIEST THING ABOUT COOKING game birds is to make sure you don't overcook them or else they get dry and iron-y and simply don't taste good. This recipe uses a technique I developed that pretty much takes the guesswork out and keeps the bird super juicy and delicate. By poaching the squab in a rich duck fat that we season almost like we would a stock, we're able to maintain the integrity of the bird while imbuing it with lots of great flavour. It's a bit like making confit, but we're just cooking the bird in the duck fat long enough to get it to medium-rare. The other special thing that I like about this technique is that you can use that duck fat over and over again and it just gets more flavourful. If you can't find duck fat, clarified butter is a fine substitute. For this dish we don't use the squab legs—we save them to make game sausage.

We have an amazing relationship with Carole Precious who runs Chassagne Farm and supplies us with just about all of our game birds. She started out raising hunting birds—Harris hawks, peregrine falcons, golden eagles and the like—and she fed them quail. The story goes that someone once said to her, "You know, the French love to eat quail. You could probably sell them." At first she laughed it off, but now she's our primary game bird provider. We get eggs from her and quail and ring-necked pheasant and, as in this recipe, squab.

SERVES 4

Infused Duck Fat

½ cinnamon stick

8 star anise

6 whole cloves

10 juniper berries, crushed

1 tablespoon coriander seeds

6 cups rendered duck fat or clarified butter, divided

1 cup thinly sliced shallots

½ cup sliced garlic

1 tablespoon fresh thyme leaves

1 teaspoon fresh rosemary leaves

4 fresh bay leaves

Poached Squab

2 fresh squab (13 ounces/370 g each), cleaned

6 cups Standard Brine (page 290)

6 cups infused duck fat (recipe above)

Jerusalem Artichoke Purée

⅔ pound (300 g) Jerusalem artichokes (about 4 artichokes)

1 tablespoon fresh lemon juice

2 cups whipping (35%) cream

1 teaspoon kosher salt

Jerusalem Artichoke Chips

2 large Jerusalem artichokes

4 cups vegetable oil, for deep-frying

½ teaspoon kosher salt

Spiced Chocolate Jus

1½ pounds (675 g) chicken wings, roughly chopped (3 cups)

Squab neck, wings and legs removed from the birds (see poached squab at left)

1 teaspoon vegetable oil

1 cup thinly sliced shallots

1 tablespoon thinly sliced garlic

½ cinnamon stick

⅛ vanilla bean, split lengthwise and seeds scraped

5 star anise

½ teaspoon kosher salt

½ teaspoon black peppercorns

10 juniper berries, crushed

2 fresh bay leaves

1 tablespoon fresh thyme leaves

½ cup port, divided

1 cup brandy

2 cups Veal Jus (page 289)

1 tablespoon grated dark chocolate

Kale Chips

1 bunch baby kale or large Kalette leaves

1 teaspoon vegetable oil

Pinch of kosher salt

Garnish

Cacao Barry Extra Brute cocoa powder

RECIPE CONTINUES . . .

FOR THE INFUSED DUCK FAT

In a medium saucepan, combine the cinnamon stick, star anise, cloves, juniper berries and coriander seeds. Gently toast over medium heat, stirring occasionally, until fragrant, about 2 minutes. Add 2 tablespoons of the duck fat and the shallot, garlic, thyme, rosemary and bay leaves. Reduce the heat to medium-low and continue to cook, stirring occasionally, until the vegetables are wilted and tender, about 2 minutes. Stir in the remaining duck fat. Bring the duck fat to a gentle simmer, then reduce the heat to low to maintain a gentle simmer for another 15 minutes to infuse the flavours into the duck fat. Remove from the heat and let the duck fat sit for 1 hour. Strain through a fine-mesh sieve or 3 layers of cheesecloth into a clean saucepan, cover and heat before serving. Discard the solids.

FOR THE POACHED SQUAB

Using a sharp knife, remove the neck, wings and legs from the birds and reserve for the spiced chocolate jus. Pour the standard brine into a container large enough to hold the birds submerged in the brine. Submerge the prepared birds, cover and leave to soak for 1 hour in the refrigerator. Remove the birds from the brine, give a quick rinse under cold running water and pat dry with paper towel. Discard the brine. Cover the birds in plastic wrap and bring to room temperature, about 20 minutes.

In a large saucepan, bring the infused duck fat to a simmer over medium heat. Add the squab and maintain the duck fat just under a simmer, cooking the birds for 3 minutes or until they reach an internal temperature of 125°F (52°C) when probed with a meat thermometer in the thickest part of the breast. Remove from the heat and allow the birds to sit in the duck fat for another 3 minutes. Remove the birds and transfer to a cutting board. Using a sharp knife, remove the breasts and return them to the pot of duck fat and gently heat before serving.

FOR THE JERUSALEM ARTICHOKE PURÉE

Working with one artichoke at a time, peel the artichokes and place them in a small bowl of water with the lemon juice to prevent discoloration. When peeled, thinly slice the artichokes and place them in a medium saucepan. Add the cream and bring to a low simmer over medium-low heat. Cook gently until the artichokes are tender, 5 to 10 minutes. Strain the cream into another container, reserving it for adjusting the consistency of the purée. In a high-speed blender, purée the artichokes, adding enough of the cream in a slow, steady stream while blending to achieve a smooth, thick, creamy consistency. Once processed, season with the salt. Strain through a fine-mesh sieve into a clean, small saucepan. Keep covered. Heat gently when ready to serve.

FOR THE JERUSALEM ARTICHOKE CHIPS

Slice the artichokes as thinly as possible on a mandoline or with a sharp knife. You'll need 8 to 12 chips per plate.

In a medium saucepan, heat the vegetable oil over medium heat to 250°F (120°C). In small batches, so the chips don't stick together or clump, deep-fry the artichoke slices until they are a rich golden colour and crispy all the way through, 6 to 8 minutes. Using a slotted spoon, transfer the chips to paper towel to drain. Season with the salt.

FOR THE SPICED CHOCOLATE JUS

Preheat the oven to 350°F (180°C). Spread the chicken wings and reserved squab pieces on a baking sheet and roast, stirring occasionally, until golden brown, about 20 minutes.

Heat the vegetable oil in a medium saucepan over medium-low heat. Add the shallots, garlic, cinnamon, vanilla bean, star anise, then add the salt and black peppercorns and gently cook, stirring occasionally, until fragrant and the shallots are wilted and tender, about 5 minutes. Add the juniper berries, bay leaves, thyme and roasted chicken wings and reserved squab pieces and stir to mix. Pour ¼ cup of the port into the baking sheet and use a wooden spoon or rubber spatula to scrape all the roasted bits off the pan; add to the saucepan. Increase the heat to medium-high, pour in the remaining ¼ cup port and reduce until almost dry. Add the brandy and reduce to almost dry again. Add the veal jus, reduce the heat to low and reduce the jus at a gentle simmer until thick enough to coat the back of a spoon, about 5 minutes. Strain through a fine-mesh sieve into a small saucepan. Discard the solids. Cover the jus and keep warm.

FOR THE KALE CHIPS

Preheat the oven to 325°F (160°C). On a baking sheet lined with parchment paper, toss the kale leaves with the vegetable oil and salt. Bake until golden and crisp, 5 to 7 minutes.

TO SERVE

Remove the squab breasts from the warm duck fat and pat dry with paper towel. Pull off and discard the skin and place the breasts on warm plates. Spoon some warm artichoke purée beside the squab. Garnish with the artichoke chips and kale chips. Stir the grated chocolate into the warm spiced jus. Once the chocolate has melted, drizzle the jus next to the squab. Dust the artichoke purée with the cocoa powder.

WINE PAIRING

In the world of pairings there are a few ways to go, but complementary pairings are the most common. With complementary pairings, you're looking for flavours and textures that work with the food. However, this dish is so savoury, rich and earthy, and there's such an iron component, I feel if you put an earthy wine with it, it will just be too much. So instead of a complementary pairing I prefer to go in the other direction and contrast. Contrast pairings can be tricky, because if you get them wrong, they're so wrong that you've done a horrible thing, but when you get them right, they are some of the best pairings in the world.

I like a really juicy, crunchy wine with this dish, something with no oak, just really fresh fruit and a super-mineral finish to it, so that when you take a bite you get this savoury rich feeling, then you take a sip and it wipes that memory and you can go back and appreciate both more. Young, fresh, bright, mineral-driven reds are going to give you that excellent contrast. I'd go to Piedmont. Barbera is lovely with this. Dolcetto works, Valpolicella works really well, or Cab Franc or a Mencia from Spain. If you wanted to go complementary here, I'd look to something like a Rioja with a bit of oak aging. Anything with a roast, crisp, caramelized finish calls for oak.

SOURDOUGH

THE SOURDOUGH BREAD WITH homemade butter at Langdon Hall is served on every table at every meal. It is uncommonly delicious and warming and everything a great bread should be. Many guests describe it as the best bread they've ever had, and more than one has smuggled a slice home for snacking on another day. Pastry chef Rachel Nicholson breaks down what makes the bread so special and how she comes up with ideas.

I find bread so fascinating, and sourdough in particular is ridiculous. It's just an amazing product. It looks like goo and it doesn't smell good at all and the majority of people tend to think it's a disgusting mess, but I love it. Once you start working with it and get to know it and let it rest, it becomes this beautiful pillow of loveliness.

My best guess is that our sourdough starter at Langdon Hall is sixteen years old. He was definitely here when I first started, so he could be as old as twenty or twenty-five. He's a grumpy man and he's finicky until you get to know him. We tend to spoil him. Depending on the weather we'll move him around from one room to another to keep him happy. I think he likes the change of scenery.

Somebody almost killed him once. By accident, not because he's grumpy. They forgot to feed him, and starters are living things, so if you don't feed them, they die. That was too close for comfort, so now we go to some trouble to make sure that never happens again. In the winter, during our annual shutdown, he goes into two different separate homes. I've frozen some and dehydrated some, so we usually have three or four backups just in case something happens.

In the summer, we'll reduce the amount of water we use to make sure that the starter isn't as active so he can eat overnight and not deplete himself. In the winter, we sometimes have to increase the water to make sure that he's a little bit more active. Sometimes we'll have to change the temperatures of the water that we add. And in the really, really cold winter, we store him in our proofer overnight. The proofer is turned off, but it's just a tiny bit more insulated than the ambient room temperature.

He's worth the trouble, because he makes a beautiful old-fashioned very sour sourdough. A true sourdough with strength and a really nice texture to it. It's an all-around great bread, soft and delicious. The flavour is there, but it's not overwhelming.

Beyond our famous sourdough, the bread program has grown a lot in recent years. We've doubled the number of bakers we have, and this gives us the opportunity to really expand our offerings. A lot of the bread is made with ingredients from the property, and we try to incorporate a range of herbs and grains. We're never at a loss for inspiration. Typically, our ideas start with going for a walk on the property, bringing back a little bit of what we find and working our way through that.

A lot of our new breads start with making something for staff meal. We have this really interesting dynamic where we have these ridiculously well-educated, food-driven culinary people in the house, but we also have all these other people who work here in different departments whose palates might not be as highly trained. Trying new ideas out on the staff gives us this great opportunity to get a generalized idea if what we're doing appeals to a broad range of people, because that's who our clients are. They also give us the ability to be a little freer, though. We can take some chances because our guests trust us.

SOURDOUGH BREAD

A STAPLE AT LANGDON HALL since the early days, the sourdough has grown to become an iconic offering from the kitchen. It is served at every service to every guest and everyone loves it. Our bakers also do other things—rosemary country loaves (page 133) or Danish ryes or breads inspired by the season, maybe a dandelion loaf or a fresh spice loaf where they get to experiment and have some fun—but the sourdough is always there. With the possible exception of the truffle soup, this sourdough with our homemade butter is a favourite with many of our guests.

This levain recipe will leave you with just under 1 cup of sourdough starter for another loaf.

MAKES 2 LOAVES

Levain

1 cup water

1 cup all-purpose flour

½ cup sourdough starter (see Tip)

Sourdough

¾ cup levain (recipe at left)

1¼ cups water

3 cups all-purpose flour

½ cup whole wheat flour

1 teaspoon kosher salt

FOR THE LEVAIN

In a large bowl, stir together the water, flour and sourdough starter with a spoon until well mixed and the dry is completely combined with the wet. Cover with plastic wrap and allow to rest overnight in the refrigerator. The levain will grow to triple in volume and then will fall to about double, so make sure to have it in a large enough container.

FOR THE SOURDOUGH

The day before baking, in a stand mixer fitted with a dough hook attachment, mix together the levain and water. Add the all-purpose and whole wheat flours and mix on low speed until the dough comes together. Cover the bowl with a kitchen towel and allow to rest for 20 minutes. Add the salt and mix on medium speed for 5 minutes. Cover the bowl with a kitchen towel and proof at room temperature for 1 hour or until the dough has doubled in size.

Turn the dough out onto a work surface and divide into 2 equal pieces. Round the loaves and let rest for 10 minutes. Shape the loaves into the desired loaf shape and place on a baking sheet lined with parchment paper, leaving 5 inches of space between the loaves so they don't grow together. Cover the loaves with a damp kitchen towel and place in the fridge overnight to proof. This step increases the flavour of the bread and gives the crust a dark, rich colour once baked.

BAKE THE BREAD

Preheat the oven to 450°F (230°C) with a cast-iron pan on the bottom rack. Remove the proofed loaves from the fridge and let them come to room temperature.

When the oven is preheated, add 2 cups of ice cubes to the cast-iron pan to create steam. Immediately score the loaves and place on the middle or top rack of the oven. Bake for 20 minutes. At the 15-minute mark, remove the cast-iron pan to develop the crust. The bread will be a golden brown colour and sound hollow when fully baked. Cool on a rack.

RECIPE CONTINUES . . .

I suggest you visit your local artisan baker and ask if you can purchase some starter to attempt sourdough at home. I have found over the years that bakers are quite friendly and are usually happy to share some starter for home bakers to experiment with. It is much quicker than trying to make your own and will be much tastier, as starters that are mature offer a much more developed character and more interesting flavour profile.

Humidity and room temperature can change the amount of flour needed in the recipe, and it may take a couple of tries to get a result that works best in your kitchen environment.

Keep in mind that all ovens are different and kitchen temperatures change throughout the seasons as well; you might have to make minimal adjustments to the water or flour amounts as you might need more flour (or less water) on hot, humid days or less flour (or more water) on cold, dry days. Temperature and bake time may fluctuate as well.

Mixing in strong herbs such as rosemary or thyme or spices like mustard or caraway will give a home baker an easy change to the bread without needing to adjust the flour/water proportions.

MILK CHOCOLATE TART
with cocoa crust and passion fruit

EASILY ONE OF MY FAVOURITE flavour combinations, this recipe utilizes our house milk chocolate and passion fruit. Passion fruit isn't necessarily something people think of as local, but we do have a passion fruit vine on a wall in our greenhouse that gives us some delicious flowers and fruit. I love its sour, tropical flavour and its incredible versatility. Passion fruit goes great with shellfish, you can use it in a vinaigrette and it even works well with truffle. In fact, this tart is one of the only times we use it in a dessert.

The recipe itself is as simple as it gets when it comes to a tart but it's super impressive. Just remember when it comes time to serve, cut the tart while it is cool and then let it temper a little bit, otherwise it will fall apart. You should end up with something that's as delicate and soft as warm butter.

MAKES ONE 12-INCH TART, SERVES 8

Black Cocoa Tart Shell
1¾ cups all-purpose flour
1 cup icing sugar
¼ cup black cocoa powder
¼ teaspoon kosher salt
½ cup chilled unsalted butter, cut into small dice
1 large egg

Milk Chocolate Ganache
24.6 ounces (700 g) milk chocolate, chopped (4 cups)
1 teaspoon kosher salt
3½ cups whipping (35%) cream
¼ cup glucose syrup

Passion Fruit Sauce
8 ripe passion fruits
2 tablespoons sugar

Caramelized Cocoa Nibs
½ cup sugar
2½ teaspoons water
½ cup cocoa nibs

Garnish
Flaky sea salt

FOR THE BLACK COCOA TART SHELL
In a stand mixer fitted with the paddle attachment, mix together the flour, icing sugar, cocoa powder and salt. On low speed, add the chilled butter, a few pieces at a time, until the mixture resembles crumbly coarse sand with a few pea-sized pieces of butter still visible. Add the egg and continue to mix on low speed just until the dough forms a ball that holds together. On a lightly floured work surface, flatten and work the dough into a ½-inch-thick disc. Wrap in plastic wrap and chill for at least 2 hours in the refrigerator.

Preheat the oven to 350°F (180°C).

On a lightly floured surface, roll out the dough into a 1/16-inch-thick 15-inch circle large enough to have some overhang once in a 12-inch tart pan with removable bottom. Roll the dough up onto the rolling pin and unroll it over the tart pan. Press the dough into the pan, pressing it into the sides with your fingers. Trim off the excess dough with a paring knife. Transfer the tart pan to a baking sheet. Prick the base of the pastry with a fork. Line with parchment paper and fill with baking beans or rice. Blind bake for 15 minutes, until the dough is cooked through on the sides. Remove the parchment and beans and continue to bake for another 5 minutes or until the dough is cooked through on the bottom and looks dry. Transfer to a rack and allow to cool completely. Once cool, remove the tart shell from the tart pan.

FOR THE MILK CHOCOLATE GANACHE
Place the chocolate and salt in a medium bowl. In a medium saucepan, heat the cream and glucose syrup over medium heat, whisking to combine, until it reaches a simmer. Pour the simmering cream over the

RECIPE CONTINUES . . .

chocolate and stir gently with a rubber spatula until the chocolate melts completely and the mixture is smooth and looks like a thick chocolate sauce.

Pour the warm ganache into the prepared tart shell, filling it up to the very top. Allow the ganache to cool to room temperature, then refrigerate until completely cool before slicing.

FOR THE PASSION FRUIT SAUCE

Cut the passion fruits in half and scrape the fruit and seeds into a small saucepan. Stir in the sugar. Over medium-high heat, bring the mixture to a boil, stirring often so the sugar doesn't burn. The mixture will be cloudy at first. When the juice starts to clear, it should thicken slightly. Remove from the heat and allow to cool to room temperature. Press the sauce through a fine-mesh sieve and transfer to a squeeze bottle or small container.

FOR THE CARAMELIZED COCOA NIBS

Line a baking sheet with parchment paper. In a small saucepan, heat the sugar and water to 235°F (113°C) over medium heat. Add the cocoa nibs and stir to coat the nibs well. Using a rubber spatula, scrape the cocoa nibs onto the prepared baking sheet and allow to cool to room temperature.

TO SERVE

Note that the ganache filling is very soft, almost like a thick pudding once it comes to room temperature. You will need to slice the tart while chilled and firm—you can even place it in the freezer for an hour before slicing—to keep the cuts clean and precise. Transfer the slices to serving plates and allow to come to room temperature before finishing and serving.

Top each slice of tart with flaky sea salt and caramelized cocoa nibs and spoon a generous pool of passion fruit sauce beside.

STEEL-CUT OATS AND HEMP
with caramelized bananas, spiced pecans and dark chocolate

THIS OLD-SCHOOL OATMEAL IS LIKE what your grandma would make for breakfast if your grandma had access to wild hemp leaves. It makes a great breakfast, but we like to serve it as dessert too. I love the density and the mouthfeel of these long-cooked grains. You can do so many things with them, whether it's savoury or sweet, in a porridge or a risotto, with a piece of roasted meat or, as in this case, a little bit of almond milk, sugar and maple.

The first time I ate this I was excited about the texture of the chocolate and the nuts but thought it needed another soft and creamy element, so we took slightly underripe bananas, dusted them with sugar, broiled them and popped them in the porridge. To add a fun element from the property, we went out to the edge of the forest and picked some wild hemp leaves. They have a nutty, grassy flavour that we accented with toasted hemp seeds. What we wound up with was this chunky monkey–type concoction with all these interesting textures that give a different mouthfeel with every bite.

SERVES 4

Spiced Pecans

1 egg white

½ cup pecan halves

1 teaspoon cinnamon

1 teaspoon brown sugar

½ teaspoon ground cloves

¼ teaspoon kosher salt

Steel-Cut Oats

2 teaspoons coconut oil

1 cup steel-cut oats

2 cups water

2 cups unsweetened almond milk

2 teaspoons kosher salt

Caramelized Banana

1 banana

1 tablespoon brown sugar

Garnishes

2 tablespoons roughly chopped
    dark chocolate

1 tablespoon toasted hemp seeds

2 tablespoons maple syrup

Hemp leaves, flowers and seeds
    (optional)

Almond milk or chocolate milk, for
    serving

FOR THE SPICED PECANS

Preheat the oven to 325°F (160°C). Line a baking sheet with parchment paper.

In a medium bowl, whisk the egg white until soft peaks form. Add the pecans, cinnamon, brown sugar, cloves and salt. Stir until the pecans are entirely coated with the spiced egg white mixture. Spread the pecans on the prepared baking sheet and bake, stirring occasionally, until lightly golden brown, about 15 minutes.

FOR THE STEEL-CUT OATS

In a medium saucepan, melt the coconut oil over medium-low heat. Add the steel-cut oats and stir for 2 minutes to toast. Add the water, reduce the heat to low and bring to a simmer. Cover and continue to simmer, stirring occasionally, for 25 minutes. Stir in the almond milk and continue to simmer, covered, for 10 minutes or until the liquid is absorbed and the oats are tender. Season with the salt. Remove from the heat and keep warm.

FOR THE CARAMELIZED BANANA

Peel the banana and slice into rounds, cubes or rectangle shapes. Sprinkle with an even layer of brown sugar. Use a kitchen torch to melt the sugar until a crispy layer of caramel forms on the surface.

TO SERVE

Spoon the steel-cut oats into warm bowls. Top with the caramelized banana, spiced pecans, dark chocolate, toasted hemp seeds and maple syrup. Garnish with hemp leaves, flowers and seeds (if using) and serve with additional almond milk or chocolate milk on the side.

SWEET HONEY TEA
with honeycomb and matcha

REMEMBER THAT CARAMEL HONEYCOMB CANDY you used to get at the hockey arena when you were a kid? This is basically a grown-up version of that. We take a simple microwave sponge cake recipe and add a little matcha tea powder, milk and honey. We serve that with a fior di latte gelato and a matcha pastry cream and finish it off with a milk and honey jam.

Incidentally, the microwave sponge cake is great. It's so simple and fast and the cake comes out really aerated. It's not like a dense regular sponge cake, though it looks like fossilized rock. Since pastry chef Rachel discovered it a few years ago, we've done several versions—pumpkin, chocolate, strawberry, even beetroot to name a few.

SERVES 6

Milk and Honey Sauce
2 cups whole milk
½ cup honey
2 teaspoons kappa carrageenan

Honeycomb
1½ cups + 1 tablespoon sugar
2 tablespoons water
2 tablespoons corn syrup
4 teaspoons honey
1 teaspoon kosher salt
1 teaspoon pure vanilla extract
1 tablespoon baking soda

Matcha Sponge
2½ teaspoons matcha powder
¾ teaspoon cream of tartar
¾ teaspoon baking soda
½ cup almond flour
¼ teaspoon kosher salt
3 large eggs
⅓ cup liquid honey
¼ cup whole milk
2½ teaspoons pure vanilla extract
2 tablespoons unsalted butter, melted

Fior di Latte Gelato
2½ cups whole milk

½ cup + 2 tablespoons whipping (35%) cream
¾ cup sugar
¼ cup glucose syrup
¼ teaspoon kosher salt

Matcha Pastry Cream
¼ cup sugar
2 tablespoons matcha powder
2 tablespoons cornstarch
2 large egg yolks
1½ cups whole milk, divided

Garnish
Matcha powder

FOR THE MILK AND HONEY SAUCE
In a small saucepan, bring the milk, honey and kappa carrageenan to a simmer over medium heat. Pour into a bowl and place in the fridge for 2 hours or until firmly set. Remove the set jelly from the bowl and cut into rough pieces. Transfer the jelly pieces to a food processor and blend until smooth. Strain through a fine-mesh sieve. Transfer to a squeeze bottle and store, covered, in the refrigerator until ready to use.

FOR THE HONEYCOMB
Line a baking sheet with parchment paper. In a medium saucepan, combine the sugar, water, corn syrup, honey, salt and vanilla. Mix well. Over medium-high heat, bring the mixture to 300°F (154°C). The

sugar will be just starting to turn to a light golden caramel. Remove the saucepan from the heat. Working quickly, whisk the baking soda into the caramel. The mixture will bubble and foam, greatly increasing in volume. Immediately pour onto the prepared baking sheet and let sit until completely cooled. Break into small pieces with a rolling pin. Store in an airtight container at room temperature for up to 3 days.

FOR THE MATCHA SPONGE
In a small bowl, sift together the matcha powder, cream of tartar and baking soda. Stir in the almond flour and salt.

In a medium bowl, whisk together the eggs, honey, milk and vanilla. Add the dry ingredients and

RECIPE CONTINUES . . .

mix together with a whisk. Add the melted butter and mix until the batter is smooth and well combined. Pour the batter into a 1-litre siphon canister, filling it halfway. Secure the lid and charge with 2 cartridges of CO_2, shaking well after each charge.

Poke several holes around the sides and bottom of six 12-ounce paper coffee cups using a paring knife to allow some of the steam to escape. Siphon the aerated cake batter into the cups, filling them about halfway. Place one cup at a time in the microwave and cook at 70 percent power for 50 seconds or until the sponge cake is nearly fully baked—moist but no longer in a liquid state. Take the cup out of the microwave and place it upside down on the countertop. The residual steam will finish the cooking. Repeat with the remaining cups. Allow to cool completely. Remove the cake from the cups and tear into small bite-size pieces. There will be leftover batter and cake.

FOR THE FIOR DI LATTE GELATO

In a medium saucepan, combine the milk, cream, sugar, glucose syrup and salt. Heat over medium-low heat, stirring occasionally, until the sugar has dissolved. Strain through a fine-mesh sieve into a bowl. Cover and chill until cold. Pour the chilled mixture into an ice-cream maker and process according to the manufacturer's instructions until the ice cream has a soft-serve consistency. Scrape into a chilled airtight container and freeze until hard, about 4 hours. Keep frozen until ready to use.

FOR THE MATCHA PASTRY CREAM

Place the sugar in a small saucepan. Sift the matcha and cornstarch into the sugar and whisk together. In a small bowl, whisk the egg yolks with ½ cup of the milk, then whisk this into the matcha mixture until smooth. Whisk in the remaining 1 cup milk. Over medium-high heat, whisk constantly until the mixture comes to a boil and thickens. Remove from the heat and immediately strain through a fine-mesh sieve into a small bowl. Allow to cool completely, then cover and store in the refrigerator. Whisk again before using.

TO SERVE

Dot the plate with the matcha pastry cream. Spoon a pool of the milk and honey sauce in the centre of the plate. Arrange alternating pieces of honeycomb and matcha sponge cake on the edge of the milk and honey sauce. Sprinkle some crumbs from the honeycomb to make a spot for the gelato to sit. Scoop the gelato and place on the honeycomb crumb. Sprinkle the dish with matcha powder to finish.

LEMON CRINKLE COOKIES

PASTRY CHEF RACHEL AND I are on the same page when it comes to lemon sweets: they have to be lemony. If people are having a lemon dessert, we want them to really taste the lemon. You need that sour element, and the balance between sweet and sour is crucial. The lemon curd in this recipe is less on the sweet side and more on the acid side, so we balance that by making the other elements just a touch sweeter. If you ate them separately it wouldn't be the same experience as when you eat them together. The cookie is a classic little thumbprint lemon sugar cookie, and when you add the lemon curd to it, that makes for a really fantastic lemon experience.

These cookies are great for breakfast or afternoon tea and would make a phenomenal addition to a petits fours plate alongside a salty, rich, buttery vanilla caramel (page 277), a chocolate truffle (page 216) and a sweet, fruity little pâte de fruit (page 213).

MAKES ABOUT 30 MINI COOKIES

Lemon Curd
½ cup granulated sugar
⅓ cup cornstarch
½ teaspoon kosher salt
2 large eggs
½ cup fresh lemon juice

Lemon Crinkle Cookies
2 tablespoons unsalted butter, at
    room temperature
⅓ cup granulated sugar
1 large egg
½ tablespoon lemon zest

1 tablespoon fresh lemon juice
1 cup all-purpose flour
⅛ teaspoon baking soda
Pinch of kosher salt
1 cup icing sugar

FOR THE LEMON CURD

In a small saucepan, stir together the granulated sugar, cornstarch and salt. In a small bowl, whisk together the eggs and lemon juice, then add to the cornstarch mixture and whisk to combine well. Place the saucepan over low heat and cook, whisking constantly, until the mixture has thickened to a curd consistency. This will take only a few minutes once the mixture is hot. Strain the curd through a fine-mesh sieve and allow to cool. Using a funnel, scrape the curd into a squeeze bottle or a piping bag fitted with a small plain tip. The lemon curd can be made a day in advance and stored in the refrigerator.

FOR THE LEMON CRINKLE COOKIES

In a stand mixer fitted with the paddle attachment, beat the butter with the granulated sugar on medium speed until creamy and pale, about 3 minutes. In a small bowl, whisk together the egg, lemon zest and

lemon juice. Add to the butter mixture and mix on low speed until incorporated well. The mixture will appear split, but it will all come together when the dry ingredients are added.

In a small bowl, whisk together the flour, baking soda and salt. Add to the egg mixture and blend on low speed until all the flour has been incorporated. Scrap the dough out into a container, cover and chill in the refrigerator for at least 6 hours or overnight for best results.

Position the racks in the upper and lower thirds of the oven. Preheat the oven to 325°F (160°C). Line 2 baking sheets with parchment paper.

Place the icing sugar in a bowl. Using a small ice-cream scoop or teaspoon, portion the dough into thirty 1-inch balls. Roll each ball in the icing sugar to coat, shaking off any excess, and arrange on the prepared baking sheets, spaced 1 to 2 inches apart. Bake for 6 minutes. At this point the cookie should be mostly baked (not browned) but still soft enough

RECIPE CONTINUES . . .

for you to gently push the end of a wooden spoon into the centre of each cookie to create a divot. Continue to bake for another 6 to 8 minutes, until the cookie has cooked through, golden and cracked at the sides, but is not browned. Remove the cookies from the oven and allow to cool on the baking sheets. Unfilled cookies can be stored in a cookie tin for up to 3 days or kept in the freezer for 2 months.

TO SERVE

Using a spoon, squeeze bottle or piping bag, fill each cookie divot with lemon curd. These cookies can sit for up to 8 hours once filled with curd.

VANILLA CRÈME CARAMELS

A FAVOURITE IN MY HOUSEHOLD and one of my dad's all-time favourite treats, these little caramels are a definite crowd-pleaser. In the dining room, we serve them as something sweet at the end of the meal with your coffee or something to take home. We're not just using sugar and cream in our caramels. We use fresh vanilla beans and some of our own estate honey to give a sense of place. We top them with a few flakes of Canadian sea salt just to tie everything together.

The only trick with these is to make sure to get the caramel just right when cooking. A little too far and they will taste bitter, and not quite far enough and you won't have that rich caramel flavour.

MAKES 18 TO 20 CARAMELS

Vanilla Crème Caramels

1½ cups whipping (35%) cream

1½ cups sugar

¼ cup honey

3 tablespoons unsalted butter, at room temperature

¼ teaspoon kosher salt

½ vanilla bean

FOR THE VANILLA CRÈME CARAMELS

Line a 9 × 6-inch baking sheet with parchment paper.

In a medium saucepan, combine the cream, sugar, honey, butter and salt. With a paring knife, split the vanilla bean in half and scrape the fudgy seeds out of the pod; add both the seeds and the pod to the saucepan. Bring the mixture to a boil over medium heat, occasionally stirring to dissolve the sugar, and boil, stirring occasionally, until the mixture reaches 242°F (117°C). Working quickly, remove the saucepan from the heat and use tongs to take out the vanilla pod. Immediately pour the caramel onto the prepared baking sheet, scraping out the pan with a heatproof rubber spatula. You want the caramel to end up ¼ to ½ inch thick on the baking sheet. Allow the caramel to cool for 1 hour. Once cool, wrap the baking sheet with plastic wrap and leave overnight at room temperature.

Using a paring knife, cut the sides of the caramel away from the pan and turn out onto a cutting board. Peel away the parchment paper and cut the firm caramel into one-bite rectangular bonbons. Store in an airtight container at room temperature between layers of parchment paper for up to 1 week.

TO SERVE

Roll the caramels in cellophane wrappers or parchment paper and twist the ends. Serve on a candy dish.

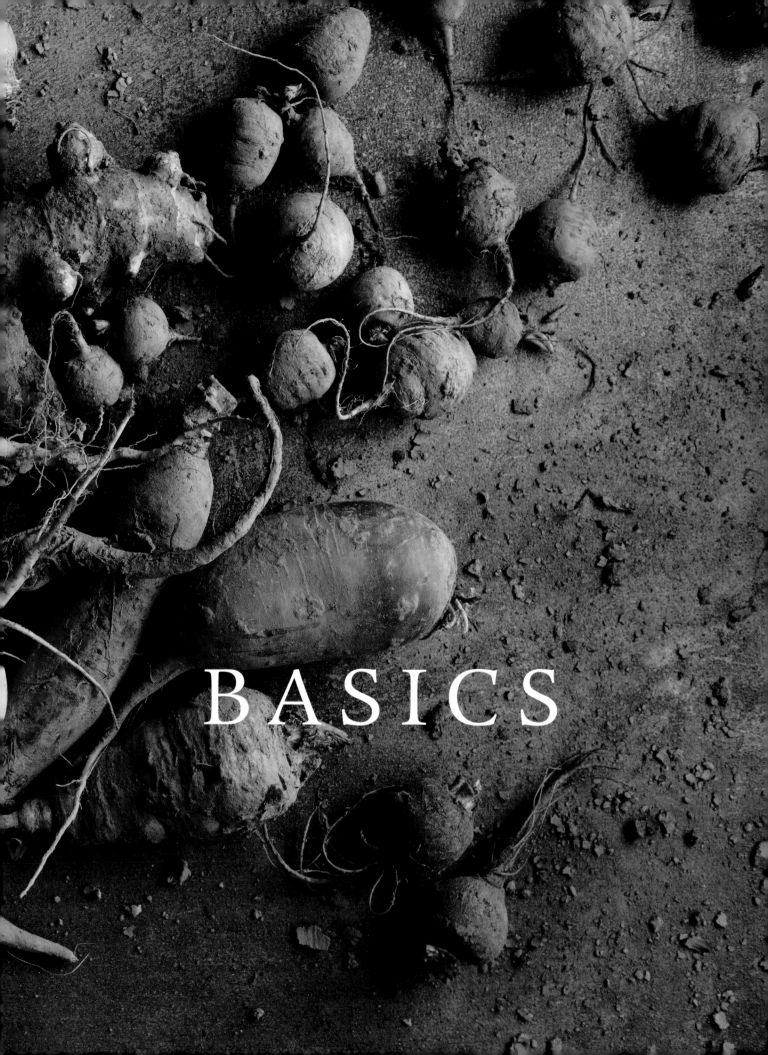

BASICS

BROWN BUTTER

I LOVE FRESH WHOLESOME BUTTER as an ingredient, and when cooked to the point of caramelizing the milk solids, creating this delicious nutty transformation, it jumps to a whole new level. You can use brown butter in desserts or savoury applications. It is great with seafood, mixed into a cake batter or spread onto some grilled corn on the cob.

MAKES ABOUT 1½ CUPS

1 pound unsalted butter, cubed

In a wide heavy light-coloured medium saucepan, melt the butter over medium heat. As it melts, continuously swirl the pan until there are no solid cubes of butter left. The milk solids will separate from the butterfat as the butter bubbles and cooks. The solids will start to caramelize and will go from brown to burnt quickly, so watch closely. Keep swirling the butter over the heat until it is light brown in colour and starts to smell nutty. The entire process should take less than 5 minutes. Pour the brown butter into a bowl. Allow to cool slightly and develop in flavour for 10 minutes at room temperature. Strain the fat from the solids through a fine-mesh sieve or several layers of cheesecloth. Discard the milk solids and allow the butterfat to cool completely. The brown butter can be stored in an airtight container in the refrigerator for up to a week.

MAYONNAISE

A STAPLE IN MOST KITCHENS, this very versatile sauce can be transformed simply by the addition of flavourful ingredients. Lemon, garlic, chili, herbs, black pepper, truffle and anchovy are among a long list of possibilities. Served with vegetables, poached fish, or simply on a sandwich, fresh homemade is the way to go; you select the ingredients, there are no preservatives and you control the final flavour and texture.

MAKES ABOUT 1½ CUPS

2 large egg yolks
½ tablespoon white wine vinegar
1 teaspoon Dijon mustard
½ teaspoon kosher salt
1 cup vegetable oil

In a medium bowl, whisk together the egg yolks, white wine vinegar, mustard and salt until well mixed. While whisking, drizzle in the vegetable oil in a thin stream, whisking constantly to emulsify and thicken the consistency. Transfer to a container with a lid and store in the refrigerator for up to 5 days.

AÏOLI

THIS COUSIN TO MAYONNAISE PACKS a garlicky punch. It's great on its own as a condiment but also is easily transformed into a dressing or dip for crudités or a salad. A favourite of many and often requested with an order of hot salty frites or on the side of a juicy Wilks' Bar burger.

MAKES ABOUT 1½ CUPS

2 large egg yolks
1 garlic clove, finely minced or grated with a microplane
½ tablespoon fresh lemon juice
1 teaspoon white wine vinegar
1 teaspoon Dijon mustard
1 cup vegetable oil
½ tablespoon olive oil
1 teaspoon kosher salt

In a medium bowl, whisk the egg yolks with the garlic, lemon juice, white wine vinegar and mustard to mix well. While whisking, add the vegetable oil in a thin stream, followed by the olive oil, whisking continuously to emulsify. The aïoli will thicken to the texture of a silky mayonnaise. If it becomes too thick, thin it with a few drops of room-temperature water. Stir in the salt. Transfer to a covered container and refrigerate for up to 5 days.

CRÈME FRAÎCHE

SIMILAR TO SOUR CREAM, CRÈME fraîche is creamier, with a higher fat content and a clean finish. A go-to as a spread or base for a dressing or dip. I often serve this au naturel with chilled seafood and as the perfect accompaniment to caviar.

MAKES ABOUT 4 CUPS

4 cups whipping (35%) cream
¾ cup plain natural full-fat yogurt (with active cultures)
1 tablespoon fresh lemon juice
½ teaspoon kosher salt

In a medium bowl, whisk together the cream, yogurt, lemon juice and salt. Transfer to a 6-cup mason jar. Cover the top with cheesecloth and secure it in place by screwing on the screw ring (without the flat lid), allowing air to travel in and out of the jar. Alternatively, you can secure the cheesecloth with string or an elastic band. Leave in an area just above room temperature (about 82°F/28°C) for 48 hours. Transfer to a clean mason jar with a lid and store in the refrigerator for up to 5 days.

GARLIC CONFIT

TO CONFIT SOMETHING IS TO slowly cook it submerged in fat, technically in its own fat, such as duck leg confit. In this version, the garlic is slowly cooked in vegetable oil. The result is a very soft clove of garlic with a softened savoury flavour and a garlic-infused oil. Both the garlic and the oil may be used together or on their own. I often add the garlic or the oil to marinades, vinaigrettes, emulsions or stews and sauces to add a punch of soft garlic flavour. When the cloves are puréed, they add a smooth, creamy texture.

MAKES 1½ CUPS

1½ cups garlic cloves
2 sprigs fresh rosemary
2 cups vegetable oil
1 teaspoon kosher salt

Combine the garlic, rosemary, vegetable oil and salt in a small saucepan. The garlic should be fully submerged. Bring the oil to a low simmer over medium-low heat. Reduce the heat to low and cook gently until the garlic is fork-tender, 15 to 20 minutes. Remove from the heat and allow to cool to room temperature. Remove the rosemary and discard. Transfer the oil and garlic to a medium mason jar, seal with a lid and store in the refrigerator for up to a week.

SHALLOT VINAIGRETTE

THIS SIMPLE VINAIGRETTE IS A workhorse in our kitchen. It is fantastic on its own with any type of lettuce, tossed with vegetables or drizzled over fresh cheese. It can be modified by adding any herb to alter the flavour. Try adding a tablespoon of chopped fresh basil, marjoram, dill or tarragon for a taste of summer when dressing butter lettuce, poached seafood or roasted garden vegetables.

MAKES 2 CUPS

⅓ cup chopped shallots
¼ cup honey
1 teaspoon Dijon mustard
½ cup red wine vinegar
½ cup white wine vinegar
1½ cups vegetable oil
1 tablespoon kosher salt

In a high-speed blender, combine the shallots, honey, mustard, red wine vinegar and white wine vinegar. Process to purée. With the blender running, add the vegetable oil in a slow, steady stream until fully emulsified and smooth. Season with the salt. Keep covered in the refrigerator for up to a week.

PICKLED MUSTARD SEEDS

I REALLY ENJOY ALL KINDS of mustards, on their own as a condiment or used to enhance other recipes, and I'll often experiment, creating combinations with such pantry items as garlic confit, honey, maple, spices and herbs. This recipe was developed for a roasted lamb dish served with late-harvest stone fruits. Use it in marinades and dressings or serve with your favourite pâté or charcuterie or, as I have done in this book, to add a fresh mustard pop to steak tartare.

MAKES ABOUT 2 CUPS

⅔ cup yellow mustard seeds
1½ cups rice vinegar
1 cup water
½ cup sugar
1 tablespoon kosher salt

In a small saucepan, bring the mustard seeds, vinegar, water, sugar and salt to a simmer over medium heat. Reduce the heat to low, cover and cook at a light simmer for 1 hour, stirring occasionally. The seeds will soften and absorb the liquid. Keep an eye on the level of liquid in the pan, and add a little more water if it is all absorbed before the seeds are softened. When done, the seeds will be soft like caviar, with a pop of texture, and lightly sweet pickled.

LIME LEAF POWDER

I ADORE THE FLAVOUR AND smell of lime leaf. It has a nostalgic effect on me, reminding me of Froot Loops, which I loved as a kid. I use this powder in many dishes that centre on citrus. It is a beautiful bright green and it explodes on the senses with citrus essence.

MAKES ABOUT ½ TABLESPOON

12 fresh lime leaves

Pick the lime leaves off the stem. Arrange them on a plate in an even layer. Microwave on 50 percent power for 3 minutes or until crisp but still bright green. Allow to cool for 15 minutes. In a small food processor or spice grinder, blend on high speed for 2 minutes. Pass the powder through a fine-mesh sieve to remove any small stems and pieces that didn't blend thoroughly. Store in an airtight container with a lid for up to a week.

SIMPLE SYRUP

A CLASSIC DESSERT BASE RECIPE typically used for sweet sauces, sorbets, dressing or poaching fruits and brushing cake layers. By playing with the ratio of sugar to water, you can make the syrup thicker or thinner depending on what you are using it for. Many flavours can be added to modify it as well. Try citrus rind, light fragrant spices, fresh mint or vanilla.

MAKES ABOUT 2 CUPS

1 cup sugar
1 cup water

In a small saucepan, combine the sugar and water. Heat over medium heat, stirring occasionally until the sugar has dissolved. When the syrup has come up to a boil, remove from the heat and allow to cool. Store in a sealed jar in the refrigerator for up to 2 weeks.

LEMON GEL

THIS IS MY GO-TO FOR adding a punch of lemon to a dish instead of using straight lemon juice. It has a thick, smooth texture and is well balanced with a sweet-and-sour flavour. Use it as a glaze for roast chicken, a base for a dressing, a jam or a condiment just as is.

MAKES 3 CUPS

Lemongrass Syrup (makes 4 cups)
2 cups sugar
2 cups water
1 lemongrass stalk, tough outer leaves and stems discarded, chopped

1 tablespoon lemon zest
6 fresh lemon verbena leaves

Lemon Gel
2 cups lemongrass syrup (recipe at left)
2½ teaspoons (7.8 g) agar powder
1 cup fresh lemon juice

FOR THE LEMONGRASS SYRUP
In a small saucepan, make a simple syrup by bringing the sugar and water to a simmer over medium heat, stirring occasionally until the sugar has dissolved, about 4 minutes. Add the lemongrass, lemon zest and lemon verbena and cook gently for another 5 minutes. Remove from the heat and allow the syrup to cool completely with the aromatics. Once cool, strain through a fine-mesh sieve and store in a sealed jar in the refrigerator until ready to use or up to 2 weeks.

FOR THE LEMON GEL
In a small saucepan, whisk together the lemongrass syrup and agar powder. Bring to a boil over high heat. Stir in the lemon juice and remove from the heat. Strain the liquid through a fine-mesh sieve, cover and chill in the refrigerator until the liquid sets to a firm, solid gel, about 30 minutes. Once set, cut the lemon gel into 1-inch cubes.

In a high-speed blender, purée the cubes into a smooth gel. Pass the gel through a fine-mesh sieve to remove any small lumps. Pour the gel into a squeeze bottle, piping bag or container with a lid and keep in the refrigerator for up to a week.

VEGETABLE AND WHITE WINE NAGE

THIS IS A RECIPE I LEARNED while cooking in Europe and I have used adaptations of it ever since. Its flavour is incredible and so fresh. It's great for poaching chicken, fish or vegetables. The acidity from the wine is interesting, but the flavour is more delicate and refined than a court bouillon. This is best once it is made. It will lose its vibrancy and freshness over a couple of days.

MAKES ABOUT 8 CUPS

6 cups sliced peeled carrots

3 cups sliced white onions

1 cup sliced leeks (white part only)

1 cup crushed fresh peas in the pod

8 star anise

1 tablespoon kosher salt

½ teaspoon white peppercorns

8 cups water

1 cup dry white wine

1 fresh bay leaf

¼ cup lightly packed fresh cilantro leaves

¼ cup lightly packed fresh tarragon leaves

¼ cup lightly packed fresh basil leaves

¼ cup lightly packed fresh thyme leaves

¼ cup lightly packed fresh flat-leaf parsley

In a medium saucepan, combine the carrots, onions, leeks, peas, star anise, salt, white peppercorns and water. Bring to a simmer over medium-high heat and simmer for 10 minutes. Remove from the heat and add the white wine, bay leaf, cilantro, tarragon, basil, thyme and parsley. Allow the nage to cool to room temperature. Cover and steep in the refrigerator for 24 hours.

Strain through a fine-mesh sieve or several layers of cheesecloth into a clean medium saucepan or a container with a lid. Store in the refrigerator and use within 2 days.

VEGETABLE STOCK

FRAGRANT AND FULL OF FLAVOUR, this stock will do just fine as a substitute for vegetarians replacing meat stocks in any recipe. Use this recipe as a guideline, and feel free to add any additional herbs or vegetables you have in the refrigerator.

MAKES 3 QUARTS

4 cups sliced white onions

2 cups sliced peeled carrots

2 cups sliced leeks (white part only)

1½ cups sliced fennel

1 cup sliced celery

1 tablespoon sliced garlic

½ teaspoon white peppercorns

4 fresh bay leaves

¼ cup lightly packed fresh thyme leaves

¼ cup lightly packed fresh flat-leaf parsley

In a medium saucepan, combine the onions, carrots, leeks, fennel, celery, garlic, white peppercorns and bay leaves. Add water to cover the vegetables by 1 inch. Bring to a simmer over medium-high heat. Simmer gently for 10 minutes, skimming any impurities that rise to the surface with a large spoon or ladle. Continue to simmer for another 10 minutes. Remove from the heat, add the thyme and parsley and allow the stock to cool to room temperature. Cover and steep in the refrigerator for 24 hours.

Strain through a fine-mesh sieve or several layers of cheesecloth into a clean saucepan or containers with lids. Store in the refrigerator and use within 3 days or freeze for up to 2 months.

CHICKEN STOCK

A STAPLE IN MOST KITCHENS, chicken stock can be made in various ways. I have worked in many kitchens, and believe it or not, the simple basic recipe was different in every one of them. This recipe makes a light base stock that is perfect for soups, sauces or braising. The important thing to remember is to cook it low and slow after it's been skimmed of fat and impurities at the start to result in a clear, tasty finish.

MAKES ABOUT 6 QUARTS

5 pounds (2.25 kg) raw chicken bones, chopped

½ cup kosher salt, for rinsing

2 fresh bay leaves

2 cups lightly packed fresh flat-leaf parsley

½ cup fresh thyme leaves

¼ cup fresh rosemary leaves

½ teaspoon black peppercorns

2 cups sliced leeks (white part only)

2 cups sliced white onions

1 cup sliced peeled carrots

½ cup sliced celery

3 garlic cloves, crushed

Using poultry shears or a paring knife, remove any bloody pieces or organ meat attached to the bones. Place the bones in a large stock pot, add the salt and rinse the bones in cold running water for 5 minutes to clean off any blood and to lightly brine them. Dump the water. Add enough fresh cold water to cover the bones by 1 inch. Over medium-high heat, and without stirring, bring the water to a boil and skim off the fat and impurities that rise to the surface with a large spoon or ladle. Reduce the heat to low and very gently simmer the stock for 10 minutes, continuing to skim. Without stirring, add the bay leaves, parsley, thyme, rosemary and black peppercorns,

followed by the leeks, onions, carrots, celery and garlic. Season with salt and continue to cook just under a simmer on low heat for 3 hours, uncovered, without stirring, and skimming occasionally. You should only see small percolating bubbles occasionally rising to the surface. It is key to cook this stock low and slow, and do not stir the stock as that may cloud the finished product.

Turn the heat off and allow the stock to settle for 20 minutes. Strain through a fine-mesh sieve into containers with lids and cool rapidly over ice (see JB's Tip, page 287). Store in the refrigerator and use within 3 days or freeze for up to 3 months.

FISH STOCK

FISH STOCK SHOULD BE MADE only with the freshest bones. For best results I prefer halibut bones as they provide the cleanest flavour. This stock is subtle, clean and delicious, not overpowering, making it a perfect base for sauces and soups.

MAKES ABOUT 6 QUARTS

4 pounds (1.8 kg) fresh halibut bones, chopped

½ cup kosher salt

¼ teaspoon white peppercorns

2 star anise

1 fresh bay leaf

½ cup lightly packed fresh tarragon leaves

½ cup lightly packed fresh chervil leaves

½ cup lightly packed fresh flat-leaf parsley

2 garlic cloves, crushed

2 cups sliced leeks (white part only)

1 cup sliced onions

1 cup sliced fennel

½ cup sliced celery

1 tablespoon fresh lemon juice or Champagne vinegar

Using kitchen scissors or a paring knife, remove any bloody pieces attached to the bones. Place the bones in a large stock pot, add the salt and rinse the bones in cold running water for 5 minutes to clean off any blood and to lightly brine them. Dump the water. Add enough fresh cold water to cover the bones by 1 inch. Over medium-high heat, and without stirring, bring the water to a boil and skim off the fat and impurities that rise to the surface with a large spoon or ladle. Reduce the heat to low and bring the stock to a very gentle simmer. Add the white peppercorns and star anise and continue to skim for another 5 minutes. Without stirring, add the bay leaf, tarragon, chervil, parsley, garlic, leeks, onions, fennel and celery. Continue to cook just under a simmer on low heat for an additional 20 minutes, without stirring, and skimming occasionally. You should only see small percolating bubbles occasionally rising to the surface. It is key to cook this stock low and slow, and do not stir the stock as that may cloud the finished product.

Turn the heat off and allow the stock to settle for 20 minutes, then add the lemon juice or vinegar and adjust seasoning if necessary. Strain through a fine-mesh sieve into containers with lids and cool rapidly over ice (see JB's Tip). Store in the refrigerator and use within 3 days or freeze for up to 3 months.

JB'S TIP

It is important to cool soups or stocks over ice, bringing the temperature down quickly prior to storing in the refrigerator. Bacteria grows between the temperatures of 40°F (4°C) and 140°F (60°C), so by chilling rapidly once completed you limit the growth of bacteria. This in turn ensures safe bacteria levels and will prolong the freshness of the finished soup or stock.

Placing hot liquids in the refrigerator to cool is dangerous; the hot liquid affects the internal temperature of the fridge, which in turn can affect the quality of other temperature-delicate items.

LAMB JUS

LAMB JUS IS ONE OF my favourite sauces to make. Lamb has such a distinctive flavour, and the roasted bones along with the garlic and rosemary are a delicious combination. The key thing to remember is to not over-roast the bones. Too much colour and caramelization will overpower the clean flavours of the jus and make the sauce bitter.

MAKES 2 TO 3 CUPS

2 cups lamb trimmings and bones
1 teaspoon vegetable oil
1 cup sliced shallots
¼ cup sliced garlic
½ teaspoon kosher salt
½ tablespoon fresh rosemary leaves
½ tablespoon fresh thyme leaves
1 fresh bay leaf
½ cup roughly chopped ripe tomato
½ cup dry white wine, divided
3 cups Veal Jus (page 289)

Preheat the oven to 350°F (180°C). Spread the lamb bones in a medium roasting pan and roast, stirring occasionally, for 10 minutes or until golden brown and caramelized.

In a medium saucepan, heat the vegetable oil over medium heat. Add the lamb trimmings and fry, stirring occasionally, until lightly caramelized. Reduce the heat to low and add the shallots, garlic, salt, rosemary, thyme and bay leaf. Cook, stirring occasionally, until the vegetables are tender and starting to colour, about 3 minutes. Add the roasted lamb bones and the tomato and cook for another 3 minutes Pour ¼ cup of the wine into the roasting pan and with a wooden spoon or rubber spatula scrape all the roasted bits off the bottom of the pan. Add this to the saucepan, then add the remaining ¼ cup wine. Reduce to almost dry. Add the veal jus. Bring to a simmer, then reduce the heat to medium-low and gently cook for 10 minutes or until the jus is well flavoured with the lamb and has a sauce consistency. Strain through a fine-mesh sieve into containers with lids. Discard the solids. Chill rapidly over ice and store covered in the refrigerator for up to 3 days or freeze for up to 3 months.

VEAL JUS

THERE IS ALWAYS A POT of this on the stove in the kitchen at Langdon Hall. It's a neutral base for so many sauces. Most chefs when they make bone sauces start with animal bones—lamb, duck, chicken—make the stock from the bones and reduce it down. For this one, what I do is create a neutral base using poultry, veal and a little pork. Nothing's roasted and there's no tomato paste, so the result is a sweet, delicate base that can go in any number of directions.

MAKES 2 TO 3 CUPS

5 pounds (2.25 kg) raw chicken bones, chopped

3 pounds (1.4 kg) veal bones, cut into 2- to 4-inch pieces

1 pound (450 g) pig trotters, split or sliced into 2-inch pieces (2 small trotters)

2 medium white onions, cut in quarters

6 garlic cloves, crushed

1½ cups roughly chopped celery

1½ cups roughly chopped peeled carrots

1 cup sliced leek (white part only)

6 tablespoons fresh thyme leaves

1 teaspoon black peppercorns

2 fresh bay leaves

2 cups peeled shallots

FOR THE STOCK

Place the bones in a large stock pot and add enough cold water to cover them by 1 inch. Over medium-high heat, and without stirring, bring the water to a boil and skim off the fat and impurities that rise to the surface with a large spoon or ladle. Continue for 5 minutes and discard any impurities. Dump the water, rinse the bones and refill the pot to 1 inch above the bones with clean cold water. Over medium-high heat, bring the water to a boil and skim the fat and impurities that rise to the surface with a large spoon or ladle. Reduce the heat to low and bring the stock to a very gentle simmer. Without stirring, add the onions, garlic, celery, carrots, leek, thyme, black peppercorns and bay leaves. Continue to cook just under a simmer on low heat for 8 hours, uncovered, without stirring, and skimming occasionally. You should only see small percolating bubbles occasionally rising to the surface. It is key to cook this stock low

and slow, and do not stir the stock as that may cloud the finished product.

Remove from the heat and allow to cool slightly. Strain through a fine-mesh sieve lined with several layers of cheesecloth into a large saucepan. Discard the solids.

FOR THE VEAL JUS

Add the shallots to the stock and simmer over medium heat until reduced by half, about 4 hours, skimming occasionally while cooking. Strain through a fine-mesh sieve lined with several layers of cheesecloth into a medium saucepan. Discard the shallots. Return the stock to the stove over medium-low heat and continue to reduce to a light sauce consistency. Strain through a fine-mesh sieve lined with several layers of cheesecloth into containers with lids and cool rapidly over ice. Store in the refrigerator for up to 3 days or freeze for up to 3 months.

TRADITIONAL COURT BOUILLON

THIS QUICK BROTH IS USUALLY made for the purpose of poaching seafood. It is loaded with fresh aromatics and acid usually consisting of citrus or vinegar and it packs a punch of flavour. See the lemongrass/ginger variation in the Marinated Shrimp recipe (page 33).

MAKES ABOUT 2 QUARTS

1 cup sliced white onion

½ cup sliced leek (white part only)

¼ cup sliced celery

¼ cup sliced peeled carrot

2 garlic cloves, sliced

4 star anise

1 tablespoon coriander seeds

2 tablespoons kosher salt

1 teaspoon white peppercorns

8 cups water

1 cup dry white wine

½ cup white wine vinegar

2 fresh bay leaves

¼ cup lightly packed fresh tarragon leaves

¼ cup lightly packed fresh dill leaves

¼ cup lightly packed fresh flat-leaf parsley

1 fresh lemon, cut in half

In a medium saucepan, combine the onion, leek, celery, carrot, garlic, star anise, coriander seeds, salt and white peppercorns. Add the water and bring to a boil over high heat, then reduce the heat to a simmer and cook until the vegetables are tender, about 8 minutes. Add the white wine, white wine vinegar, bay leaves, tarragon, dill and parsley. Squeeze the lemons, add the juice and lemon halves to the pot, and continue to simmer for 8 minutes. Remove from the heat and strain through a fine-mesh sieve and allow to cool. Transfer to containers with lids and store in the refrigerator for up to 3 days or freeze for up to 3 months.

STANDARD BRINE

PORK AND CHICKEN ALMOST ALWAYS get a brine bath in my kitchen. Once you have tried it you'll see why. The brine seasons and flavours the meat as well as helps to keep it plump and juicy during cooking.

MAKES ABOUT 4 CUPS

4 cups water

¼ cup kosher salt

2 tablespoons sugar

⅓ cup sliced garlic

½ tablespoon fresh thyme leaves

2 star anise

2 fresh bay leaves

In a medium saucepan, bring the water, salt and sugar to a boil. Remove from the heat, add the garlic, thyme, star anise and bay leaves and allow the brine to cool to room temperature. Store the brine in an airtight container in the refrigerator for up to a week.

TRADITIONAL METHOD OF BRAISED BEEF SHORT RIB

FOR THE SOUS VIDE RECIPES we use boneless rib, but if you are braising the traditional way, bone-in will give you a more beefy flavour. The only difference will be the colour of the flesh once sliced, and the texture will be slightly different. Short rib is quite fatty, but braising melts much of the fat away into the cooking liquid. Skim it off as you would a stock or sauce before serving, or let the braise chill overnight in the refrigerator. The fat will solidify on the surface and be easy to spoon off.

SERVES 4

1 boneless beef short rib
   (1 pound/450 g)
2 cups thickly sliced white onions
1 cup thickly sliced peeled carrots
½ cup thickly sliced celery
1 tablespoon sliced garlic (2 cloves)

1 fresh bay leaf
¼ cup lightly packed fresh thyme
   leaves
¼ cup lightly packed fresh flat-leaf
   parsley
2 cups dry red wine

1 tablespoon kosher salt
1 teaspoon freshly cracked black
   peppercorns
1 tablespoon vegetable oil
2 cups Chicken Stock (page 286),
   beef stock, veal stock or water

Place the beef short rib in a large bowl and add the onions, carrots, celery, garlic, bay leaf, thyme, parsley and red wine. Cover and marinate in the refrigerator for 8 to 12 hours.

Preheat the oven to 325°F (160°C).

Strain the wine through a sieve or colander into a medium bowl. Reserve the wine. Separate the vegetables from the herbs and reserve both in separate bowls. Pat the beef dry with paper towel and season well with salt and pepper. In a large Dutch oven or saucepan, heat the oil over high heat. Sear the beef until golden brown on all sides, 1 to 2 minutes per side. Remove the beef from the pan and rest on a small baking sheet.

Reduce the heat to medium and add the reserved vegetables and garlic. Cook, stirring frequently, until the vegetables are golden brown, about 5 minutes. Return the beef to the pan and add the reserved herbs and red wine. Bring to a boil over medium-high heat and reduce the wine by half. Add the stock and bring to a boil over high heat. Reduce the heat to low and

allow the liquid to come to a gentle simmer. Cover the pan, place in the oven and cook slowly for 2 to 3 hours or until the meat is fork-tender, turning the beef and basting with the cooking liquid every 30 minutes. The braise should be at a very gentle simmer, so adjust the temperature of the oven if needed. Do not boil.

When cooked, adjust the seasoning with salt and pepper, if needed, and cool the beef to room temperature in the cooking liquid. Cover and store in the cooking liquid in the refrigerator for up to 3 days.

For the Beef Short Rib and Caviar dish on page 55, you will need to cool the braise in the cooking liquid overnight. When ready to serve, remove the cold meat from the liquid and slice it ¼ inch thick and to the dimensions of the brioche batons. Warm gently in a medium pan over low heat in a few tablespoons of the braising liquid. When warm, carefully transfer the slices to a plate lined with paper towel to absorb some of the juices and then place the short rib on the prepared brioche.

FARMERS' NOTES

Kolapore Springs Fish Hatchery

Sean Brady at Kolapore Springs has a really special setup. His fishery is located at the top of the watershed, where it's fed by all this moving clear water. He's got all these different types of trout—speckled trout, rainbow trout, brown and tiger trout—and he just turns out a beautiful product. When a supplier cares so much about what they're doing and puts so much effort into the product that they want to deliver and they stand behind it and the quality, you just can't beat it. And that's the thing with all our suppliers—they're all a pleasure to work with. Those are the people you want to be in business with, that you want to form a relationship with. There's a face, there's no middle person, no big sixteen-wheeler coming and dropping off the stuff, they're delivering it in person.

"Langdon Hall is synonymous with high quality and consistency. They're such strong supporters of local product, and Jason is always focused on putting great food out to his customers day in and day out. And he can trace that food all the way back into the ground of the community—or in our case under the water. Having our product on the menu there is really special, because Jason and the great owners at Langdon Hall are committed to exceptional ingredients. We don't spend a lot of time on marketing and sales because those guys have done all the heavy lifting for us. It's a blessing to be associated with Langdon Hall." —SEAN BRADY

Soiled Reputation

Antony John at Soiled Reputation is pretty much the one guy who's been really experimental and really pushing the boundaries of what people can grow around here. His varieties of winter squash are incredible, and he's got these amazing cellar sprouts and pretty little coloured zucchini and eggplants—things you wouldn't necessarily find at the farmers' market. Lots of interesting heirloom or heritage varieties, really interesting, uncommon stuff. He's almost like a mad scientist and he's always trying something new just to see if it works. His care and

attention to detail in everything that he does is incredible, and as a result the products are always outstanding.

"It is a tremendous honour and a pleasure to be able to provide ingredients to Langdon Hall. In a sense, we're the first line of editing for the produce that they want, so we're already doing that selecting based on Langdon Hall's standards of quality. We have a personal investment in the team and think of ourselves as an extension of that team." —ANTONY JOHN

Murray's Farm

Murray Thunberg at Murray's Farm is someone we work really closely with. He started his farm around the same time I started at Langdon Hall, so we've kind of come up together. This was a guy who just showed up one day in a pickup truck with a pig in the back and said, "Do you want my pig?" That's how I met him. He was only doing pork at the time, and I think he was the only farmer in Canada with a registered herd of Gloucestershire Old Spot and Hereford pigs. Even then, though, he had big plans to grow the best heirloom tomatoes and potatoes, and now he's got cows and chickens and we get beautiful eggs. You can't really just order from him. He'll just call up and say, "I've got a pig ready," and we have to take the whole thing.

"It's a feather in your cap to have Langdon Hall serving your products. It's huge. But making sure that the product stays good is also really important. You've got to have integrity with the product. I grow between thirty-five and forty varieties of tomatoes every year from about seventeen hundred plants—Matt's Wild Cherry, Black Beauty, Oxhearts, Kellogg's Breakfast—but we still pick everything by hand. We can literally pick a tomato and it can be on somebody's dinner plate at Langdon Hall within two hours. Our eggs usually arrive in forty-eight hours." —MURRAY THUNBERG

ACKNOWLEDGMENTS

THIS PROJECT WAS MADE possible thanks to the passion and collaboration of many highly driven, supportive and talented individuals.

First and foremost, thanks to the entire team at Langdon Hall, everyone from the owners and managers to the cooks, dishwashers, porters, gardeners, service teams and maintenance personnel. Every individual in some way has helped to make this property the extraordinary place it is today and has helped to bring this cookbook project to life. Braden Bennett and Mark Steenge, thank you for believing in this project and for the unwavering support and guidance. Jennifer Houghton, Anna Hewat and Sara Norman, thank you for keeping us on track and helping to organize all the parts that were less fun than digging in the dirt, visiting farms and cooking delicious food.

Special thanks to our incredibly gifted and loyal kitchen brigade: Chefs Philippe de Montbrun, Rachel Nicholson and Daniel Angus, along with the entire culinary team who worked diligently on this book and were vital to the development and success of this project. To sommelier Faye MacLachlan and her team for their dedication to the wine program and the informative pairing notes written throughout these pages. To long-time Food and Beverage Director Virgilio Vea and the entire dining room team for consistently pushing for perfection. To the grounds crews who keep Langdon Hall looking her best and provide the kitchen with some of the earth's best ingredients.

Thanks to all our purveyors, especially farming friends and producers Antony John, Bryan Gilvesy, Murray Thunberg and Carole Precious for being so awesome at what you do. The relationships we have built with our farming communities help us showcase the importance of knowing where good food comes from.

For the early-morning chats, insightful essays and knowledgeable cookbook writing guidance, writer Chris Johns. It has been a pleasure working with you on this project.

For the beautiful props and photography by the Geary House crew, perfectionist photographer Colin Faulkner and his assistant team, along with props expert Lara McGraw and the much-needed organizational talents of Alison Lovell, thank you.

Thanks also to Conestoga College's Brad Lomanto and his dedicated group of up-and-coming culinary students who worked with us to test the recipes outside our kitchens and provided such detailed and constructive recipe feedback.

Mentors and friends who offered insightful quotes and introduction—Anton Mosimann, Afrim Pristine, Anita Stewart, Michael Bonacini, Daniel Boulud, David Kinch, John Higgins, Kevin Chan and Philippe Gombert. Thank you for writing such lovely words and being a part of our story.

Andrea Magyar, our editor at Penguin Canada, for seeing the potential in this project and helping to guide it to completion.

To my family: Stacey, Sebastian and Christian. A project like this, on top of being the chef at Langdon Hall, requires a lot of attention and sacrifice. Thank you for your support.

To the founding owners, Bill Bennett and Mary Beaton. This book exists because of the vision you both had for this property. In realizing your dream, you created something beautiful that truly represents the best of refined countryside luxury lodging, fine dining and exceptional hospitality. Thank you.

INDEX